The Narcissist Trap

Also from Dr Supriya McKenna

Divorcing a Narcissist: the Lure, the Loss and the Law

Narcissism and Family Law: A Practitioner's Guide

(with legal contributions from Karin Walker)

The Narcissist Trap

The Mind-Bending Pull
of the
Great Pretenders

Dr Supriya McKenna

Copyright © 2023 Supriya McKenna

First Paperback Edition September 2023

ISBN 978-1-7394936-0-8 (Paperback)
ISBN 978-1-7394936-1-5 (Ebook)
ISBN 978-1-7394936-2-2 (Audiobook)

Published by Tavistock Publishing
www.tavistockpublishing.com

Dedication

For my children, India and Theo, and
my mother, Shashi.

In honour of all the half-lived lives and stolen dreams
of those who only knew the dark.
For the reluctantly brave and quietly heroic.
And for those who try to turn on the light.

"Once you've seen narcissism, you can't ever really unsee it."

Contents

ACKNOWLEDGEMENTS

Thanks to Dr Elinor Greenberg, whose prolific body of writing about narcissism for the public has inspired me so much. Our transatlantic chats, on and off the air, have been fascinating and full of humour, and I'm pretty sure I also owe you for your help in coming up with the title of this book.

Thanks also to Dr Craig Malkin, from whom I learnt a great deal during our interviews, and whose work on the Spectrum of Narcissism has been so valuable.

I'd also like to thank Dr Geoffrey Harvey for reading and critiquing every chapter of this book, and editing, correcting and proofreading it. Your enthusiasm and encouragement for this project has been unfailing, and I am delighted that you have been able to identify Tennyson's Ulysses as a narcissist, as a result. I'm guessing you must be absolutely sick of narcissism by now. Which is a shame, because there are a few more books I've been thinking of writing...

Thanks also to Mabel, my Labrador, who lay right next to my desk for the entire writing process, occasionally sighing (in an effort to guilt trip me into taking her for a walk), but mostly just being pleased that I have hardly left the house.

Finally, thank you to all my clients. The insights I have gained from you have not only been humbling, but have been the making of this book; they have breathed life into it. Together we have turned your experiences into a platform, to raise public awareness of the many narcissists all around us. I hope I have done you proud.

Foreword

I am delighted to contribute a foreword to what I believe, in the field of narcissism, will be a stand-out book; possibly the book of the decade. As an academic and university teacher of English literature (and editor of a number of major literary works), what has struck me, quite unexpectedly, is how many literary characters, in drama, fiction and poetry are (I now know!) clearly narcissists. These 'Great Pretenders', as Supriya McKenna calls them, are so because their pretence creates drama for themselves, and havoc in other people's lives, and so they offer themselves readily to the writer.

Dr Supriya McKenna is well known as a best-selling, gifted writer - not for her the dullness of academic discourse! Her writing is lively and hugely engaging, as she leads the reader along a fascinating pathway of discovery and understanding. Her narrative voice is that of a friend and counsellor, who asks the reader questions, and openly draws on her own experiences. Unexpected, perhaps, but most welcome, are her flashes of sardonic humour. Warm and informal, she offers insights, knowledge, wisdom, compassion and hope.

The Narcissist Trap is a comprehensive examination of how precisely the 'Great Pretenders' go about entrapping their victims, with suggested strategies for escape, and mechanisms for coping. The wealth of detailed information and advice is also brilliantly organized, which makes for effortless reading.

Dr Supriya's book is founded on her work as a former GP, her lectures, her close involvement with the cases of hundreds of clients, and her own deep personal experience. It demonstrates how the misery caused by Narcissistic Personality Disorder is not only spread through family clusters and social communities, but is passed down through the generations. But this book seeks to reveal and explain; it is not judgmental; compassion for victims is balanced by the recognition that narcissists do not choose a disorder that shields a vulnerable personality.

Descriptions of the various types of narcissist and their behaviours are illustrated in a wonderfully imaginative way, through a cast of recognizable characters. Their life stories are placed in dramatized situations from everyday life, to which the reader can easily relate.

The book uses the metaphor of the solar system to suggest a gravitational relationship between the narcissist and their victims, in the way that the various planets orbit the sun. So nearest to the 'Great Pretender', and most affected by them, will be their spouse or partner, and in the furthermost orbit will be the postman, or a man in the pub. Reference is continually made back to these orbits and characters, so that the various narcissistic behaviours are deconstructed for the reader with a deceptive ease.

Dr McKenna is notably impatient with the inadequate recognition of the prevalence of narcissism in the medical and legal worlds. She also calls for greater awareness of Narcissistic Personality Disorder as a global phenomenon, in which a significant number of heads of state put their nations and peoples, who are trapped in the ultimate outer orbit, at risk from their narcissistic behaviours.

This is a truly remarkable book, and an eye-opening and compelling read.

Dr Geoffrey Harvey

Introduction

J onathan Delaney is 48 years old, and is the headmaster of an upmarket school in the South of England. He believes himself to be an exceptionally fine looking man (even though he is a little rotund). Having said that, charisma does ooze from his every pore and, should you ever meet him, you would definitely find yourself chortling at his jokes, even if he does seem a little 'full of himself'.

His grand oak panelled office is the most salubrious room in the whole school, and it is filled with impressive leather-bound tomes of everything from literary classics to science books. Jonathan is a self proclaimed 'polymath', and he'll tell you that he has read every single volume on those shelves. But Jonathan will be sure to inform you that he takes no credit for his extraordinary intelligence, and that it was inherited from his great grandfather, a renowned intellectual, whose stone bust takes pride of place by the fireplace.

A staunch traditionalist, Jonathan is rarely seen in anything other than his trademark three-piece pinstriped suits, which are custom tailored in London. If you are a prospective parent, viewing the school for your child, he will sweep grandiosely into the marble floored waiting room, with a huge beam on his face, and call out your name in his unmistakable booming voice. And, if you happen to be extremely observant, you might glimpse Mollie, his new receptionist, swooning just perceptibly as he vigorously shakes your hand. You might also notice the two secretaries behind the glass partition to the office exchanging the tiniest of withering looks.

Jonathan will insist on giving you a personal guided tour of the school, chest puffed out as he struts like a peacock past the 'biggest swimming pool in the area', the 'finest squash courts' and the 'most well-equipped science labs'. Taking barely a breath between sentences as he leads you onwards, he will regale you with stories of his own school days, the well-known people he associated with whilst there, and the prominent alumni of this school. But, to his credit, he's good with the 'little people' too, as you'll discover when he regally waves at the school gardener, and bestows upon him a "Morning Phil! Excellent work, marvellous, marvellous! Do carry on!"

If you chance upon any pupils during your tour, he will be sure to make you aware that he knows their names. "Which lesson are you off to now, Harry?" "What about you Mimi? Very good, very good..."

And as you scurry after him (he's remarkably quick-footed for a man of his diminutive height), you may momentarily lose sight of him, as he unexpectedly bursts into classrooms where lessons are in progress. The sound of the scraping of chairs across the floor will guide you to him at such times, as pupils reflexively jump to their feet and stand to attention.

"Fourth Years!", he will boom with a flourish of his hand, looking terribly pleased at being greeted in this way, "Do sit." You might feel a little flustered at suddenly having the eyes of twenty adolescents upon you, but Jonathan will be oblivious to this. Instead, he'll subject you to a display of lighthearted banter with the awkwardly smiling teacher, who is having to play along with the imposition. There can be absolutely no doubt that Jonathan Delaney loves an audience, and being the most important person in the school.

Jonathan doesn't really have many teaching duties these days, and so when he isn't striding around the school, chatting with staff, or having appointments with parents, he spends his time playing golf and hobnobbing with the wealthy locals at the golf club. He considers himself to be the highest authority on all things to do with education, and his ambition is to be interviewed on the TV or radio, like another local headteacher. At headteachers' conferences he genially slaps this particular chap on the back and ingratiates himself with him, but behind his back he tells others that he is just an attention seeker, who is actually jealous and in awe of *him*.

Jonathan very much thinks of himself as a 'man of the people'. He is a regular at the local village pub, where he is treated like a hero. Jonathan likes to think he can talk to anybody from any walk of life, and in the pub he greets people loudly, and claps them on the back whilst waiting for his drink. After some raucous banter, he will always make his way to the winged chair that seems to be reserved for him, lean back expansively in it and hold court. The locals love it, and they hang upon every word of this man of superior intellect, feeling flattered that he talks to them. After all, he's a local celebrity.

I do not expect you to be surprised to hear that Jonathan Delaney is a narcissist — he fits the commonly held stereotype perfectly. He's vain, extroverted, charismatic, self-important, attention seeking and a name dropper, just for starters. But this type, referred to by psychologists as the 'Exhibitionist Narcissist', is actually just *one of four types* of narcissist — and the other three are very much harder to spot, and just as prevalent.

We'll reconvene with Jonathan (and the people who orbit him) later on. However, it may be useful for you to know that this book is not about harmless people who are just vain or selfish, as Jonathan might, at first glance, appear to be. Nor is it the opposite — a book intent on making you believe that there are 'evil' people lurking around every corner, luring you into their web of lies and deceit, so that you quake in your boots, too terrified to leave the house.

But it *is* a book that exposes a global phenomenon which hides in plain sight, adversely affecting individuals and society alike. The fact is this: narcissists trap people and behave badly towards them. At best, they cause confusion and pain. At worst, they devastate the lives of those around them, causing irretrievable damage to their physical and mental health.

True 'narcissism' is actually Narcissistic Personality Disorder (NPD), which is a real, diagnosable personality disorder. And it's *much* more common than you probably think, affecting a staggering one in 20 people. Narcissism does not discriminate. It transcends gender, socioeconomic groups and cultures. It can afflict the leader of your country. The local bag lady. Your doctor, your builder, your refuse collector. Your friendly neighbourhood policeman or your yoga teacher. Your 'nasty' boss or your 'nice' co-worker. Your hot date. The people you love — your mother, your father or your sibling — and even your soulmate.

Meet Laura, who I sat next to on an interconnecting flight to South Carolina some years ago.

Laura was in her early sixties, perfectly turned out, and had a soft Texan accent. In London, if you speak to a stranger on any form of public transport you are regarded as a dangerous lunatic and instantly shut down with an incredulous, frosty stare — so it was a pleasant surprise when this lady with the warm smile was up for a chat to pass the time.

But it became noticeable that between 'normal' bouts of conversation, Laura kept on referring to her *mother*, a retired secretary, whom she spoke of with a mixture of pride and disappointment.

She talked about the things her mother had done and the things she had said. Of the disapproval she would have to endure if her mother found out that she was on her way to a solo beach holiday, even at her age. Laura disclosed that her longest relationship had lasted five years, but that her mother had felt that the man in question was 'not good enough', and so it had come to an end. Several times Laura insisted that she was happy single and childless (although she did later admit that she was thinking about joining a dating agency, just to 'see what's out there', and it was impossible not to notice how taken she seemed with the sweet little baby across the aisle from her).

It transpired that Laura's mother had brought her up believing that her father had left when she was a few months old, and that he had wanted nothing to do with her. But when, out of the blue, he contacted Laura when she was 18, she heard a different version of events — that her mother had ended the relationship and kept Laura away from *him*. He claimed that her mother had left him for her wealthy (and married) boss, but when the brief relationship failed, she had demanded that he come back and 'try again'. Her fury at his refusal meant that, despite his efforts, he was completely shut out of his own daughter's life.

Laura, distressed and confused, had done what any eighteen-year-old would do, and angrily confronted her mother. But she denied it all, and wept disconsolately, telling Laura that she felt betrayed by her only daughter. How could Laura be so ungrateful to the person who had brought her up and given up everything for her? What was the point of her going on living if this was how she was to be treated? Laura, distraught at causing her mother so much pain, agreed to never speak of her father again, and when he died a few years ago she found out by stumbling upon his obituary in the newspaper. She told me that a day hadn't gone by in her recent years that she hadn't regretted not getting to know him.

When the airplane snack arrived, a pastrami sandwich, Laura guiltily divulged that her mother had raised her as a strict vegetarian, and had no idea that she ate meat. She was never going to tell her, seeing as her lifestyle was already subjected to intense scrutiny and criticisms of unhealthiness. From the fatalistic way in which she spoke, it seemed that on some level Laura actually *believed* these criticisms, and was expecting to drop dead at any minute. It seemed unlikely, given her commitment to being teetotal, her athletic frame, her running habit, and the dubious-sounding green vegetables she said she juiced into her drinks.

Not having the strength to stand up to her mother was clearly a recurring theme throughout Laura's six decades of life. But, oddly, even when telling this tragic story, she didn't speak of her mother with a resentful tone — but with one more of helplessness, mixed with admiration.

This is exactly the sort of tale that causes the familiar sirens to wail in anyone who is interested in NPD. The criticisms, the put downs, the

9

invalidation. The controlling behaviours, the victim playing, the lies and the gaslighting. Not to mention the obvious fact that Laura's world had been revolving exclusively around her mother for the whole of her life — so much so that her nagging, critical voice accompanied Laura everywhere she went, no matter how far apart they were, even at altitude.

Laura thought that her mother had got worse with age, and described how these days she would call her up and demand that she drop whatever she was doing to help her organize something, or make a lunch for her and her friends. How she would fake having a poor memory to get attention, and even arrange herself at the bottom of the stairs in a crumpled heap when she knew Laura was visiting, for maximal effect and sympathy.

If you didn't know about narcissism, as Laura didn't, it would be easy to assume that her mother was 'complicated', just 'not very nice' or 'a bit mad' — all labels that would not only be *wrong*, but unhelpful.

Laura had thought for all her life, as most do, that it was her *own* fault, and that she should keep trying harder to please her mother. That she was all the things that her mother told her she was. That she didn't have the right to start living her life on her own terms.

I had had many casual conversations with those in relationships like this prior to this interaction with Laura, but, as a family doctor, I had always been plagued by a deep discomfort about 'diagnosing' someone I had never even met. This had always prevented me from sharing my suspicions. But over time, I had come to realize that narcissists, like psychopaths, hardly ever present to professionals to get a diagnosis of their own volition. After all, a narcissist's narcissism usually *works for them,* as I will explain later. So, was it morally right for me to continue to keep my counsel in these situations, knowing what an enormous difference one word could potentially make to these people's lives?

By the time the plane had begun its descent through the cloudless sky into Charleston, phone numbers had been exchanged and Laura was clutching a paper napkin with the question 'narcissistic personality disorder?' scrawled on it. Although the professional guilt weighed heavily on me, the thunderbolts I was waiting to be struck by never came.

And, a few months later, I heard from Laura. She told me that, having researched narcissism, she was having therapy with an American psychologist who understood the condition. She was full of gratitude, and said that she had been 'set free'. She was finally able to understand what she had been subjected to her whole life, and how it had affected her ability to form close relationships with others. She was learning to set boundaries with her mother and had even started to date again.

Laura proved to me, back then, that it's never too late to benefit from understanding NPD, and this was the turning point for me, as well as her. It marked the time when I decided to exclusively focus on educating and helping the unwitting victims of those who would qualify for a diagnosis of narcissistic personality disorder (whether or not they had received a formal diagnosis). I'm pleased to report that the thunderbolts still haven't got me.

But how might this be relevant to *you*? I've thought a lot about the messages we constantly receive these days, in our inboxes and social media feeds. We unwittingly consume a diet of toxic positivity. We are told to be unfailingly kind, forgiving and compassionate, even to those who do us wrong. We are given messages of 'empowerment' and told that only *we* hold all the cards to our life. That *we* spin the wheel of our fortunes. That the only thing holding us back is *ourselves*. But what is the deeper implication here? To my mind, what this is really telling us is that if we mess things up, it's *completely on us*.

Now all this stuff is well and good in a narcissist-free world. But shouldn't we be allowed to entertain another notion too? The notion (and I say this in a whisper) that *other people in our lives* might be partially to blame for our failures, our disappointments and our pain?

Shouldn't we be allowed to take a closer look at the seemingly 'complicated' people we know — who blow hot and cold, who disparage us and hurt us, but then win us over time and again? The people we constantly try so hard to please? The people who make us feel confused? Fed up? Not good enough? Uncherished, even? The people we forgive, and maybe even rescue, endlessly? Shouldn't we be allowed to at least consider whether *they* have more to answer for than we previously realized?

> *"True 'narcissism' is actually Narcissistic Personality Disorder, a real, diagnosable condition."*

I believe that millions of us across the globe have inadvertently fallen into The Narcissist Trap. Could it be that *you* have too?

I invite you on a voyage of discovery, during which I will introduce you to the different types of narcissist who may be passing below your radar. I'll deconstruct their behaviours, and show you how to protect yourself from them. I'll help you to *understand* these types — because, as you will learn, they rarely have insight into themselves. Perhaps you will learn that the 'complicated people' you know are actually not so complicated after all.

1

The Great Pretenders

Do *you* secretly feel as though you are a bit special? At the beginning of my talks I often ask the audience for a show of hands from 'all those who secretly feel as though they are a bit special'. I'm sure it will come as no surprise to you that hardly anyone ever puts their hand up, and that instead I am met with a very nervous collective titter. Let's face it, very few people are going to admit to such a thing in an auditorium, whether it's full of colleagues or strangers — but it helps me make an important point.

Because here's the thing. Research has shown that *most people* secretly feel as though they are a bit special. This phenomenon is known as the 'better than average effect'. And in fact, believing this about yourself has been proved to actually be good for you. It leads to better physical and mental health, better relationships and it may even mean that you live longer.

So, if *you* secretly feel as though you are a bit special, you can now breathe a sigh of relief. And, you can be fairly sure that this means that you are not a narcissist. *Because narcissists secretly feel as though they are <u>not</u> special, regardless of how they might present themselves to the world.*

Think back, if you will, to Jonathan Delaney, the pompous but superficially likeable headmaster you met in this book's introduction. On the surface, his grandiosity looks real. He looks like he believes himself to be special — superior even. But, as with all types of narcissist, this is merely a defence.

All narcissists actually have low self-esteem and feelings of underlying shame and unworthiness, mostly as a result of their difficult childhoods. They do not feel like they are truly 'enough'. However, narcissists cannot bear to *actually feel* these feelings. To them, feeling this way threatens their very existence — it feels like an existential crisis, a thing to be avoided at all costs.

And so narcissists construct a 'false persona', which they hold up to the outside world, and hide behind. And the four types of false persona look very different from each other indeed.

The false persona of the Exhibitionist Narcissist might come across as jokey, extrovert and charming, like headmaster Jonathan Delaney. They might be visibly vain and haughty. They might work hard to achieve status and wealth and rise to positions of great power.

The Closet Narcissist constructs a very different false persona to hide behind. They do not like to be seen to be openly hogging the limelight, and can seem introverted, shy and self-effacing. They may play the victim with quiet aplomb, with mystery illnesses, pain, or difficulty coping with the unfairness of life's vicissitudes. They usually attach themselves to someone who they, or society, see as special.

The Devaluing Narcissist (also known as the Malignant Narcissist) hides behind a different false persona altogether. This type comes across as being openly toxic — shaming, ridiculing, badmouthing and criticizing others with abandon.

And the final type, the Communal (or Altruistic) Narcissist, portray themselves as the consummate do-gooder, through charity work, public acts of benevolence, religion, or perhaps by working in the helping professions.

Narcissists are the Great Pretenders. Their false personas are, for the most part, utterly convincing. But narcissists require external validation from the outside world to keep this false persona going – they need other people to believe in their false persona, *so that they can believe in it too.* This image that they put out to the world is like a suit of armour — it prevents them from having to feel their true feelings of shame, worthlessness and inadequacy.

So narcissists do *not* feel special at their core — and they spend their entire lives trying to get this feeling of specialness from *others*, in sneaky (and not so sneaky) ways. Narcissists exploit others and, very often, even *abuse* people to this end.

> *"The image that they put out to the world is like a suit of armour — it prevents them from having to feel their true feelings of shame, worthlessness and inadequacy."*

Would you know a narcissist if you saw one?

Having briefly read about the four major false personas that narcissists employ, you may now be questioning your previous beliefs about narcissism. When I ask most people to think of a narcissist, and describe the kind of image they conjure in their mind's eye, I get a variety of responses, many of which are at the extreme end of narcissism or even psychopathy. Dictators, cult leaders and crazed megalomaniacs are commonly mentioned. Serial killers and perpetrators of mass genocide usually make an appearance — and politicians always do.

But if I asked you to summon images from closer to home, who might you suspect? The pouting girl in the tight top, splattering pics of herself all over your Instagram feed, all collagen and false eyelashes; the sort whose self-esteem seems to be dependent on 'likes' and comments from people she barely knows? The chap who ghosted you after three perfect dates, driving off into the sunset in his flashy car? Your egocentric sister, with her penchant for designer bags and social climbing? Your aggressive ex-wife, who took you for everything you had, just like she said she would?

Are these people narcissists? Well, possibly yes — but also possibly no. Firstly 'everyday narcissists' are often far less obvious than you might think. But secondly, looking at the examples above, it's important to realize this: you can be vain and not be a narcissist. You can be mean and not be a narcissist. You can be selfish and not be a narcissist. You can covet high end goods and an affluent lifestyle and not be a narcissist. You can even be all of these things combined, and *still* not be a narcissist.

The fact is this — not everyone who is superficial, egotistical, unpleasant or unreliable is a narcissist, and nor is every great leader, public speaker or extrovert.

The 'buzzword' factor

We also need to talk about the 'narcissist' word itself, because we have been using it incorrectly in recent times. Even the gold standard book of words and meanings, the Oxford English Dictionary, mis-defines a narcissist as '*having or showing an excessive interest in or admiration of oneself and one's physical appearance*'.

I'd give that definition a two out of ten, and would scribble lengthy corrections all over it in red pen (if I hadn't already set fire to the relevant page).

For those of us working in the field of narcissism, battling these misconceptions is a constant endeavour. But you may be wondering why I seem so miffed that our modern culture has misappropriated the term. Well, I believe that in doing so, we have *undermined the seriousness of what true narcissism is and how dangerous it can be.*

It matters to know when you are dealing with a real narcissist (a person who would qualify for a diagnosis of Narcissistic Personality Disorder) because they behave in ways which require a specific action plan, so you don't get drawn into the manipulations and the mind games. You need to be able to recognize them in order to protect yourself from their subtle exploitation, which can do so much damage to your life and your mental and physical health, *without you even realizing it*.

Whether your connection is personal or professional, the fact is that you can forget about authentic, mutually fulfilling relationships with a true narcissist, and you can forget about ever getting closure, or an apology, if you walk away from one.

These ubiquitous narcissists are dream-stealers. They are saboteurs. Little by little they erode their victims' self-esteem and they turn them into shadows of their former selves, especially those closest to them. They will make you question your competence and abilities — and ultimately your *reality* — so that you come to doubt yourself.

They will control you, usually covertly. They will trample right over your boundaries, and exploit your generous, kind or forgiving nature. They are 'future-fakers', keeping you hooked with false promises they have no intention of really keeping. They seek out your vulnerabilities under the guise of caring and then they weaponize them against you. They can lie to you with complete conviction because they believe their lies at the time they are telling them, often using a nugget of truth to add credibility.

They lack empathy, and so they cannot feel your pain. And because they cannot feel your pain, they cannot really *care* about you. Most devastating of all, if you are the partner or child of a narcissist, and contrary to everything you might hope and believe, they cannot love — not as you can, anyway.

We will look at how narcissists are created in Chapter 3, but for now let's meet Lina, our Closet Narcissist. This subtle type of narcissist very often goes unrecognized for the whole of their lifetime, as they go about trying to obtain their feelings of specialness in covert ways.

THE CLOSET NARCISSIST

Lina is 42 years old, but her combination of South Asian skin and a rigorous skincare routine means that she could easily pass for a 32-year-old. These days she speaks the King's English in a soft, slightly breathy voice, which belies her working class roots, and she looks up at people through her long eyelashes shyly, with her head tilted ever so slightly downwards. At first, it's endearing, how self-effacing and demurely she comes across, and her occasional childlike giggle is initially rather sweet. Lina has never been one to stand in the spotlight, and you can't help but be drawn to her quiet and easy manner when you first meet her.

When Lina brought Raj home to meet her parents, they were delighted — a handsome dentist, who was in the process of setting up his very own dental surgery! Lina's shopkeeper parents had worked hard all their lives, but they had always wanted so much more for Lina. But Lina had never been an academic girl, and university had never really been an option, so they were particularly thrilled at the thought of Raj as their son-in-law.

Things had been hard for Raj in recent years, as he had lost both parents to cancer. To make matters worse, when Raj met Lina, he had just come out of a six-year relationship with his dental school sweetheart. When his fiancée had broken off their engagement to take up a dentistry job in the USA, his heart had been shattered. He hadn't been ready for a new relationship, but he had agreed to meet Lina on a blind date anyway, expecting nothing to come of it.

Lina was the very first person that he had dated after his breakup, and he found himself opening up to her about his heartbreak. She listened intently, and consoled him for his losses. She was kind and caring, and she understood that he needed time to heal before he even thought about another relationship. But Raj was lonely, and he found himself spending almost every evening with Lina, just talking and walking arm in arm in the warm summer evenings.

Lina was an excellent cook, and Raj very definitely was not, so as the evenings drew in they would meet in the supermarket after work, buy ingredients and go back to Raj's flat, where Lina would cook delicious Indian food, as Raj caught up with paperwork. Gone were the instant noodles and the takeaway kebabs, replaced with fare that even Raj's mother would have been pleased with. Then they would talk, late into the night, about what they both wanted from life — and Raj was surprised and pleased at how similar their visions of the future were.

Things were easy with Lina, in contrast to with his former fiancée, who had been hotheaded and competitive. Here there was no competition. Lina had her role, and Raj had his. After just four months, now head over heels in love, Raj decided to ask Lina to move in with him, and they married a year later.

Lina, a Hindu, would tell him in the early days of their relationship that Parvati, the Goddess of love, would visit her in her dreams, and tell her that she had been sent to heal Raj of his pain. And to Raj, meeting this compassionate, shy person who couldn't do enough for him, did indeed feel like fate.

Two pregnancies and births quickly followed, and Lina outwardly relished her role of mother and housewife. By this time Raj's dental practice was up and running, and the money was coming in – and for the first time in her life, Lina told Raj, she felt that she was where she truly belonged. The truth was that Lina had secured the status that she had always secretly believed she should have.

She would buy the children and Raj expensive clothes from Harrods, and Raj was surprised to discover that the children's pushchair with all its attachments cost nearly as much a secondhand car would have. But Lina's parents would always thank him for making her so happy and her father would slap him on the back, beaming, congratulating him on his success. They were, after all, *his* family now.

If Raj ever brought up her spending, Lina would point out that *she* only wore modestly priced clothes herself, often bought from sales racks or the supermarket, and this was true.

Lina piled on the weight after her pregnancies, and would complain of sore knees and feet, and Raj would often come home to a bomb site. Lina would be sitting in front of the TV, toys strewn everywhere, with the children in dirty nappies, running amok. She'd rarely have anything prepared for the children's meal, and Raj would find himself giving them cheese on toast, and then bathing them, ready for bed. "What a day it's been," Lina would say, "I'm exhausted." She rarely cooked now, and Raj either cobbled something together or they would have a takeaway. Lina would be in bed by 9 pm, snoring away. How different things were from just a few years ago — but Raj just put it down to the pressures of parenthood.

When it was Lina's turn to host a mother and child coffee morning, however, things were very different. The house would be gleaming. The children would be dressed in their best clothes, hair shiny and neat, and Lina would have made her own cookies, cakes and pastries, which would be laid out in tiered displays on her dining room table. Tea would be drunk out of the fancy china cups that she had always aspired to own, with matching side plates. Lina even had tasteful cake forks and crisp cotton napkins at the ready. "Oh this!" she would say with coy modesty, "It's nothing! Please — do try a millefeuille! Or perhaps one of these Indian sweets?" She made it look easy on the surface, but no one had seen the stressed days of preparation that had preceded such events. And it was Raj who was always tasked with the clearing up, once he had returned from work.

And when it came to the children's birthday parties, Lina would really pull out all the stops. Children's entertainers, jugglers, bouncy castles and face painters would take up residence in her enviable garden. She would prepare an impressive buffet, and everyone would comment on her wonderful hostess skills. The thought that they were secretly jealous pleased Lina, but she would never dream of saying anything, other than to her mother. "You're a lucky man, Raj!" his friends would tell him.

But Raj did not feel so lucky. Apart from when anyone else was looking, Lina was lazy and messy. Both spare rooms were piled high with clothes that didn't fit, that she had bought in the sales but couldn't be bothered to return. The kitchen was always in a state, the bins overflowing and the dishwasher not loaded. The interiors magazines that she was so fond of were strewn about, open, and the doorbell would constantly be ringing with deliveries of things they didn't need, including clothes and shoes for himself.

Raj also noticed that Lina really didn't like it if he didn't wear the exact combination of clothes she had put out for him to wear the night before. She considered it to be part of her role, as a wife and mother, to remove this burden of having to choose what to wear from her family. He tried to feel grateful, but sometimes he just wanted to wear what *he* wanted to wear without having to justify it, and without being made to feel guilty for not appreciating Lina's efforts. As the children got older this became a problem for them too, as their own choices in clothing were deemed to be 'common' and 'low class'.

In the toddler years Raj would often come home to find that Lina was out shopping, and his mother-in-law was babysitting, washing, ironing and sweeping. Raj was mortified at times like this, but Lina refused to let him get a cleaner. "I don't want strangers coming in here," she would argue. "I have my pride…" Raj felt as though they were exploiting her ageing mother, however, and took even more upon himself to assuage his guilt.

Even though Raj was run ragged, if he was so much as to leave a damp towel on the bathroom floor by mistake, Lina would sulk. "I do so much for everyone," she would sniff. "Nobody appreciates what I do." "I've only ever supported you in whatever you want," she would say, tearfully, feeling well and truly taken advantage of. She would follow this up by moving to the spare room for two or three days, barely speaking to Raj, so deep was her resentment and hurt.

And Raj didn't like the way she could be with the children either. Arun, the oldest, was the apple of her eye. "One day you are going to be a dentist, just like your Daddy!" she would tell him, from the day he was born. "Or maybe even a doctor! Even better!" Whatever Arun did, he was the best at, in her view. She enrolled him in cricket lessons as soon as he could walk, and got him into the junior chess club from the age of five, where he did very well, much to Lina's delight.

But it was a very different kettle of fish for their daughter, Laila. Laila was a skinny little girl, who needed glasses from an early age, and had the great misfortune of having darker skin than her brother. In Lina's culture, fair skin was associated with beauty and status, and Laila was a desperate disappointment in this regard. Where Arun could do no wrong, Laila could do no right, and Lina would shame, ridicule and criticize her constantly. "Arun was reading fluently at your age," she would say, when Laila was just five. "I suppose I shouldn't be surprised that you didn't win," she once sighed, when Laila came second in the egg and spoon race. "So unathletic…"

Arun's drawings would always get pride of place on the fridge, whereas Laila's would be tossed into the recycling with barely a glance, and a 'hmmph' at best. "You'll never amount to anything if you keep going like this," she would tell her all the way through her childhood, slathering sun lotion on her all year round, in a desperate bid to stop her from getting even darker. "Eat, eat!" She would shout impatiently at her, even when she was being spoon fed in her highchair, "People will think I am starving you with those skinny legs…"

Today Laila is fifteen and suffers from anxiety, depression, and anorexia nervosa, but Lina refuses to believe these diagnoses. "You are just a moody teenager…" she will tell her dismissively. "Happiness is a *choice* — you should just snap out of this nonsense." "Stop pushing your food around on your plate and JUST EAT. Do you know how long it took for me to make this? I have toiled all of your life, just giving, giving, giving, and *this* is how you repay me?"

When Laila rebelled against her mother's insistence that she wore her hair long, getting it chopped into a pixie crop one day after school, Lina was predictably apoplectic with rage, but the usual pattern followed, as Raj stepped in on Laila's behalf.

At these times, Lina retreats into hurt mode, piling on the guilt. "What did I do wrong? Tell me where I went wrong? I have sacrificed so much for this family, for you. Only Arun appreciates me. You would all be better off without me. Is that what you want? For me to just go? You will be sorry when I am dead..." she sobs, as if her whole world has come tumbling down. At these times everyone jumps to console her, ashamed that they have hurt her so badly, proffering tissues, tears and hugs.

But whilst Lina is intolerant of anyone else's illnesses, her own are a different matter, and she groans and sighs with every minor movement. She is in constant pain from her knees and feet, although the doctors haven't been able to find the cause. "I am an enigma," she regularly says, shrugging with a hopeless air. Lina also insists that she can't eat wheat or dairy, that caffeine doesn't agree with her and that she is pescatarian.

If she goes out for a meal, in addition to these dietary requirements, she will always ask for an alteration in some way, smiling sweetly at the waiter. "I'll have the fish, but could you put the parsley in a little dish on the side, finely chopped?" "Would you make sure the baby new potatoes are peeled?" And could I have rocket in the salad instead of the lamb's lettuce?" The more salubrious the restaurant, the more modifications will be required.

When Raj's 40th birthday came round, Lina's mystery aches became too bad for her to be able to organize a celebration, so the staff at the dental practice decided to throw a surprise evening party there instead. Laila and Arun were enlisted to help, and the practice manager ran things with military precision, organizing food, music, decorations and tasteful invitations.

Somehow, however, Lina let it slip to Raj that this was being arranged, spoiling the surprise, but Raj was delighted anyway. Lina had been tasked with getting Raj to the party, but on the day, everything seemed to go wrong. Raj's car keys had somehow fallen under the sofa, and took ages to find, and Lina couldn't decide which dress to wear and kept changing. She curled her hair but then decided it would look better straight, and so had to re-wash and dry it. Raj was getting more and more impatient as the time ticked on, and an argument ensued, much to his regret. When they eventually arrived at the party, they were over an hour late — but all was forgiven when Lina limped in on crutches, ahead of Raj, smiling shyly. Raj duly feigned surprise, and the party was off to a start.

Brave Lina, incapacitated by pain, was waited on hand and foot by the practice staff, who even opened up the drug cupboard to get her some painkillers — but in the end the pain won out and she was driven home early, by one of the nurses. When Raj returned from the party she was in the spare room again, refusing to answer him in anything other than monosyllables. Days later he found out that he should *never* have danced 'in that way' with his receptionist.

In spite of the terrible time Lina had had, she was still able to post lovely pictures of the event on Facebook, with the caption "My wonderful husband's surprise 40th birthday! Thank you to everyone who came!" The 'likes' came flooding in, as they always did for Lina's posts, which portrayed her family life as one of wealthy, happy perfection. It was interesting that she didn't correct anyone who assumed that *she* had planned the party, though. And why was it that, although Lina had hundreds of friends on Facebook, they were conspicuously few and far between in real life?

Technology has been a mixed blessing for their family. Lina insists upon tracking everyone through their phones, on the grounds that she is 'worried about them', and will ring and message them several times a day. If they don't reply immediately, and she can see that they are online or have read her message, her texts will become more insistent and demanding. Lina is not very good at being on her own in the house, and every now and then she will imply that there is an emergency, and then switch her own phone off. One of them still rushes home, worried that this could be the time she's not actually crying wolf.

Even though she's still young, Lina has given up driving completely. It happened slowly — first she said she was too scared to drive at night. Then driving on motorways was out. After this, turning right became an issue, leading to tortuous lengthy routes having to be planned out. Raj wonders whether he is being uncharitable when he feels a bit used and controlled by Lina's insistence that he drive her everywhere. "Jenni's husband doesn't mind driving *her* around" she will say, of one of the dads from school, who looks like a younger version of George Clooney. In fact, Raj has noticed that it's always 'Jenni's husband this' or 'Jenni's husband that' these days — but he knows that Lina would never have the courage to speak to the man, and he is just the latest in a line of men that she has worshipped from afar. *She just needs more attention and sympathy from me,* he chastises himself at these times, disappointed with his own inadequacy in making her happy.

Lina sees herself as the very model of empathy and generosity. If someone she barely knows dies, she will comfort the relatives with zeal, taking meals to the widowed person and trying to help with the funeral arrangements. She will visit the bereaved family daily and speak to their other relatives on the phone, choking up as she offers her condolences. She will mourn their loss as one might mourn the loss of a best friend, and Raj and the children know better than to question this, even though it seems odd and over-the-top. They just wish that she could be quite so understanding when one of *them* is poorly — and it hasn't escaped their notice how her *own* ailments increase at these times, inevitably requiring much fuss and attention from everyone.

The Closet Narcissist — the poor put-upon victim, who struggles on in the face of adversity, caring and giving. Secretly needing to believe themselves to be special and important, but staying away from the limelight. Basking in the glow of another's status and specialness. Disguising control as 'worry,' and seeking attention in covert ways, such as through mystery illnesses and dietary fads. Portraying an image of the perfect family life, whilst intolerant and dismissive of any of the children's imperfections. Favouring a 'golden child' over the other. Concerned about image and appearance. Jealous of others, but at the same time believing others to be jealous of them. A propensity for social climbing. Selfish, with a belief of being entitled to special treatment. Happy to exploit others behind closed doors, and to take the credit for other's hard work. Although afraid to openly seek attention themselves, resentful when others do. A lack of real empathy for others. Manipulativeness, disguised as 'rescuing' and a desperate need for approval and validation.

2

What's it all about?

The word narcissism, used correctly, actually refers to those with Narcissistic Personality Disorder or NPD, as defined in the Diagnostic and Statistical Manual of Mental Disorders (5th ed.; DSM-5; American Psychiatric Association, 2013). This is the tome in which the official diagnostic criteria for Narcissistic Personality Disorder are laid out. It's the book that psychiatrists and psychologists would use to make a diagnosis of NPD (were a narcissist to present to them for a diagnosis in the first place — altogether another issue, which we'll discuss in a while). We will be heaving it onto the table, blowing off the dust and taking a look at it a bit later on, but for now, let's start with the important basics.

To distill NPD right down, there are four major things that those with NPD exhibit:

- An inability unable to see people (including themselves) as a blend of good and bad traits — they fluctuate between viewing people as either 'all good' or 'all bad' (going from 'hero to zero').
- Low empathy
- A sense of entitlement
- An addictive need to chase feeling special

As I have already mentioned, regardless of outward presentation, *all narcissists actually have very low self-esteem*. Grasping this concept is crucial, because this underpins *every single thing that a narcissist does*.

Think back to Jonathan Delaney, our Exhibitionist Narcissist headmaster. He comes across as arrogant, haughty and self-assured. He struts around, full of confidence, with charisma seeping from every pore. He's a know-it-all, a mansplainer who voices his opinions with unshakeable confidence. It's very hard to see that, beneath that outward image, he is actually a very fragile creature indeed, as a result of how he reacted to his upbringing. His superficial acquaintances would be very unlikely to see that Jonathan, deep down, has a core made of colossal shame, unworthiness and a sense of 'not being enough'.

But critically, this is why he has created his grandiose 'false persona', to project out to the world. Lina, our Closet Narcissist, who you met in the previous chapter, is also hiding behind a false persona — she's superficially sweet, shy and self-effacing.

"Everything a narcissist does is a bid to get external validation."

All narcissists need you, and everyone else, to *believe* in their false persona. To believe that they are all the things that they purport to be. Because if *you* believe in it, *then they can too.*

And they *need* to believe in this false image that they are projecting out to the world, because believing in it stops them from having to face their real feelings of shame, and unworthiness. This facade they hide behind acts as an armour of sorts — protecting them from their own sense of inadequacy.

But although the narcissist's armour has an important function, it doesn't come without its own problems. For a start, it's *inflexible*, restricting the narcissist in all sorts of ways in life, with knock-on effects for those around them. There are things that narcissists simply can't do — such as have true empathy for others, or care deeply about how others are feeling. And secondly, it's designed to be impermeable in *both* directions. So, while it doesn't let the narcissist's true feelings about themselves *out*, it also doesn't really let the world or people *in*.

Narcissists don't have deep friendships, and they are unable to be truly emotionally intimate with others.

But there is an even bigger problem here too. The narcissist's facade, their false persona, this armour — is intrinsically *weak*. It only survives in the presence of external validation. It needs other people to believe in it and constantly validate it to keep it going. Imagine a suit of armour that is continually rusting. You need to keep welding metal over the rust patches and holes to keep it intact, but if you stop, even for a second, the rust holes just keep on coming.

In the same way, the narcissist's false persona needs *continual* propping up from the people around them, to keep it intact. And that can come in the form of attention, adoration, drama, conflict or from other people's fear.

I cannot emphasize the importance of those last sentences enough. Because everything, *everything* a narcissist does is a bid to get that external validation. And attention, adoration, drama, conflict, fear and any other emotional response are what gives the narcissist the thing he or she needs most. This is known as 'narcissistic supply'.

Narcissistic supply is like fuel to a narcissist. They need narcissistic supply like an ordinary person needs oxygen, or food. For a narcissist, if their narcissistic supply is cut off, their false persona becomes weakened and holes develop in the armour. And then it can no longer function as a defence against them feeling their true feelings about themselves.

So, imagine you were to ignore a narcissist, for example. Or inadvertently slight them in some way — maybe you praised someone you didn't know they were jealous of. Perhaps you have shamed them, or even abandoned them. It doesn't have to be intentional, and it doesn't have to be big. What you will have done is injured their false persona — you have inflicted a 'narcissistic injury' upon it. So now it can no longer do its job.

Now the narcissist is being forced to feel their true feelings of shame, inadequacy and worthlessness. And this literally feels like an existential crisis to them. To take a look at what lies within is just too much to bear — so they react in a very predictable way — with 'narcissistic rage'.

Narcissistic rage

This is one of the hallmark behaviours of a narcissist, and you'll definitely know it when you see it. A narcissist in the throes of narcissistic injury and consequent rage gets two things out of it. Firstly, it's a great way to quickly distract themselves from their own inner wounds. And secondly, it's a very effective way of securing a giant hit of restorative narcissistic supply from anyone who might be watching. Imagine you are the partner of a narcissist who is hurling the wedding china across the room, or slashing the sofa, for example. Of course you will be reacting in some way, and the narcissist will be feeding off your reaction. The narcissist's rage will have got them attention, caused drama, and probably caused fear in you — three of the five major sources of narcissistic supply.

These meltdowns can present in various ways, and can resemble toddler style tantrums (tellingly, partners of narcissists often describe them as being like an extra child). A narcissist's rage might also present as open aggression, and may even tip into physical aggression, directed at a person or at objects. Door slamming, wall punching, mug throwing and ripping up other people's work are all examples, but narcissistic rage doesn't have to be physical in nature — it can be a quiet, chilling sort of fury. And it doesn't have to last long either — it can be over in a quick, but scary flash. But it always goes well beyond anger, and it always provokes emotion in the onlooker. But for now, let's meet our next type of narcissist.

THE NARCISSIST TRAP

THE DEVALUING NARCISSIST

Oonagh Campbell-Jones is now 51, and you will never see her without a full face of makeup and perfectly coiffed hair. Born as just plain Oonagh Campbell, she firmly believes that the best thing her poor, put upon husband Geoff ever did for her was to give her a way to hyphenate her surname. Oonagh was brought up on a small farm in Ireland where money was tight, but she knew she was destined for greater things. When she announced her engagement and intended new surname, she was met with squeals of delight from her many younger sisters. "Campbell-Jones — it sounds dead aristocratic!" and "Our Oonagh's an *English lady* now!"

Her father, always one to pour cold water on things, simply looked up from his paper and muttered "Well girls, our Oonagh's always had ideas above her station, so she has…"

And indeed, Oonagh *had* decided that she wouldn't be sticking around in rural Ireland for the rest of her life. She left school aged 16 and, much to her father's disgust, rather than help on the farm, she secured a job in the university library. Come rain or snow, she would cycle three miles down to the bus stop, lean her rusty old bike up against the hedgerow, and catch the first of the three buses she had to get on, in order to reach the city. She quickly became an expert at piling on her make-up on the way there, and wiping off all traces of it on the way home, and she'd spend the rest of the journey absorbed in the books she had borrowed from work. Oonagh was on a mission to 'better herself', and no one was going to get in her way.

After two years, Oonagh's persistence finally paid off. She quite literally bumped into Geoff in the student library, when he took a few steps backwards into her, causing her to drop the enormous pile of books she was carrying. Englishman Geoff was older than Oonagh, and had come to Dublin to do a PhD in Biology. But despite his age, Geoff was awkward and shy, and had never had a real relationship.

31

Flustered, he helped Oonagh pick up the books, thinking that such a beautiful girl like her would never be interested in someone like him.

But Geoff was wrong — she was indeed interested, and he couldn't believe his luck. She was everything he had ever dreamed of. Well-read with a sharp wit — and stunning too, with her flame-red hair, which fell to just above her tiny waist, in natural corkscrew curls.

They soon started spending every lunchtime together, and meeting later too, at the library after she finished work. They'd often go back to his student flat for an early dinner, eating to the soundtrack of his favourite classical music (which no other girl had ever been interested in), until it was time for Oonagh to catch the bus home.

By the time they met, Oonagh had learned how to dress to emphasize her physical attributes. She'd carefully observed the city girls, and devoured the fashion magazines in the staff coffee room where she had been eating her sandwiches. Her hemlines and heels were carefully chosen to show off her long, shapely legs, which she would cross and uncross provocatively, and wide necklines would 'accidentally' slip every now and then, to give a tantalizing glimpse of an alabaster shoulder or cleavage. Oonagh was the sort who just could not stop playing with her red locks either — twirling them in her fingers or pinning them up, only to release them a few minutes later to toss around. And when she ate —well, it was sensuality personified. Geoff, quite understandably, found himself driven wild with desire.

Oonagh made Geoff feel manly and sexy – with her he felt like the best version of himself. She listened to his hopes and his fears, with rapt attention. She even adored listening to him play his violin (he played first violin in the university orchestra and was very accomplished indeed). Geoff had met his soulmate, and according to Oonagh, she had too.

After a month, Geoff took Oonagh to England to meet his parents, who were utterly charmed by the Celtic beauty with the soft accent, who hung upon their son's every word, and gazed at him adoringly.

Looking back, Geoff now knows that he missed a red flag in those early days of their courtship. When Oonagh's younger sister got engaged to her childhood sweetheart of five years, Oonagh was incensed. "How *dare* she? I'm older than her…She should have waited for *me* to get married first…"

Geoff's attempts to rationalize with her, and to calm her were met with footstamping and tears. "You English people don't know anything about it! It's how we do things in Ireland. Who does that Billy White think he is, proposing without even checking with me first? How *dare* he? He's made an utter fool out of me…"

Was she right? Perhaps he *didn't* have the right to comment about her culture. As she raged and ranted, lovestruck Geoff found himself telling himself that she was just a fiery redhead, and that that was what he loved about her. Was he being a fool, getting down on one knee and proposing to her, right then and there, in the university park, with a ring pull from a can of cola for a ring? Was two months just too soon? It didn't feel like it, especially when her tears of frustration turned to those of joy and she declared her undying love for him.

Oonagh got her way, and they married before her sister, just six months later, in a small ceremony in front of only their parents and Oonagh's immediate family. When he asked her why she wasn't inviting her old friends (whom he had never met), should he have considered her responses more carefully? "They're jealous of me. They can't stand the fact that I'm leaving this shithole and moving to London. They just don't know how to be happy for me. They are all losers anyways. I just wouldn't want them there, spoiling our day. Honestly Geoff, they'll just be embarrassments, so they will."

Geoff decided that if she wasn't inviting her friends, he wouldn't invite his either, in solidarity. They'd be able to celebrate properly with them once they were living in England, he told himself.

Oonagh's sister's wedding took place two months later, but Oonagh continued to refuse to be her bridesmaid. "Sure Geoff, I can't condone it — I really can't. That Billy White is just a nobody. She deserves so much more. I just can't go against my principles. I've got to be true to myself, you know?" Geoff was still blinded by love, and decided that it was not his place to interfere. But did he genuinely believe that Oonagh was 'just making an effort for the wedding' when she booked a hairdresser and make-up artist for herself for the day, and put on a show-stopping, figure-hugging white dress? Today he'd hang his head in shame and tell you that he was so smitten that it really did not occur to him that Oonagh was upstaging her sister, on the biggest day of her life.

These days, 30 years on, things are a far cry from those heady days of youth. In fact, things began to change on their honeymoon. Just the day after their wedding, Oonagh started criticizing Geoff's prowess in the bedroom, when she'd never complained before. He was utterly wretched — why was she saying these things? She started ogling other men on the beach, commenting on how muscular they were, knowing perfectly well that Geoff was a bit touchy about his lanky frame. She'd always been more interested in his intellect than his looks — so why the sudden change? But when he looked hurt she just laughed it off dismissively. "Sure Geoff, stop being so oversensitive, will you? It's very unattractive, you know. And anyways, there's nothing wrong with just looking." And she was right. Wasn't she?

Once they moved to London, little by little things continued to deteriorate — so slowly that Geoff just accepted them as normal. The occasional weekends that the couple had enjoyed visiting Geoff's parents got further and further apart. Oonagh would always have something else to do, or worse, cancel at the last minute. Geoff tried everything to encourage her to go, especially as his parents thought *she* was wonderful, and he was their only child.

When Oonagh gave the excuse that the food they served was unpalatable, he'd suggest going out for dinner with them instead. When she said that they were boring, he'd try to entice her with a designer shopping trip at the outlet mall near to their house. When he suggested that they came to visit them instead, so that she could do her own thing whilst they were there, she'd mess up the house in the preceding days and refuse to help him tidy it in preparation. And if Geoff went to see them on his own, Oonagh would be cold and silent toward him for at least a week afterwards, all the while claiming that 'nothing was wrong.' These silent treatments were agonizing for Geoff, and he found himself fawning over Oonagh to try to get back into her good books — bringing her cups of tea, cleaning her car, buying her flowers — but nothing worked. These moods were so destabilizing and upsetting that Geoff started to see his parents less and less, effectively allowing Oonagh to isolate him from them — one of his biggest regrets today.

It became obvious early on that Oonagh was an ambitious lady, and despite her lack of formal qualifications, she climbed the corporate ladder in marketing quickly. It also became clear that, to her, Geoff's job came second. When he was promoted to Head of Pharmacokinetics at a big pharmaceutical company, he came home with a special bottle of champagne, sure that Oonagh would want to celebrate. When he got the text from her saying that she would be a little late, he decided to start making a special celebratory meal — steak, Oonagh's favourite. Although lateness was what he had come to expect from Oonagh, he was sure that today would be different. But he waited. And waited. And waited. She seemed to be receiving his messages on her phone, but she wasn't responding to them, and he was starting to get worried. What if she'd been mugged on the way home, and someone else had her phone? Anything could have happened, especially as no one was answering the office line.

By the time Oonagh rolled in at 10.30pm that night he was so beside himself with worry that he didn't notice that her normally perfect lipstick was a little smeared. Whilst it wasn't unusual for her to work late and not tell him what time she would be home, this was a *special occasion,* and he was sure that something bad must have happened. But no. Oonagh just yawned and said that she'd had important work to do that night, and that it wasn't her fault that it had taken so long. "If I hadn't had to read all those messages from you, I'd have been finished way sooner…" she even had the gall to say.

"God almighty. This steak's dry as a bone. I can't be eating this." Oonagh then complained, prodding it with a knife. "Why'd you keep it in the oven for so long? Anyways, we had pizza in the office, so I'll pass and head on up to bed. And can you turn that bloody classical music off? You know I can't stand it…" Geoff was utterly deflated, and the champagne remained unopened until Oonagh grandly presented it to her company's CEO at his summer barbecue, to much appreciative 'oohing' and 'aahing'.

When other people congratulated Geoff for his promotion in front of Oonagh, she would wrap her arm around him, beaming, and say how proud she was. *Phew!* Geoff would think, relieved — *she does appreciate me after all! I was just being touchy before.* But then, behind closed doors, she would scoff, with a snigger, "Ah Geoff, I think we both know you're not a *proper* scientist."

These occasional public displays of affection, interspersed with humiliations, were all very confusing for Geoff. But Oonagh had had a terrible childhood of harsh poverty, made worse by a vile father. She was *wounded*. Geoff had made his vows — he just had to love her more and everything would eventually be okay. Besides, he was pretty sure that Oonagh was a bit autistic and this explained why she could behave so oddly at times.

But why, although *she* was often late back from work, would *he* be questioned at length about his whereabouts, if he was even five minutes later than expected? At first Geoff had been flattered by this, thinking that it showed how much she cared and worried about him. But as the years wore on, the hypocrisy of it did slowly dawn on him. He would often have to put up with embarrassing tirades over the phone from her, whilst his colleagues tried not to exchange glances at each other, pretending not to hear her vile accusations that he was 'f**king some slag'. At those times he really wished the ground would just swallow him up. And when he did get home, did he know just how abnormal Oonagh's interrogations were? He knew he was terrified of her at these times, that's for sure, especially when she would tell him that his fast breathing rate and increased swallowing was proof that he was lying to her. "Don't think I don't know exactly what is going on in that tiny mind of yours, Geoff" she would say to him at these times, with an intense and chilling steeliness.

At some point in their relationship, Oonagh completely stopped taking her house keys out with her when she left the house, on the grounds that they jangled annoyingly in her bag and the sound gave her intense migraines. In reality, this meant that Geoff had to be home before Oonagh, to let her into the house, if he was to avoid her wrath at being made to wait outside. He had suggested hiding a key for her outside, or giving a key to a neighbour for the rare occasions when he couldn't get back in time for her, but she was adamant that this was completely unsafe and that they would be asking to be burgled. Geoff never did cotton on to what an excellent way she had found to covertly control his movements.

One year he resolved to join a cycling club, after she accused him of 'letting himself go' by putting on a bit of extra weight. The people were welcoming and fun, and he realized how much he had let his social interactions slide. Oonagh didn't actively discourage him until she realized that women were also involved in the club, and that after the cycle ride they would all eat lunch together at a cafe. She was furious with him, and told him that the reason she had agreed to him joining was on the grounds that he would be attending purely for his physical health, and that having lunch with them ('if that was even what he was *really* up to') was ruining their own 'quality time' together. He doesn't quite know when her jealousy stopped feeling like love and turned into an inescapable oppressive weight, but he remembers feeling as if he had no choice but to leave the club, and to forget about ever doing anything outside of work that didn't involve her.

Speaking of social interactions, Oonagh had the remarkable knack of being able to completely change her accent, and her range was impressive. She could go from southern Irish farm girl to English landed gentry in the space of a heartbeat, with all the gradations in between. She could speak softly and liltingly, or at great speed, with machine gun precision, depending on what was required. "Oonagh is like a box of chocolates," Geoff once tried to explain to his mother, misquoting a famous film, "You never know what you're going to get next…"

But one thing never changed — Oonagh believed herself to be vastly intellectual, and she had the bookshelf to prove it. "I'm living proof that university is an utter waste of time," she would declare, in clipped British tones, at the dinner parties they were rarely invited to. "Geoff will tell you — won't you Geoff? What I haven't read simply isn't worth reading."

Oonagh would then go on to quote obscure poetry and literature to prove her point, and then feign incredulity when people didn't recognize the source. "Surely, you can't be telling me that you don't recognize *Ulysses*? Seriously now? And you've a *Master's* degree?" During one such conversation she even proclaimed "I made a decision a long time ago that the day Geoff reads Proust *in French* will be the day that I take his intellect seriously!" She'd then let out little peal of laughter, "And I think we all know that *that* day won't be coming anytime soon, don't we?" Needless to say, the invitations dried up almost completely over time.

She got even worse after a few glasses of wine. At Geoff's pharmaceutical company's Christmas dinner, which she felt very aggrieved at having to attend, she loudly held court. "Tell me, do all of you with PhDs call yourselves 'doctors'? Geoff does. Honest to God, people actually think he's a *real* doctor. I tell you, we were on a plane this once, and he was asked to revive a woman who'd collapsed. It was utterly mortifying, having to explain that he's just in pharmaceuticals. I nearly died *myself* — of the sheer embarrassment!"

And what could Geoff do, other than to sit frozen and red-faced, when she leant conspiratorially over to his boss, with her ample cleavage in full prominence, and whispered, sotto voce, "You know, I used to think that with Geoff, 'still waters run deep'. But I've come to realize that those waters are actually just still…Tell me, Brian…are *you* deep? I bet you are…"

Geoff tried harder and harder, but no matter what he did, as the years wore on he, and almost everyone else they knew, was treated with increasing ridicule and contempt. Nothing anyone did or said was good enough, apart from the occasional new person at work or in the neighbourhood, who Oonagh would idolize, and talk about endlessly in glowing terms — until they too fell off their pedestals and became 'losers'.

She would complain ruefully about anything she could, looking up from whatever classic masterpiece she was reading, as Geoff cleaned up around her, or brought her wine and snacks, tiptoeing around her. One time, she knocked the wine glass (that he'd carefully set in the usual place on her side table) with her elbow, spilling red wine everywhere. "Oh you idiot!" she roared at him, "What a stupid place to put it — that close to me, when I'm busy reading!" Everything had to be his fault, even innocent accidents.

If he ever asked for help with the household chores, she would reply, "I will not be stereotyped Geoff — you know that. We women have to make a stand. We've been the underdogs for far too long, and you should respect my position as a feminist." Was she right? Geoff couldn't tell for sure these days.

But every now and then everything would change, and Oonagh would make him a romantic dinner, and her criticisms would stop for a while. They'd even curl up on the sofa together and watch movies, just like they used to, and go for walks, hand in hand. Oonagh would even ask Geoff to play her something on his violin at these times, something he rarely now did because of her 'sensitive ears.'

See Geoff? he used to say to himself at these times. *Everything is okay after all!* It took decades to accept that these reprises would never last — and that her scorn and mockery would inevitably return.

Geoff's greatest sadness was that they had never had children. When they first met, Oonagh had told him that she dreamed of having a boy and a girl, just as Geoff wanted. She painted a picture of wanting to be a stay-at-home mother, at least for a few years whilst the children were young. They had even talked about baby names in that first year, and they bought a house that had enough rooms for the children. But as the years wore on it became clear that Oonagh's career was more important to her than a family. At first, she simply said that she was not ready to have children, but later, when she was 35 and time was running out, she delivered her biggest blow.

"Oh, come now Geoff, you call yourself an intelligent man. The world's overpopulated for God's sake. It's *unfair* to bring children into it. You're thinking about it all wrong — and you've absolutely no right to tell me what I should do with my womb. Just get a bloody dog if you're that broody…"

Heartbroken, Geoff did just that. And it was from Maisie, a dainty black and white mongrel that he, at last, received the unconditional love so missing from his marriage.

"She never comes to meet *me* at the door when *I* come in…" Oonagh would complain, jealous of their bond. When Maisie grew old and grey, she would tell Geoff that it was 'cruel' to keep her alive. "If it were down to me, I'd just shoot the bloody thing…" she'd say every time she saw Geoff giving Maisie her thyroid tablets. But when the time did eventually come for Maisie to be put to sleep, Oonagh made a big show of tearily leaving work to go home to say her goodbyes.

And when the vet and nurse arrived at the house, brimming with kindness and sympathy, Oonagh took one look at them, and curtly said, "Listen. I grew up on a farm. You don't have to pretend to be sad on my account, okay? So how about I give you permission to drop the act?" Did she notice their eyes widening in dismay? Yes, she did. But she smugly misattributed this to her belief that she had correctly called them out on their insincerity.

At least Oonagh had the decency to stand back and allow Geoff to rest his head on Maisie's and whisper reassuringly to her as she fell asleep for the final time.

But when he let the tears roll down his face, something he had been careful to avoid doing in front of Oonagh for decades, she just stared at him, as though he was a science experiment.

"It's just a *dog*. You can't *love* a *dog* for God's sake…" he heard her muttering incredulously, as she left the house to go back to the office, where she sniffed and dabbed her dry eyes, and basked in the glorious sympathy of anyone who felt brave enough to approach her.

Oonagh has threatened to leave Geoff countless times. He used to feel as though he simply couldn't live without her, and so each time he would beg her to reconsider. But he has finally made his mind up. The next time she brings up leaving, he will agree with her. After years of being told by Oonagh that 'no one else would ever be able to love him', he fully expects to be alone for the rest of his life, but he's accepted that. His bigger problem is his fear of how she will react when she realizes that he is actually leaving — but even he, familiar though he is with her rages and cruelty, won't be prepared for just how bad things will inevitably get when he does finally make a break for it.

The Devaluing Narcissist. Critical and demeaning. Invalidating other people's achievements. Putting people down in order to feel more special themselves. Name-calling ('losers'). Gaslighting others so that they question their own self-worth, their emotions and their opinions. A sense of entitlement resulting in not having to pull one's own weight. Exploitative behaviour. A need to believe that one is intellectually superior. Lateness as a devaluation and control tactic. Silent treatments, as a method to punish and control, and to acquire narcissistic supply from the fawning that results. A cyclical pattern of abuse followed by a period of respite. Love bombing occurring at the beginning of the relationship. A tendency to see people only as either 'all good' or 'all bad'. A pattern of isolating the victim from others. Nonsensical assertions, made with absolute conviction. Control and jealousy. Rage when things do not go their way, or their image of themselves is threatened. A profound lack of empathy, and inability to care about the feelings of others. Derision, ridicule and contempt. Future faking, inventing a dream of shared goals and visions, but never delivering upon it. Destroying the victim's self-esteem so that they feel too weak to leave the relationship. A complete inability to love.

It's time to hit the textbook

According to the Diagnostic and Statistical Manual of Mental Disorders (5th ed.; DSM-5; American Psychiatric Association, 2013), at least five of nine criteria need to be met in order to diagnose NPD. To paraphrase these, the things to look out for are:

- Grandiosity with an exaggerated sense of self-importance. This can show up in outwards behaviours, or can be in fantasy. For example, they might exaggerate their talents, or expect others to recognize them as being superior, regardless of their actual achievements.
- Being wrapped up in thoughts of success, beauty, power or a romanticized notion of love.
- A view that their specialness and uniqueness means that only other people who are special (or who have high status) can understand them, and that they should only be involved with people or institutions of this nature.
- Feeling entitled to special treatment, and for people to simply comply with their wishes.
- Exploiting others, taking advantage of them for their own gain.
- Low empathy, with a limited understanding or concern for other people's needs or feelings.
- Being envious of people, and/or believing that other people are envious of them
- Behaving in an arrogant and haughty way, or having attitudes of this nature
- Needing excessive and constant admiration from others.

If you think back to our Devaluing Narcissist, Oonagh, and consider this list, it's pretty clear that she qualifies for a diagnosis of NPD — there is very little that is subtle about *her*.

But what about Lina, our Closet Narcissist, who you met in Chapter 1? The Closet Narcissists don't want others to see them as arrogant or haughty, but the obvious 'yeses' for Lina include that

- she married Raj, a dentist, because of his high status
- she doesn't really have true empathy (shown by her unwillingness to care for others when they are ill)
- she exploits her mother and Raj who do the housework for her
- she needs to be admired by the other mothers (so hosts impressive coffee mornings and children's parties to gain this admiration)
- she believes that people are secretly jealous of her

It gets a bit trickier when it comes to her grandiose sense of self-importance, because the Closet Narcissists try to hide this from the outside world, but you do get a sense that Lina wants to be recognized as being superior by others, and probably fantasizes about it. We can see that she goes about getting this sense of superiority in sneaky ways, such as through 'bigging up' her son's achievements.

Lina's sense of entitlement also makes an appearance through her manipulation of others. She expects her family to respond to her messages immediately, and ensures that she gets special treatment by feigning mystery illnesses.

The DSM-5 also has an alternative model for diagnosing NPD, which we'll take a very quick look at later on.

3

Where did it all go wrong?

Narcissistic Personality Disorder is thought largely to be a condition that people *develop* in childhood, as a result of their upbringings — although studies involving twins separated at birth also show that some people are genetically predisposed to it. Many things that we humans suffer from are as a result of the combination of nature and nurture, but it seems that in most cases of NPD, it's the nurture element that is most important.

Let's take a trip down memory lane with Jonathan Delaney, our Exhibitionist Narcissist.

Twelve-year-old Jonathan was nervous. Very nervous, in fact. Holding his cricket bat tightly, he took up his position and said a silent prayer to a God he wasn't sure he believed in. This was the second time he had tried to get into the prestigious county cricket team, but he knew that, this time, failure was not an option. His mother would simply do her nut, and his father, who prided himself on his sporting prowess as a young man, would probably say absolutely nothing, but clench his jaw in that way he did when he'd been hopelessly let down. Jonathan didn't know which reaction he dreaded most.

The truth was that Jonathan was *tired*. Life had always seemed to be just one endless loop of activity. He wanted to be able to lie on his bed and stare at the ceiling, just for a bit. But there was always something to do and someone to compete with. Three times a week he would be roused at 6 am to be at swim club by 6.45, where he'd be critiqued, timed and shouted at by Mrs Douglas, his swimming coach (who he'd never actually seen in the water herself). *I bet she can't even swim, the silly cow*, he always thought to himself, as he lowered himself into the pool, teeth chattering. But at least Jonathan had made it into the national squad. His mother had squealed with delight, and phoned everyone she knew, and his father had slapped him on the back, beaming. "I'm proud of you, son" he had said, after taking the obligatory photo for the dining room wall, opposite the trophy collection. But did young Jonathan *himself* feel pride? Or was *relief* the emotion he most commonly felt, each time he successfully met his parents' ever upward-spiralling standards?

Jonathan also excelled at rugby. He much preferred football, but there wasn't time to do both, and he knew that expressing a preference would fall on deaf ears, despite the fact that painful sprains and rugby injuries were a constant issue for him. So Saturdays were always spent in the car, en route to some match or competition or other, his father driving as his mother relentlessly tested him on his Latin, or his French or whatever else he needed to learn to perfection for the following week. Jonathan was in the scholarship class at school and the academic pressures were high, but if he failed to beat Spencer Williams in every test, his mother's disapproval would be palpable. And Jonathan could have sworn that he actually saw her spitting blood when Spencer was given the lead role in the school play over him. He'd felt so ashamed on that occasion that he'd pretended to have a stomach ache, so he didn't have to face their forced conversation at the dinner table. "After all the opportunities we've given him…" he'd once heard his father complain, when he thought he was out of earshot.

And then, to top it all off, there were the extracurricular music demands. But being in the chamber choir (which he hated) and playing the bassoon in the school orchestra was not enough for either of his parents. Auditions for the city choirs and orchestra had already gleefully been put on the kitchen calendar.

But today Jonathan batted like a pro, and sailed into the county cricket team. Giant hugs and smiles were forthcoming, and neither of his parents stopped telling him how much they loved him for the entire evening, repeatedly tousling his hair and planting smiley kisses on his forehead. But Jonathan's mind was already on the next day's maths challenge, which he had to win, if he was to represent the school in the national finals.

Jonathan came to believe that he was only worthy of love and attention if he achieved great things — and specifically only things valued by his parents. He learned that parental love is *conditional*.

These hardworking children, like Jonathan, develop a sense of emptiness and low self-esteem within. They feel they need to appear perfect and successful to the outside world, and they learn to construct an image in line with this. They grow up needing the approval of their parents to feel okay. As adults, they rely upon external validation from everyone else to prop up the image they have created of themselves — so that they can feel emotionally safe.

But what about Lina, our Closet Narcissist? Next, we wind back the clock to visit her in Bradford, in the north of England, just before her tenth birthday.

The sign outside Romesh Mehotra's convenience store simply said "Bradford's Best Shop." He was a man of superlatives, especially when it came to his own endeavours and achievements.

"I came to this country with one pair of trousers and a T shirt," he would tell little Lina, gesturing grandly to his surroundings, as she restocked the cramped shop's shelves with toothpaste, carbolic soap and tampons. "And look at me now, hey?"

Lina adored her father. Even aged nine she loved to be in the shop with him, watching him interact with the customers, and listening to his anecdotes. She was quite sure he was the cleverest man in the whole world.

A little bell was attached to the shop door, heralding the arrival of each customer, and Romesh would quickly arrange his features into a wide toothy smile every time it rang. He knew the names of all his customers, and had a special greeting for every single one of them. "Mr Singh, you old dog, eh?" he said every week, as he handed over a bottle of whiskey in a brown paper bag to the local tailor with a huge wink. "Don't worry, your secret's safe with me, my brother!"

"Mrs Banerjee! Welcome, welcome!" he would bow to the old lady as she squeezed her ample frame past the tinned tomatoes, "Tell me, how can it be that you look more beautiful with each passing day?" Although Mrs Banerjee would be tutting with mild embarrassment, Romesh knew that she was secretly flattered. "Just the five samosas today?"

"You see Lina?" he would say, once the shop was empty again "*This* is how you do customer service." Now run upstairs and tell mama that we need more samosas. Quick, quick."

Lina was a sweet looking thing, with huge brown eyes, a delicate jawline and long black pigtails. One Saturday she'd got her mother to put big ribbons in her pigtails, at both the top and the bottom, and gone downstairs to the shop. Her new look had gone down a storm with the customers, and drew many comments such as "Little Lina you are too cute! I could just eat you!" and the like. But with each comment her father seemed increasingly displeased, and eventually ordered her to take the ribbons out. "What is all this, look at me, look at me, eh?" he spat at her, meanly. "Get upstairs, now. And don't let me see you looking like this again."

Lina's father was an Exhibitionist Narcissist, and Lina's role was clear — to worship and adore him, and never, ever to take the spotlight away from him. These children are taught that seeking admiration for themselves will be punished by criticisms, and that they must never out-do their narcissistic parent, on any front. When they toe the line, they are rewarded with praise, attention and validation but, at the same time, they unconsciously learn narcissistic behaviours. They desperately want to be special, and may fantasise about feeling this way, but they learn to achieve this feeling of specialness by obtaining external validation in *covert* ways, including by playing the victim, to gain attention and narcissistic supply.

In adulthood they shy away from the spotlight, instead associating with others with status, so that the other person's specialness rubs off on them. But, because they are relying on the other person's specialness, perfection and uniqueness to feel okay themselves, they are disappointed when the other person's human flaws come out. They are more prone to bouts of depression than the other types of narcissist because of this.

And what was life like in 1970s rural Ireland, where Oonagh Campbell-Jones, our Devaluing Narcissist, started off life?

Campbell's Dairy Farm had been ailing for years, and farmer John Campbell was permanently exhausted. Cows would need to be retrieved from fields and ditches at all hours, when fences came down in storms. Milking times were frequent, and at antisocial hours, and the continual hard labour of cleaning up cow excrement whilst being lashed by the rain was not for the fainthearted, leading to a high turnover of farmhands. And during calving seasons even less sleep was to be had, as one never knew when a birth would have complications.

Perhaps it was no wonder that John Campbell was continually on edge and irritable. Born and bred in southern Ireland, he came from a long line of dairy farmers, each as moody as the last, and each with a taste for liquor. But he knew where he came from, and was proud of it. John Campbell had never left Ireland, and he saw absolutely no reason to ever do so.

It continually irked him that his wife had only produced girls — and seven of them, at that. "What f**cking use is this lot gonna be to me, you stupid bloody woman?" he had angrily asked his wife after the third daughter was born, whilst she was still lying spreadeagled on the kitchen table, waiting for the midwife to finish delivering the placenta.

Oonagh was the oldest daughter, which meant that she was put to work on the farm before the others. She started by cleaning milk pails at seven years old. By the time she was 13, she hated her life, and longed to escape. She would moan to her sisters about her father's demands on her. "Sure, at least Daddy knows your *name…*" some of the younger ones would occasionally retort.

Their mother was a kind woman, but with serial pregnancies and hungry babies, she was busy, and meeting Oonagh's emotional needs was not high on her list of priorities.

There was only one thing that Oonagh could do — escape her dreary existence by retreating into a fantasy land. She was an avid reader, and read and re-read every story book in the village school. Her nose was stuck in a book whenever it could be. She'd even read whilst milking the cows, irritating her father immensely.

"Who do you think you are?" he would ask, clipping her ear if she had been too engrossed in a book to hear him. "Fancy yourself as Margaret Bloody Thatcher, do you?" "Too important to listen, are you now? UPWARDLY F**CKING MOBILE, ARE YOU?"

One day I'm going to be rich. One day, I'm going to move to England. One day I'm going to marry a Lord. Oonagh would drown out the sound of his ridicule with mantras like this, repeating them over and over in her head.

One day, when she was sixteen, her father was drunk and on the warpath once again. "Too good to be a Campbell, are you, you little bitch?" he was bellowing in her face, with the stench of whiskey on his breath. Holding back the tears, Oonagh mentally said her biggest prayer yet, begging for a solution to present itself. And the very next day, it did.

The local priest had heard about Oonagh's literary interests, and after church, he told her about a job in the university library in Dublin. The farm was in dire financial straits. They needed a steady income. If she took it, she could escape the farm life, better herself, and help her father with his financial struggles, in one fell swoop.

"It's win win, Daddy," she had told him that afternoon, crossing her fingers behind her back. It turned out that even John Campbell couldn't argue with logic like that.

Oonagh grew up in a house of ridicule and humiliation, with a father whose explosive outbursts could not be avoided. Was he himself a narcissist? Perhaps — or perhaps not. But belittling parents like these invalidate their children, who tiptoe around their moods, try to placate them or zone out. They internalize the message that they are 'not enough', 'bad' or 'useless', but try to avoid these feelings by vowing to prove to the world that their parent was wrong. It's no wonder that they are often highly driven to achieve status, wealth or power, as a way to gain the admiration of others and justify their existence. If they have learned to put other people down as a way of inflating their own shaky self-worth, they can turn out as Devaluing Narcissists, as Oonagh did — but these children can also go on to become any of the other types of narcissist too.

You haven't yet had the opportunity to meet Marcus, our Communal Narcissist as a grown up. But here I introduce you to his background, in London, England, and the final type of parenting style that can lead to narcissism.

When Dianne Brown told her mother that she had fallen pregnant through a one night stand with a black man, she really didn't know how she would react — but frankly, at 37 years old, it hardly mattered. But all her mother cared about was that God had given her daughter the only gift she'd ever really wanted, and that she was radiantly happy. They hugged each other tightly as they laughed and cried.

Dianne was a midwife at St.Thomas' hospital, in London, and her busy career had meant that she had never found the right man to settle down with. It was her last day in Jamaica, holidaying with girlfriends, when Daniel, the hotel pool-boy, had flashed her a wide smile, and stuck a paper napkin under her drink, with the words 'Age is just a number, right?' scrawled on it. He was a mere 21 years old, with long dreadlocks, defined muscles and perfect dark chocolate skin.

After Dianne's announcement, mother and daughter immediately started planning. It was agreed that Dianne would move back into the house in South London with her mother, where she had grown up. She would rent out her own small flat in trendy Clapham, and this would provide the income to enable her to work part time, while the baby was little. It was agreed that she and her mother would bring up the baby together, and never divulge to anyone the story of his origins.

Baby Marcus was the light of their lives. He had Dianne's pale blue eyes, which, in combination with his brown skin, drew admiring comments from everyone who stopped to look at him. "My darling little prince!" Dianne would call him, and "My little miracle!" He was her raison d'être, and the most special person the world had ever known. When he gurgled and babbled at just a few months old, Dianne was sure that she could discern words, and she would boast about it to anyone who would listen. "He's practically speaking in full sentences!" she would excitedly say. "Oh yes, he's very musical — he was humming 'twinkle twinkle little star' in his cot the other day…" Marcus was loved like no other baby, and lauded for every single thing he did. His grandmother and mother would spend hours intently watching him, lavishing praise on him for his every movement. "Oh look! He kicked his legs! Clever boy!!!" they would coo in unison.

This was a pattern that continued throughout Marcus's upbringing. Regardless of how well he actually did, he was told that he was a 'genius', 'the cleverest little boy in the whole wide world' and the 'most talented' at everything. When he wasn't offered the part of Joseph in the school nativity play, aged five, Dianne stormed into the school to complain, and told the headmistress that 'Marcus could one day be the world's greatest actor'.

Dianne also felt that Marcus deserved the best of everything. When they went to restaurants he would be allowed to choose the most expensive thing on the menu. If he didn't like the food, he would be allowed to choose another meal — and if he *did* like the food Dianne would insist that the chef came out to see him, so that Marcus could give his compliments in person. She liked to dress him in little buttoned shirts and waistcoats for such excursions, with the occasional bow tie, so he looked like the 'little gent' she believed him to be.

When his school grades were underwhelming, Dianne heaped praise on him, and told him that the testing system failed great minds like his, and were designed for 'just the average Joe'. When he played his guitar (hesitantly and badly) Dianne would listen with rapt attention, barely holding back her tears of pride. In company, even with adults, if he was speaking Dianne would shush everyone in the room, so that he could be heard. Dianne believed he was the wittiest, the strongest and the bravest child ever, as well as being the kindest and sweetest.

Dianne was not a narcissist, but she needed to believe that there was no area in which Marcus did not excel. It's no surprise that Marcus himself grew up needing to believe it too.

These overvaluing parents do love their children, but seem to genuinely see them as unique and superior. The child comes to believe that they are entitled to special privileges, but as they grow up, faced with   reality, they struggle. They therefore develop narcissistic defences to protect themselves from having to accept the truth. Their parents may well continue to brag about them forever, inflating their achievements and attributes throughout their adulthood.

Are Narcissists 'evil'?

Narcissists do behave badly — very badly in fact — but perhaps you can now see, from how they are made, that their narcissism is far from their fault. These tragic children developed their narcissistic defences partially because they unconsciously learned them from their parents (if they were narcissists themselves), and partially as a way to cope with life as a result of their upbringings. The workarounds that they develop to protect themselves essentially become 'wired' into their developing brains, causing them to become narcissists themselves in later life. This is why many psychologists consider NPD to be a personality '*adaptation*'.

During my work with the adult victims of narcissistic relationships, I've never heard of a situation where the narcissist in their lives didn't come from a background of abuse, neglect, conditional love or being 'overvalued'. What is interesting, though, is that although in most cases the narcissist has a *poor* relationship with their family of origin, in some cases, the adult narcissist continues to idolize their parent.

So, to answer my own question, 'are narcissists evil?' — *I* think not but, if you are on the receiving end of their behaviours, it can certainly feel like it, believe me.

But what about siblings? How can two people have exactly the same upbringing, and one turns into a narcissist but the other doesn't?

This is a question that I get asked all the time, and it's a good one. But I believe that *no two people have the exact same upbringing or environment.*

Firstly, in any family, how you are treated by your parents depends on a huge number of factors, unconscious and conscious. Different genders may be treated differently, and have to fulfil different expectations. There may be different stresses on the family at different times, so a younger sibling may be treated differently as result of this. Birth order may also have a part to play

"The workarounds that they develop to protect themselves become 'wired' into their developing brains. This can lead to them becoming narcissists themselves in later life."

in how you are treated — we've all heard of 'middle child syndrome', for example. Your own inbuilt temperament may affect how you are treated, or how you are affected by such treatment. You may be naturally more resilient than your sibling, or more sensitive.

Your parents' biases will play a role too, whether they realize it or not, and there's little you can do about these. Do you remind them of their great aunt Susan (who they hated) because of the shape of your chin, so they treat you accordingly? Are you naturally able enough to become the school chess champion, as they desperately want you to be, whereas your disappointing sibling simply doesn't have what it takes? Do you remind them of *themselves* as children perhaps, so you get off lightly, whereas your sibling does not?

Then there's the consideration that 'it takes a village'. You might have supportive adults or role models in your life that your sibling doesn't have — a teacher perhaps, who validates you and sees you as an individual. You might have close friends to confide in, whereas your painfully shy sibling does not.

We'll take a deeper look at how narcissists affect their children later on, but for now, it's time to meet our final type of narcissist as an adult, — the Communal Narcissist. So how exactly did Marcus, brought up in London by his adoring mother and grandmother, turn out?

THE COMMUNAL NARCISSIST

Marcus is now 30. Being mixed race is a big part of how he sees himself, and you'll be mesmerized by his unusual blue eyes, which he uses to great effect by holding your gaze for just a little too long.

If you ask him about himself (and even if you don't) he'll tell you, in his deep slow drawl, that he's 'one of life's good guys'. He'll nod earnestly as he speaks, and occasionally flash you a disarming smile, revealing all his perfect white teeth. It can feel a little discombobulating, for some reason.

"You know, I've done a lot of things in my life…" Marcus likes to arrange his athletic 6 ft 4 frame on the chair with deliberate intention, leaning back, and resting one ankle on the other thigh. It's an open posture, one you might find yourself unconsciously mirroring, as he continues, "but it's time for me to 'give back', you know?"

And indeed, Marcus's social media profiles corroborate his varied skills. He has a 'broad range of expertise in a variety of fields.' He's an 'innovator', a 'thought leader', an 'entrepreneur', a 'family man', a 'philanthropist', and a 'sportsman'. "But I'm a Christian first, you know? That's what keeps me on the path — the righteous path…"

Marcus married fairly young, as he believes all good Christians should. "Irina is like…she's like a guiding light to me, you know?" he speaks with great fervour about his Romanian wife, who is six years his senior.

Irina was a struggling single mother when they met, balancing cleaning jobs with caring for her eighteen-month-old son, Janis. But handsome Marcus was not put off, and swooped in to rescue her and Janis. When Marcus's grandmother died, she had left her four bedroom Victorian home in Camberwell, South London, to him. It was the house both he and his mother had grown up in and was, by this time, worth a very sizeable amount. They'd only known each other a month when Marcus asked Irina to move in.

If you mention this generosity, Marcus will nod thoughtfully and say "Yeah, well you know — if you've got empathy, that's all you need in life. Yeah. I guess I was lucky like that — I've got empathy levels off the scale."

These days Irina runs a small cleaning firm, with four staff. They clean affluent South Londoners' houses, but it's a stressful business which nearly went under during the COVID-19 pandemic. The clientele can be rude and demanding, and they frequently complain and withhold payment. Irina also often finds herself having to step in for absent staff members at the last minute.

She'd like to go to university and then train to be a psychotherapist, but Marcus tells her that even if she *did* have the brain for it, they wouldn't be able to afford it, even though they have no mortgage. And it's true — they can't afford it. Money just seems to drain away, as fast as it comes in. She knows that his penchant for all the latest designer trainers isn't helping, and she despairs at the size of his collection (which has taken over the spare room). But Marcus is clear on this point. "They are an important part of my cultural identity as a black man," he tells her, with absolute conviction, making her feel as though she is a racist. She hasn't heard of 'gaslighting'.

Marcus is keenly involved with the local football club, where he coaches the youngsters, including twelve-year-old Janis, every week. To onlookers, he's taken on the role of stepfather admirably.

His voice is naturally deep and resonant and so travels great distances without him having to shout. "That's it Janis, my main man…hook it under, yeah, cool one…" "Harris, dude — you've got this…save! Result, man…badass…" There have definitely been more mums on the sidelines since Marcus started football coaching in his shorts and tight T-shirt.

Janis finds these public displays of 'encouragement' excruciating, and he's fully aware of the fact that his 'cool' stepfather is nothing like this when no one else can hear or see him. When he picks him up from school, Janis usually finds him intensely interacting with one or other of the mums, who usually seems flustered or giggly. Marcus takes his kit bag from him as he fist-pumps him, and then encases him in a giant, over-the-top bear hug, which Janis surrenders to. He knows that the car journey home will probably be in silence.

Marcus talks a lot about his work, through his church, in helping disadvantaged children — although if you actually followed him around for a few days, you'd be hard pushed to work out what he actually does in this regard.

You might note that he has worked his way through various churches, falling out with the pastors and other members. The last time this happened, Marcus insisted that he could take over from the lead guitarist of the church band, who was emigrating. No one questioned his ability until their first practice, when it became painfully clear that, although he had an incredibly expensive handmade guitar, he could barely play it, and just mis-strummed chords randomly. The pastor was enlisted to ask him to step down, but Marcus raged so frighteningly that the police were nearly called. He accused the terrified pastor of racism, and of using his white male privilege against him. "God is going to pay you back for this, you f**king nobody…" were his parting words as he stormed off. But when he got home, he was so depressed he could barely speak, and he didn't get out bed for three days. He told Irina that the luthier, who had made the guitar specially for him, had 'made it wrong' on purpose, to sabotage him, and that it was all his fault.

He's the sort who gives twenty pound notes to the homeless (if he happens to have an audience) with a "Peace, brother…" and when you comment on his generosity, he'll dismiss it modestly, with a wave of his hand.

But Marcus feels his greatest altruistic achievements have come through Instagram, where he has over 100,000 followers. Every other day he posts a short video starting with the words, "Greetings, fam. Marcus Brown here, sharing with you my thoughts. It's my intention to make the world a better place, by spreading peace and light."

Marcus mostly lifts his content from other people, including from his own pastor's weekly sermons. He is so good at passing off other people's work as his own that he even gets away with using old or obscure poems or song lyrics, which he delivers slowly and with great intensity.

Irina doesn't quite know what to make of the fact that he has set up a permanent studio in a corner of the dining room, with lighting rigs, a boom microphone and an eye-wateringly expensive camera and teleprompter. She and Janis know to tiptoe around the house whilst he's 'in session', as he calls it, recording himself time and time again until he gets it just right. But then again, she hasn't been allowed to put her own stamp on any part of the house since she's lived here, on the grounds that she'd be 'violating the memory of his grandmother' if she did.

Marcus ends his videos with a little outro. "I hope that's given you either food for thought, or comfort or joy. Once again, I'm Marcus Brown. Follow me here or on Twitter, if you'd like to be part of my growing community of thinkers and changers. Peace and love, fam."

Marcus makes sure he responds to every single comment he receives in response to these videos. "It's practically a full time job," he once told Irina, when she had the audacity to ask him if he could load the dishwasher. These days she can't help but feel irritated when she comes back from work and finds his cereal bowls and mugs littered around the place, the washing not done and the fridge bare. There's only so much his winning smile can make up for, she has realized in recent years. It's particularly annoying as she knows he's very capable – if anyone visits he will make a big show of wiping down surfaces and drying dishes, or whipping up a delicious meal. But as he points out, she should be *grateful* to be living there. "Don't forget where you'd be if it wasn't for *me*," he growls at her, if she steps out of line.

When Irina heard rumours that Marcus was having an affair with Loretta from their latest church, she was confused, and nearly brushed it off as ridiculous. Marcus had always displayed a zero tolerance approach to infidelity in everyone he came across, so she was stunned when he eventually came clean and admitted that the unlikely rumours she'd been hearing were true.

Irina was absolutely distraught, her pain amplified by the humiliation of realizing that everyone in the community had known except her. But, somehow, Marcus had persuaded her to give him another chance. In couple's therapy, he blamed his indiscretions on the fact that Irina was often working, leaving him feeling lonely and isolated. The therapist agreed with him and spoke of the value of forgiveness. Irina felt terrible guilt, and agreed to try again.

Only she knew how loving and sweet he could be when he was on form, and how he had begged her not to break up their family unit, even saying that he didn't think he would be able to go on living without her. It got to the stage where he was so scared about her leaving that he would whisper into her ear, when he thought she was asleep, over and over again "You will *not* leave me…"— proof of his enormous regret, or so she thought.

"He's such a great dad!" the other mums will say to her, who know him from his football coaching. But Irina knows that Janis only plays football because it is what *Marcus* wants. Marcus is always trying to 'bulk' Janis out too, breaking raw eggs into glasses of milk for him to drink, which he hates, and mercilessly criticizing his match performance once they get into the car.

And when Janis broke his leg in a school football match that Marcus was watching, Irina was appalled to hear that he had refused to call an ambulance, instead making him wait in the car for an hour until the match was over, with no painkillers. "The body is a miracle of God" he had drawled, when she had confronted him about it that evening. "It produces *natural* painkillers, and heals itself…"

Irina also can't understand why Marcus is so disbelieving of Janis's asthma. He sometimes has an attack when exercising in cold weather. If there are people present, Marcus will rush over to give him his inhaler, concern etched on his face. But once, when he didn't think she was around, she heard him saying angrily, through gritted teeth, "Just breathe *normally*, you little idiot…" When he turned around to see her standing there, with a horrified expression, he quickly laughed it off. "I was only joking!" he said, with his trademark winning smile.

And why, if he is such a charitable man, is he always so very rude to waiters? Why does he get fidgety and edgy if he ever has to wait in a line? Why does he always point out overweight people in restaurants, and tell her that they put him off his food? Why, on the rare occasions that she goes out with a friend for lunch or a glass of wine after work, does he text her continuously throughout, and ask her for a blow by blow account of the conversation afterwards? Why is he so damned *jealous*? Forever suggesting that he has seen her looking over at some man or other with interest, or that she is having an 'emotional affair' with someone she barely knows. He seems so sure that she's even started to question herself, even though she knows, deep down, that she's never been unfaithful to Marcus.

Every evening Marcus insists that Irina sits with him to watch TV, because 'time spent together is essential to keep a marriage healthy'. She used to think that this was a sweet sentiment, but the sports programmes that Marcus makes her watch are just not her cup of tea at all, and he never lets her choose what they watch. The one time he acquiesced, and she put on a period drama that she'd been dying to watch, he shifted around impatiently, yawned loudly, and kept looking at his phone. She felt terrible that he wasn't enjoying it, and after twenty minutes she handed him the remote control, when she could bear the guilt no more. Irina realizes that it is easier to just sit beside him and let her mind wander. And if he happens to fall asleep on the sofa, as he frequently does, she can sneak off to get on with the piles of business invoicing and paperwork that is necessary to keep funding their lives.

In recent years Irina has also noticed that Marcus just doesn't listen to her any more, dismissing her worries or feelings as ludicrous or invalid. If she tries to state a point of view, he will always have the opposite view, and she finds this exhausting and predictable —every conversation is hard work. In fact, nowadays he goes through cycles of being frosty and dismissive when behind closed doors, although she has noticed that, if she ever meets him in public, he will grandly kiss her on the cheek, hold her hand and smile affectionately at her once again, as if they are the world's biggest love story. In her heart of hearts, Irina feels completely unloved and uncherished.

This type of narcissist, also known as the Altruistic Narcissist, hides beneath a facade of being a do-gooder but, sadly, their wonderful image is merely skin deep. They often derive their all-important feeling of specialness by portraying themselves as the

"Narcissists have low empathy — one of the most important features of narcissism."

most kind, the most empathic, the most generous, the most pious or the most spiritual person you will meet. So whilst they *do* carry out good deeds, their motivations are far from pure – because, yet again, they are driven by their need to secure narcissistic supply. You'll find them in all sorts of environments and in all sorts of roles — in charitable, religious and environmental organizations, and as therapists, spiritual teachers, vicars and doctors. This sort of narcissist often loves sitting on committees and fundraising, but they are highly territorial about their philanthropic endeavours. Beneath the false persona, the usual narcissistic behaviours are in play — in Marcus's case, a sense of entitlement about not having to work or do chores; degrading others; a lack of empathy for another's pain; denial or invalidation of other people's feelings; lying, gaslighting, and using the family as image props; a tendency to play 'devil's advocate'; seeing children as mere extensions of themselves, so being unable to tolerate their imperfections; exerting control over others; applying high moral standards to others but not to themselves; blowing hot and cold; a marked tendency to be easily angered; and a masterful ability for impression management.

In the previous chapter we took a look at the diagnostic list of features in the DSM-5, and how they applied to Lina, and Oonagh. But the textbook actually has two ways of defining NPD, the second of which describes NPD as a moderate or severe impairment in personality functioning, with difficulties in two or more of four areas (identity, self-direction, empathy and intimacy). Grandiosity and attention-seeking behaviour also has to be present.

Let's take a brief look at how this might apply to Marcus. We can see that he is grandiose from his social media profiles, where he describes himself as a 'thought leader' and an 'innovator', amongst other things. His Instagram videos are clear attention seeking behaviours, and it is also clear that his sense of identity is abnormally dependent on how other people view him, and can fluctuate wildly, depending on what they think of him. His rage at being seen as not good enough for the church band, and his subsequent depression, alludes to this.

He also has difficulties in 'self-direction'. This can play out in two ways. Some narcissists set standards for themselves which are very high, and can be extremely motivated to achieve them. These high-achieving narcissists do this so that other people see them as exceptional, once they have achieved their goals. And this, in turn, allows them to *see themselves* as exceptional. Jonathan and Oonagh fit into this type. However, the opposite can also be true: some narcissists, like Marcus, have no motivation to achieve. This type believes, as a result of their sense of entitlement, that *others* should provide for them. This explains why narcissists can either appear to be high achievers or parasitic spongers — which, on the surface, might look like a bit of a paradox.

And what about empathy? This is one of the most important features of NPD, in my opinion. Narcissists have low empathy — they can't step into another person's shoes and feel their feelings or pain, so they can't recognize another person's needs. However, they can be attuned to the *reactions* of a person towards *them*, but only if it matters to them. They also aren't very good at recognizing how much they affect other people — they often either think they have much more of an effect on others than they actually do, or they underestimate their effect on others. Marcus quite clearly has low empathy, leaving poor Janis waiting in the car with a broken leg for an hour.

Difficulties in intimacy is another area to be considered. This isn't really about sexual intimacy, but emotional intimacy. Sadly, narcissists can only really have *superficial* relationships, although, certainly at first, it's easy to be fooled otherwise. Narcissists actually only have relationships to make them feel good about themselves — they don't really care about others' experiences. The big clue here is how Irina feels unloved and uncherished by Marcus. There is no way to sugarcoat this — if you have deep feelings for a narcissist, I'm afraid they are just not mutual.

4

Are *you* trapped in a narcissist's orbit?

Think of a narcissist as a sun surrounded by planets, if you will. Of course, with a *real* sun, it's the sun's gravitational pull that keeps the planets trapped in their orbits — but a narcissist uses other methods to create the pull which traps their victims, which I will expose in the next chapter. Let's now take a deeper look at the various orbits of a narcissist.

- The person (or people) in the closest orbit to the narcissist are the narcissist's partner (or partners)
- Circling the narcissist in the next orbit might be the narcissist's children
- Further out still might be the narcissist's friends and other family members
- In the next orbit out, you might find the narcissist's work colleagues
- In the very last orbit, the narcissist's casual acquaintances will be found, such as the postman, the builder and the shopkeeper

All of the people in a narcissist's orbit are there for a reason — even you. You see, the narcissist needs *everyone* who orbits them to give them external validation, that fuel that a narcissist must have to survive emotionally, which you already know is called 'narcissistic supply'.

The DSM-5 describes NPD as a 'pervasive' pattern (meaning that the patterns of behaviour and the way a narcissist thinks are present in all areas of their life). In other words, narcissists don't just cause problems with their nearest and dearest, behind closed doors, like other types of abusers do. They affect *everyone* they come into contact with to some extent. How much you are affected depends on how close you are to them in daily life, and how much exposure you have to them.

When I am helping the spouse or partner of a narcissist, I always ask them how their narcissist gets on with the people they work with. The answer is always the same. Although they usually have a small fan club of adoring people at work, over time, most people come to despise them and try to keep their distance. Essentially, these people eject themselves from the narcissist's orbit as much as they can.

> *"Narcissists affect **everyone** they come into contact with to some extent."*

I also question them about the narcissist's friendships. It is very rare indeed for a narcissist to have long-term friendships with emotionally healthy individuals, although they often blur the boundaries with work colleagues (especially subordinates) and turn them into friends. Here they have metaphorically pulled the grateful subordinate into a closer orbit, albeit usually only temporarily.

So even though everyone in a narcissist's orbit, to a greater or lesser degree, is being used by the narcissist for narcissistic supply, *it can take a long time for them to realize it.* To understand this, let's take this metaphor one step further.

Blinded by the light (and feeling the heat)

Imagine that you are in the closest orbit to the narcissist's sun. Perhaps you are married to them, or you are having an affair with them. You are so close to them that you are being dazzled by their brightness, to the point of being blinded by it. But your proximity to the heat source also means that you are being *burned* (by their behaviours) — but still you cannot see these behaviours for what they are.

The closer a planet is to the sun, the more it will feel the heat. And the closer you are to a narcissist, the more abusive behaviours you will be subjected to. And this abuse will allow the narcissist to procure their fuel, their 'narcissistic supply' from you — through your reactions to his or her behaviour.

It stands to reason that you will feel the heat of their adverse behaviours *less* if you are further away from them. This explains why the partners of narcissists are subjected to the difficult behaviours the most, the work colleagues less so, and the casual acquaintances less still (often to the point where they are largely unaware of them). Even though you are less dazzled in these outer orbits, you are still unlikely to see their true nature, and be taken in by the false image that they put out to the world.

But let's say that you are all the way out in the fourth orbit of your narcissistic co-worker. It's pretty likely that, once they start to take credit for your work and badmouth you behind your back, you will see things for what they are pretty *quickly*, because you are not blinded by their light. But that's not to say that all will be smooth sailing from that point, as anyone who has been in this situation will know.

> "The closer you are to a narcissist, the more abusive behaviours you will be subjected to."

Gravitational pull

Pretty much everyone who has been in a very close relationship with a narcissist will describe how very difficult it was to extricate themselves from the relationship — and they will usually relate to the metaphor of an attraction of *gravitational proportions* holding them in the narcissist's orbit. Again, the closer your orbit, the stronger the forces of attraction are. We will explain how this almost inescapable gravitational pull (which is actually a chemical 'addiction' to the narcissist) arises later on, and how it's all related to the victim's brain chemistry.

How serious is this?

If around one in 20 people are narcissists, and each narcissist has many people in their various orbits, it does beg the question *how many people are unknowingly being damaged by a narcissist's behaviours?* I trained as a family doctor (GP) many years ago and did not come across NPD in my training. Sadly, even today's young doctors are not learning about it, as I am frequently told when they come to see me as clients, each as flummoxed as the last as to why this personality disorder is not an essential part of medical training, given its reach and effects.

Knowing what I now know, I wonder just how many of the patients I saw during my own days in clinical practice with anxiety, depression, eating disorders, addictions, and chronic illnesses (such as autoimmune conditions and even cancers) were actually suffering at the hands of a narcissist? It's little excuse, but the pressure of being limited to five minute consultations meant that I rarely asked the questions that I wish I had. "How are things at home? How are things at work? Do you feel troubled by difficulties in any of your relationships?"

Does the narcissist care about the people in their orbits?

This is another question I commonly get asked, usually with wide-eyed hope, by someone who has threatened to leave their relationship with

> *"To a narcissist, you are just a fuel source, from whom they can procure narcissistic supply, so that they can stay feeling emotionally safe."*

their narcissist, and been met with protestations of undying love (if the narcissist is their partner), or desperate pleas for them to stay (perhaps from their narcissistic boss, upon handing in their notice). Surely this is evidence that the narcissist *does* care about them? The answer is absolutely, yes. Narcissists *do* care about the people in their orbits, but not for the reasons you might hope.

Narcissists simply aren't *able* to see people as equals, with their own wants, needs, dreams and lives. Rather they see their 'orbiters' as two-dimensional cardboard cutouts, who exist solely in relation to them. To a narcissist, you are just a fuel source, from whom they can procure narcissistic supply, so that they can stay feeling emotionally safe. You are just an 'it' to them, but they care about you staying, because they *need* you.

The bucket with a hole in it

Imagine that each narcissist stores their narcissistic supply in a bucket, but that the bucket has a hole in it. Clearly, the narcissistic supply will constantly be draining away. Now, it's crucial that the narcissist keeps their narcissistic supply at a certain level in their bucket, because if it falls below that level there won't be enough to keep their armour, their false persona, strong, whole and impermeable. And if that happens, they will be forced to feel their true feelings of shame, worthlessness and inadequacy, which is the very thing they are trying to avoid at all costs.

You can see why the bucket will constantly need refilling from the top, to prevent this drop in level. So now picture several watering cans pouring narcissistic supply into the bucket, at the same time. The biggest watering can, pouring at the fastest rate for most of the time, is likely to be the narcissist's primary partner. The smallest watering cans, just pouring in every now and then, will be the narcissist's casual acquaintances, those in their outer orbits, perhaps providing an occasional hit of narcissistic supply through a jokey interaction or an admiring glance. But everybody has some role to play in contributing to the total level in the bucket.

If you remember, narcissists obtain their narcissistic supply in five major ways — through attention, admiration, drama, conflict and by instilling fear into others. Any of these can be used at any time, with *anyone* in their orbit.

But for some narcissists, this need for narcissistic supply is like an addiction. And just like with any addiction, you often need more and more of the substance to get the same effect from it, as you develop a tolerance to it.

Imagine that with every passing year the narcissist's bucket gets bigger. They are going to need more and more attention, admiration, drama, conflict and fearful reactions from others to keep their level of narcissistic supply constant. It's no wonder people who have been in long-term relationships with narcissists begin to feel as though they can never be 'enough' for them.

You may have noticed that we haven't delved into our Exhibitionist Narcissist Jonathan Delaney's life as deeply as our other types of narcissist. If you need to remind yourself of him, feel free to revisit the introduction of this book, before you read on. Because, in this next part, we are going to look at the people who are circling him, in his closest orbit. Let's start with his wife, Brigitte.

SUPRIYA MCKENNA

THE CLOSEST ORBIT

Brigitte Delaney is Jonathan's wife, and a French teacher at the school. They met at a mutual friend's wedding, and have been married for 23 years. She has not been happy for a very long time, but hasn't told a soul. After all, on the surface she has it all — a successful, funny, clever husband, a meaningful job, a lovely house and a son. What right does she have to feel sad? When she burst into tears at her doctor's office a few years ago, she was prescribed antidepressants. Brigitte was shocked, but at the same time felt relieved — perhaps depression was to blame for her low mood, tearfulness and feelings of worthlessness after all.

She's been on the tablets ever since, but she's never really made it back to being the person she was when she met Jonathan all those years ago — the fun-loving, carefree optimist, surrounded by friends. No wonder Jonathan has a roving eye, and a penchant for flirting with the younger female members of staff — it is her fault, and she accepts it. But at least Brigitte can be reassured by Jonathan's high moral standards, and zero tolerance for those who fall short of them. She is pretty sure that this means that he himself would never actually stray.

And Jonathan still bows with exaggerated chivalry if he passes her in the crowded school corridors, and bellows "Ah there she is, the radiant Madame Delaney! Make way for her, children, make way!" Brigitte still feels momentarily flattered and relieved by Jonathan's public displays of affection. But these feelings never last long, and more and more she finds herself asking why these days he's only affectionate when they have an audience.

The truth is that Brigitte mostly feels like an accessory — someone who is expected, in public, to merrily laugh at his jokes, be a supportive, doting wife and to look good on his arm. And, in private, to play the role of uncomplaining domestic servant, sex kitten and private secretary. She doesn't want to admit it to herself, but Brigitte is feeling resentful — and if she ever shows it, Jonathan will coldly tell

70

her to 'go and take a happy pill.' Her heart will sink at these times, but she knows better than to show her pain. Jonathan can be so careless with her emotions, and throw them back at her as ammunition when she least expects it.

"I am enough" is the positive affirmation she repeats over and over to herself in the bathroom mirror — but she doesn't feel that way. She's definitely not enough for Jonathan. But that's *her* fault, not his.

When Jonathan became headmaster, Brigitte was thrilled. Finally he had achieved the goal he had talked about incessantly for years, and at last they would be able to focus on other things. During the preceding school holiday she took on the refurbishment of his office for him, making sure she incorporated everything he asked for. Despite the modest budget, she had managed to include the floor to ceiling antique books he had insisted on, which she had procured in bulk from an old manor house that was being turned into a nursing home. The Victorian stone bust of an anonymous gentleman Jonathan had wanted was another success — it took weeks of visiting architectural salvage yards to find. The whole thing was a triumph, but when she had excitedly revealed the transformation to Jonathan, he looked like he was trying to put a brave face on his disappointment, and when pushed for a reaction, he simply said "I mean, it's not *terrible*..."

The headmaster job had come with a house on the school premises, but it wasn't at all to Jonathan's taste — far too poky and dark, with 'simply no architectural merit'. Jonathan was the first headmaster in the history of the school to opt to live out. Brigitte had known there would be no point arguing once his mind was made up, but did feel slight resentment that they would have to use the bulk of the money that she had inherited from her parents to fund buying a house in the village. After months of looking, whilst temporarily staying in the house on the school site, Jonathan had found a house which he considered to be worthy of his status, although it did need complete refurbishment. But rather than continuing to live in the headmaster's house at the school, he had insisted that the family move into their new home immediately, and live with the inconvenience of the renovations being done around them. Brigitte had felt she had little choice other than to agree.

For years Jonathan had been promising her the role of head of modern languages at the school, and rightly so, as Brigitte, a native French speaker and experienced teacher, was the natural choice. She was devastated when he promoted Fiona Jones to the job instead of her. Fiona had been teaching for ten years less than she had, but it seemed it was her turn to be in Jonathan's mutual fan club. At home it was all "Fiona said this" and "Fiona said that", and when Fiona wanted new equipment for the language lab it was instantly bought, even though Brigitte had been putting her case to him for it for years.

Brigitte was further flabbergasted when Jonathan asked Fiona to co-host the prize-giving ceremony with him at Sports Day instead of her, and could hardly bear it when she overheard a parent, who didn't know who she was, commenting to his wife on the 'chemistry' between the pair. Red-faced and fighting back the tears, Brigitte felt humiliated and wished the ground would swallow her up.

Of course, Jonathan denied any impropriety, and told Brigitte that good chemistry between staff members was essential to staff well-being, and she should be ashamed of herself for not prioritizing it as he did. It all sounded terribly convincing — and, as usual, Brigitte ended up apologizing for her churlishness and oversensitivity.

To make up for it, Brigitte spent the remaining money she had inherited from her parents on a surprise Easter week away for her and Jonathan, in the Caribbean. Jonathan was pleased, and for a while, all was forgotten. Brigitte loved these times, when things were almost as they used to be and they were getting on. He was the life and soul of the party when on holiday, and he would chat to wealthy holiday makers at the bar and by the pool, and make them laugh with his obtuse humour and his jokey demeanour. Brigitte felt proud to be with him at times like this, and as usual, hoped that things would stay like this forever.

Sadly, once back home, things took the inevitable nosedive. Brigitte went back to cleaning up around him, doing all the housework, cooking, sorting out the bills and doing all the shopping, whilst Jonathan relaxed for the remainder of the holiday, surfing the internet, playing golf, watching TV and visiting the local village pub. Once term restarted, she had all this to do and more — and she'd stay up late into the night marking her pupils' homework, whilst Jonathan concentrated on 'raising his public profile' on Twitter by commenting on education issues and the 'state of schooling today', in an erudite sounding tone. He was an important chap, after all, and had his mind in higher places than the mundane — but Brigitte still resented the fact that he had dropped all domestic duties as soon as they were married, leaving them entirely to her.

When her little car eventually gave up the ghost, Brigette would have been perfectly happy to replace it with a newer version of the same model, but Jonathan had other ideas. He insisted that she move with the times and buy a hybrid electric car 'for the sake of the environment', and that they sell his car too, and just have one car between them. He was so keen that he even did all the research and took her to various car showrooms to test drive the different options. The car he wanted was much bigger than Brigitte felt they needed, but Jonathan was adamant that it was the one for them, and reeled off various figures to do with 'carbon neutrality' and 'pollution indices' to convince her.

When the car arrived, it certainly did look quite impressive, but because it ran on electricity and switched to expensive petrol mode when it ran out of charge, Jonathan insisted that Brigitte drove it so it never ran out of electric charge. This meant she wasn't ever allowed to have the radio or the heating on, to preserve the electricity for as long as possible, even in bitterly cold winters. Worse, there was a setting which meant that Jonathan could check to see how economically the car had been driven in his absence, and he would regularly haul Brigitte over the coals, telling her that she was 'killing the planet'. Eventually she stopped driving it altogether, and just let him drive, and the rare times she went anywhere without him she would use public transport.

Why didn't she leave him? Because Brigitte was a fighter, and she was fiercely loyal. She wasn't going to give up on Jonathan like his mother had, when she left him as a teenager. He'd jumped through hoops for that woman, trying to be everything that she wanted him to be. Every success he had had (and there had been many of them) she had claimed as her own. And his father had hardly been any better. Jonathan becoming a headmaster was the ultimate disappointment to his father — even though it was far in excess of anything *he* had ever achieved.

Brigitte had promised Jonathan that she would never abandon him. And honestly, she felt sorry for him. She knew that under his bluster and bravado stood a sad, deserted child, with his toddler-style tantrums and episodes of deep dejection. What Jonathan needed was more love, because love can conquer all. And when things were good, which they sometimes were, she felt that she was succeeding in helping him to heal from his upbringing. One day they would get back to the idyllic times of the past, she was sure. Poor, misunderstood Jonathan, so vulnerable and yet so brilliant. Her heart bled for him.

The thing about orbiting a sun is that you can have no idea that another planet is also in your orbit, if it is revolving at the exact same speed as you, constantly out of view, behind that sun. On that note, meet Mollie.

Mollie is the school receptionist, and she is waiting for the day that Brigitte is expelled from the orbit they share, so that she can have Jonathan all to herself. She's 32 years old and lives with her parents, who she can't wait to introduce him to, once he has divorced Brigitte. Mollie first met Jonathan whilst working at the reception of his golf club. She'd always been attracted to older men, with their worldly-wise ways, but Jonathan was without doubt the one for her. He knew exactly how to treat a lady, and she knew, from the time they agreed to have coffee, that things would go further between them. The second time they met, the sexual energy was so great between them that she didn't think twice when Jonathan suggested she procure the keycard for the rarely used golf club bedroom suite, for a passionate, clandestine liaison. To this day Mollie doesn't know how she was found out — but the very next morning she was sacked. Management never did discover who she had been entertaining in the suite though, and Jonathan, with his nine lives, remained a valued member of the club.

When Jonathan suggested she work for him as the school receptionist, she was delighted at the thought of being able to see him every day. To her, he is everything a man should be — suave, sophisticated and debonair, with the kind of arrogance that she finds irresistibly sexy. When he looks intensely into her eyes, for just a little too long, she finds herself forgetting to breathe, and she lives for their weekly evening hook-ups in the empty headmaster's house on the school site, where they have passionate sex on the brown corduroy couch that came with the house. These are the nights she longs for — she barely lives in between.

In public, sometimes his hand brushes against hers at the reception desk and she feels an electric current passing between them — the attraction is visceral, and powerful. If he walks behind her, she feels his approving gaze on her legs. Mollie, flattered and eager to please, has taken to wearing the shortest skirts she can get away with in a school, with plunging necklines that Jonathan can ogle, as she leans over her reception desk when he walks by.

Mollie finds it funny how pathetic Fiona Jones, the French teacher is, when she knocks on Jonathan's door at break-times with a tin of biscuits. Jonathan has told Mollie how Fiona is desperately in love with him, and that he doesn't have the heart to tell her to go away, so he puts up with the unwanted attention. They laugh about 'chubby Fiona' during their secret times together, and Jonathan seems to be especially passionate with Mollie during their lovemaking if they talk about all the women who want him, as part of their foreplay. But Mollie doesn't mind — she knows that *she* is his chosen one, and she feels incredibly lucky.

Jenny and Pippa, who work in the school office, have seen it all before. They know what happened to the last receptionist and why she left without giving notice, because the glass partition between their office and the school reception desk gives them a bird's eye view of the headmaster's interactions with all the simpering, pouting girls he employs in that role. But no one will ever tell Brigitte Delaney — they value their jobs far too much, and they just don't want to get involved.

So Mollie goes on believing Jonathan's tales of how 'his wife doesn't appreciate him', and how selfish she is — apparently she won't even have a meal on the table when he gets home. They haven't even had sex for two years, he has told her, but he is staying with her because she has threatened to kill herself if he leaves.

Mollie knows that he is waiting until Brigitte's mental health is stronger before he leaves her, because he is such a caring man, and he can't bear to have his son motherless. And Mollie has decided that she is going to wait for him. After all, they are in love. She knows it won't be too long until she is the new Mrs Delaney — because Jonathan has promised.

Some thoughts about the first orbit

Not every narcissist is unfaithful to their partner, but a good number are. If they are getting enough narcissistic supply in other ways they may well stay faithful, particularly if that narcissistic supply is coming from the attention and adoration of their partner. In this case, however, Brigitte knows in her heart of hearts that she is 'not enough' for Jonathan. It's interesting that she is on antidepressants, and I can't help but wonder whether she would need them if she wasn't married to Jonathan.

It's also worth pointing out another narcissistic behaviour here — that of 'triangulation'. Here the narcissist openly brings a third person into the dynamic to make their victim feel inadequate, insecure and off-balance, playing the parties off against one another. Fiona Jones is the hapless third party in this case. The drama this creates is a good source of narcissistic supply, and it is also a 'devaluation' tactic, designed to erode Brigitte's self-esteem further, so she loses even more power and agency in the relationship.

Jonathan's sense of entitlement is also clear to see in his approach to domestic duties, in the way that he, like so many narcissists, only do the work that brings in easy wins, in narcissistic supply terms, leaving the mundane work to others. Most partners of narcissists feel 'run ragged', and you will have noticed this in all our different types of narcissist. Having said that, it *is* possible for narcissists to do mundane chores *if they can procure narcissistic supply from doing them*, perhaps by being known and admired for having the cleanest house, being the best cook, or being the most organized person.

I also want to point out some of Brigitte's characteristics which have contributed to her not leaving Jonathan. Believing that 'love conquers all' is a commonly held belief amongst the long-term partners of narcissists, as is having high levels of empathy for the narcissist, leading to repeated forgiveness. This is not to blame the victim at all — there can be no doubt that these characteristics are *positive* attributes in the right hands — but they are ripe for exploitation where a narcissist is concerned.

And what of poor Mollie? She is simply another victim, who has been taken in by another classic narcissistic behaviour — that of 'future faking'. Jonathan will not deliver on his promise of marrying her unless Brigitte finds out about her, and leaves him. In those circumstances, he may try to save face by marrying Mollie, but otherwise, she is likely to be discarded when she stops being compliant. But now let's take a look at Jonathan's second orbit.

THE SECOND ORBIT

Max is 20, and is Jonathan and Brigitte's only child. He couldn't wait to leave home and start university, mostly because he is sick of his father, who he hasn't felt aligned with since he was a little boy.

He regularly rings and texts his mother, Brigitte, who he is close to, but it annoys him when she tries to hand the phone over to his dad, or asks him to just text on the group chat, because his father 'feels left out'. "Your dad loves you very much, you know," she will often say to him, when mildly berating him for the lack of effort he makes with him.

But Max doesn't feel loved by his father. After all, he's been told so many times that he is a disappointment to him. Jonathan was angry when he chose to study Psychology at university, branding it a 'useless degree, unless you want to be a shrink, like the rest of the world'. He wanted Max to do a chemistry degree, like he did, at the same university he went to, and just could not seem to hear (or care) that Max wasn't interested.

As a small child Max struggled at school, even though he was obviously intelligent. He would talk incessantly in class and keep leaving his seat to mess around, distracting the other children. He'd always been a handful, even as a toddler, and Brigitte hadn't been able to take her eyes off him, for even a second, if she didn't want to find him climbing something dangerously, or playing with the toilet brush. By the time he was nine, she was becoming concerned, and thought that they should have him assessed by an educational psychologist.

Jonathan was completely opposed to this, and point blank refused. "There is absolutely nothing wrong with him!" he said, angrily banging his fist on the table, one morning at breakfast. "He just needs to try harder and stop being lazy. He seems perfectly able to concentrate on playing the piano, doesn't he? So it's pretty obvious that this is just a question of *motivation*. Max only does what Max wants to do, quite clearly."

When Brigitte tried to explain to Jonathan that this 'hyperfocus' was actually another reason to get Max assessed, Jonathan turned to her and snarled, nastily. "Er, I think *my* credentials, when it comes to education and children, trump *yours*, don't you?"

Brigitte was flabbergasted, but, as usual, she gave in. It had always been planned that Max would attend Jonathan's school at the age of eleven, but it slowly became clear that he would not pass the entrance exam, and it was only at this point, faced with the shame of this, that Jonathan agreed to him being assessed.

It was no surprise to anyone, least of all to Max, that he received a diagnosis of ADHD, and although Jonathan still refused to believe it, his mother supported him in taking medication for it.

Max still remembers how the effect of that medication was instantaneous, slowing down his racing brain, and helping him to think clearly. He had told his mother after his first dose, "Mum — I can think in a straight line!"

Much to Jonathan's relief, Max passed the school entrance exam with flying colours but, curiously, Jonathan continued to insist that Max did not have ADHD, despite all the evidence to the contrary. Although he didn't stop him from taking the medication, Jonathan just didn't ever want the word mentioned around him. It almost felt like a 'dirty little secret' to Max and Brigitte.

Max was a was hugely creative child, with fantastic musical ability. He was naturally drawn to the piano, which he begged his parents to let him play at the age of six, before his ADHD diagnosis. Brigitte was delighted at his interest, but Jonathan hated the idea of it, and tried to get him interested in a variety of alternative instruments. "You should learn the saxophone" he would tell him "or the guitar." "The piano is such a girly instrument — and you wouldn't want to be called a *girl,* would you?" This was another occasion when Max remembers Brigitte standing up for him. He turned out to have exceptional talent, and it was one of the few things that he was able to focus on for hours on end.

Luckily, he was so engrossed when he played that he never really noticed Jonathan putting his headphones in, if he was practicing in the house — and nor did he hear his irritated mutters, such as "That bloody boy is butchering Beethoven…He'd be turning in his grave if he could hear him…"

It was a very different story in public though, and Jonathan would make sure that Max played a solo at every school open day, and during school concerts. At these events he would beam with pride, give him a standing ovation with loud 'bravos' and mutter "chip off the old block!" just loudly enough for those around him to hear. He even had a large black and white photo of Max, seated at a Steinway grand piano, on his office wall, near to the bust of the man Jonathan claimed was his great great grandfather. It was rather confusing for Max, to say the least.

At the age of nineteen, Max plucked up the courage to tell his mother that he was gay. Of course, Brigitte embraced his sexuality and was pleased that he had been able to tell her, but expressed sadness at how he'd felt he'd had to keep it from her for two years. It was an emotional day, but Max was adamant that he didn't want to tell his father himself, and that he'd rather Brigitte did it when he was back at university. He knew that his father would have trouble accepting it, and would see it as a flaw — and he was right.

At first, Jonathan was incensed that Max could bring shame upon them in this way, and called him a 'pervert', and numerous other expletives. He refused to believe that Max knew what he was talking about, and accused him of 'jumping on the homosexual bandwagon'. He had shaken with anger when Brigitte told him, full of rage that Max had decided to tell *her*, but not him.

Max, feeling guilty that he hadn't treated his parents in the same way, phoned Jonathan several times, but he refused to take his calls. Jonathan completely shut him out for a whole year, sending only one message in response to Max's frantic communications. It simply read "You are dead to me now. I have done my grieving."

His father was also angry with Brigitte for maintaining contact with her only child, but Max knew that she would never agree to cut him off. Sadly though, she did feel she had to hide her phone calls and messages to him, which made them less frequent, and she didn't feel able to visit him at university, as Jonathan always insisted on being able to track her location though her phone 'for safety reasons'. It meant a lot of sneakiness — Max could only visit her when Jonathan was away at a teachers' conference, and they couldn't go out in public in case word got back to Jonathan.

When Max's cousin Charlotte got married, things got more awkward still. Charlotte and Max and been exceptionally close throughout their lives but Jonathan made it clear, via Brigitte, that Max should not attend the wedding, as he and Brigitte would be going. Max was in a dilemma. He didn't want to cause tension on Charlotte's big day, but he also knew that she would be upset if he wasn't there. He felt he had little choice but to come clean to Charlotte about the issues he was having with his father. She was shocked at Uncle Jonathan's behaviour, but insisted that she wanted Max to be there and that she could seat them on different tables.

The day came after a sleepless night for Max, but nothing could have prepared him for his father's bizarre behaviour. He acted as if absolutely nothing was wrong, hugging him with giant smiles, and proclaiming "Ah there he his, my boy!" He even looked utterly charmed when Max danced with his mother at the wedding after-party. However, when they happened to bump into each other in the privacy of the hotel lobby restroom, when no one else was there, Jonathan completely blanked him, with barely suppressed fury emanating from him. Max had known for a long time that his father prioritised maintaining a perfect facade above all else, but even he was surprised (and hurt) by this episode.

However, a year later, Jonathan had seemed to completely forget that he was ever disgusted by his son's sexuality. In fact, he was openly embracing all things LGBTQ, and insisted that the school have a morning assembly on the subject, and a special LGBTQ after-school club for pupils. He asked Max to speak at the assembly, and was genuinely surprised and offended when he declined, branding Max as 'oversensitive'. But finally Jonathan had found the subject that saw him secure interviews on the TV and radio. LGBTQ rights in schools became the subject he tweeted about the most, and he was even quoted in a national newspaper.

Brigitte, ever the enabler, was thrilled that Max was back in the fold, and told him, "See — I told you that it would all blow over. Time heals all wounds!"

Not this wound, Max thought to himself, saddened by Brigitte's invalidation of his feelings. But he knew that he would never stop hoping that he could have a meaningful relationship with his father — and maybe one day even gain his approval and love.

A word about how narcissists behave towards their children

Narcissists see their children as *extensions of themselves* — they do not see them as being separate from them. And what that means is that their children should have to *be* what they want them to be, *do* what they want them to do, and *have* what they want them to have. This is plainly evident in the way that Jonathan disapproves of Max's university choice, and his choice to play the piano.

But this inability to see them as being separate from themselves also means that a narcissistic parent cannot tolerate imperfections in their children. Remember that narcissists need others to see them as unique, and perfect. So if their *children* are not perfect, then this directly affects how others see *them*. Learning issues, such as ADHD and dyslexia are commonly seen as imperfections by narcissists (even ones who work in education). They simply cannot be taken on board, unless they stand to gain narcissistic supply from them in some way. Similarly, Max being gay is another 'imperfection' which Jonathan could not tolerate, until he could turn it to his own advantage. If we think back to our communal narcissist, Marcus, he was unable to tolerate the imperfection of his stepson, Janis, having asthma. This is a surprisingly common feature of narcissistic parenting, which can have dangerous consequences for the child, for example when treatment for their condition is withheld.

"A narcissistic parent cannot tolerate imperfections in their children..."

Becoming a narcissist's enabler

I also want to draw your attention to the way in which the non-narcissistic parent often enables or minimizes the unacceptable behaviour of the narcissist towards their children. Brigitte has no idea that Jonathan is a narcissist. She believes that Jonathan is a loving father, because 'all fathers must love their children', according to her belief system.

Our tendency to project our own qualities, values and belief systems onto others works against us when it comes to narcissists. It clouds our judgment and prevents us from seeing things clearly. It means that we assume that another person's driving forces must be as wholesome as our own. And it leads us to make excuses for exploitative, uncaring, 'odd' behaviours over and over again.

I have never met a parent who shares children with a narcissist who hasn't fallen into this trap, at least for a time — and they inevitably feel horrified and full of shame when they realize it. That they have invalidated their children's feelings about their narcissistic parent's treatment of them and normalized the narcissistic parent's behaviours can be difficult to accept. There's a lot of self-forgiveness involved in being a narcissist's enabler, especially when you are a parent.

But now let's see how Jonathan affects his work colleagues, in particular Fiona Jones, who is occupying his third orbit.

THE THIRD ORBIT

Fiona used to think Jonathan Delaney was brilliant. When she first took the job at the school, they quickly became inseparable. They just 'got on'. He would come to find her in the staff room, notably at the times when Brigitte Delaney was teaching, allegedly to discuss how to improve the French department. Jonathan confided in her that Brigitte, although a good teacher, just didn't have the creativity required to really take things further, but that Fiona was clearly 'a woman of great talent'.

They had great banter, and the pair quickly became firm friends. "Fiona, come to my office for a cuppa this break-time, would you?" Jonathan would ask, and Fiona would oblige. She would make an extra portion of her homemade flapjacks for these occasions, and Jonathan would munch on them enthusiastically, admitting that Mrs Delaney 'wasn't much of a baker'. Fiona was secretly flattered to have been selected to be the headmaster's special friend, and felt as if they had probably met in another life, as their connection seemed so strong. That said, she was happily married, although to a far less charismatic man than Jonathan, and she had absolutely no romantic designs on her boss.

Whilst she felt she should be delighted when she was promoted to Head of the Language Department, a big part of her felt guilty. Jonathan announced it with great fanfare at the staff meeting, and she was as surprised as anybody. Worse, she could sense the instant tension in the room, and she didn't miss the momentary disappointment on Brigitte's face, nor the way she quickly rearranged her features into a benign smile. The awkwardness was palpable, but Jonathan seemed oblivious to it, and he made her stand up so that the staff could applaud her. It was excruciating, and she could feel her face blushing fiercely. Fiona knew that the job should have been Brigitte's — and so did everyone else.

When she confided in Malcolm, her husband, that she didn't feel experienced enough for the role and that perhaps she should turn it down, he dismissed her worries. Ever her cheerleader, he told her that she wouldn't have been given the job had she not been suitable, and that she was probably just suffering from imposter syndrome. Malcolm thought Fiona was fantastic, and felt thrilled that she was being recognized. Fiona decided that perhaps he was right, and resolved to put her doubts to one side.

But things did not run smoothly. People would suddenly stop talking if she walked into the staff room, and everyone seemed to be making less eye contact with her. When she tried to arrange departmental meetings, often staff members would be unable to attend, or they would turn up and scroll through their phones for the duration of the meeting. Resentment was running high, and Fiona felt isolated. Only Jonathan would speak to her normally these days. She decided to talk to him about the issues he was facing, expecting support, encouragement and some strategies from him. But she was flummoxed and confused when Jonathan cut her short, and started to talk about the speech he was writing for a big headteachers' conference, and how he'd like her to provide some specific ideas for it, in writing, by the following week. She felt shut down, slightly humiliated and hurt.

This seemed to be the new norm. Fiona's new role meant that she would often have to stay late, planning lessons and holding meetings, but Jonathan would often monopolize her time, asking for her ideas on various educational issues of the day, and scribbling them down. Occasionally he would ask her to present her ideas to him as powerpoint presentations, and on one such occasion she put forward her ideas for an assembly on inclusiveness in schools, including LGBTQ issues. He seemed angry, and dismissed her hard work outright, but a few months later he gave the exact presentation in a school assembly, with no mention of her. There was a buzz in the staff room afterwards, with many hailing the talk as inspirational and forward thinking. Fiona kept waiting for Jonathan to publicly acknowledge her role in it, but he never did, and when he announced that he would be speaking about the issue on national radio, she felt churlish for feeling used.

The worst thing of all was that she had no one to confide in at the school. She was exhausted from the long hours, and from battling the lack of co-operation from her staff in the language department. She was completely unable to get support from Jonathan, who was still insisting that she brought her homemade biscuits and cakes into school for them to share at break-times, whilst refusing to talk about her worries. Only on one occasion did she feel that she had got through to him, as he appeared to listen, but she was dismayed when he told her that she was 'thinking about it all wrong' and that, as she had received a small pay-rise for her promotion, she 'didn't really have the right to complain'. Fiona, like the other victims in this book, was also completely unaware of the word 'gaslighting'.

Malcolm was starting to become concerned about Fiona. She had gone from a happy-go-lucky, energetic partner to a quiet, anxiety-ridden introvert. He was annoyed with Jonathan for failing to support her and exploiting her — although Fiona always stuck up for him when he broached the subject. Malcolm felt that she should resign from her job, have a couple of months break and then find another, whilst he took up the additional financial strain. In truth, Fiona was relieved, and tendered her resignation to Jonathan the next day, by letter. She was not expecting the reaction she received.

Jonathan begged her to stay, with tears in his eyes. He told her that her support was the only reason he could keep going. He told her that he was depressed, and that his son had shut him out of his life. "You are my *best friend…*" he proclaimed, dabbing at his eyes with his handkerchief and sniffing, "please don't desert me now". Jonathan promised Fiona that he would take some of the additional responsibilities away from her, and would speak individually to her departmental staff about co-operating with her. He even suggested that they gave their LGBTQ inclusivity talks jointly. Fiona withdrew her resignation immediately, relieved. *Everything is going to be alright*, she told herself. Although she didn't know it, she had fallen for a standard narcissistic ploy — that of 'hoovering'.

And for a short while, it was. The banter and hilarity resumed, and Jonathan was true to his word about speaking to the staff. But after just a few months, things were even worse than before. The deputy head had resigned, and even more work was heaped onto the plates of the heads of department, but especially onto Fiona, on the grounds that she was the only one Jonathan really felt 'he could trust.' Meanwhile, he was swanning off to talk about inclusivity in yet more media interviews, picking Fiona's brains on the subject for additional ideas, and then completely failing to give her any credit. The joint talks never materialized, and when Fiona tentatively mentioned the subject to him he told her, albeit with a huge smile on his face, that she 'might want to think about about taking a public speaking course' if she really wanted him to consider it.

When Fiona finally realized that Jonathan really didn't care about her or anyone else, she resigned once again, but nothing could have prepared her for his reaction. He turned on her with a venom that she could never have foreseen, and hissed angrily at her that if she left he would make sure that she never got a decent teaching job again. He declared that he would give her the worst reference imaginable, and contact every school to warn them about her incompetency, and maybe even suggest that she had embezzled money from the school. Her heart raced and she felt sick. She barely recognized the person in front of her. She fled, and went off sick for the remaining month of her contract, on the grounds of stress. The secretaries in the school office

"Narcissists take credit for other people's work, and exploit people to do their work for them."

watched her hurried, tearful exit and exchanged looks. Fiona Jones wasn't Jonathan Delaney's first casualty, and she certainly wouldn't be the last.

A word about narcissistic bosses

Jonathan Delaney is a classic narcissistic boss. He picks a favourite, and he idealizes them, telling them how wonderful they are. Of course, the recipient of this attention is flattered, and so allows their personal and professional boundaries to be crossed. In Fiona's case, the fact that Jonathan made her feel special led her to bake treats for him, and meet up with him for chats. Fiona had no idea that she was actually a victim, as the fact that she had been placed on a pedestal made her think the exact opposite.

But this favouritism will, of course, backfire on the victim, and the narcissist will gain huge narcissistic supply from watching the drama unfold. Tensions between work colleagues will rise and the victim will be ostracized by them, just as Fiona was. Eventually, Fiona came to realize that the 'gift' of being promoted to head of department was actually a poisoned chalice.

Narcissists also take credit for other people's work, and exploit people to do their work for them. If they *do* make a show of publicly acknowledging another person's role in a project, they will still be gaining something from it — and undoubtedly more than the other person will be gaining. Unsurprisingly, resentment runs high in the victims of workplace narcissists.

Abandonment

Interestingly, if a narcissist is abandoned (by *anyone* in their orbits) they do not react well. Jonathan's pity plays are a classic narcissistic reaction to being abandoned. They try to suck the person back into the relationship, in any way they can (so-called 'hoovering'). If tearful begging, or promises of more money, or better treatment don't work, they resort to threats. To Jonathan, Fiona is merely an excellent source of narcissistic supply. She is not a person in her own right, and she has no right at all to deprive him of his fuel by exiting his orbit.

But how do narcissists affect their casual acquaintances? Can they also cause carnage and chaos in *their* lives, given that they are such a long way away from the narcissist's sun? Builder Rodney provides us with Jonathan Delaney's final cautionary tale.

THE FOURTH ORBIT

Rodney is a carpenter and builder. He'd met Jonathan at the local village pub, and been sucked in by his charisma instantly, as everyone in the pub had. When Jonathan asked him to quote for a job that needed doing in his house, he was flattered, and really keen to get the job. After all, Jonathan was becoming a regular on news shows — think of the stories he could tell his mates about working for a minor celebrity! It was a smallish job, just taking up an old floor and laying a new one, but Rodney made sure he quoted as competitively as he could.

"He's just a normal bloke!" He would tell his wife, when he returned. "Made me a cup of tea himself and everything!" When he landed the work his friends teased him — "Ooh, too good to hang out with the likes of us now, aren't you?!"

Rodney found himself in stitches at Jonathan's anecdotes, and felt himself really drawn to him. "I know we come from different walks of life and everything, but I really feel that we could be mates — it's like I've known him for years! He even helped me bring my tools in from the van!"

The job came to an end, and Jonathan paid Rodney promptly. A few months later, he called upon him again, this time to quote for a small extension. Again, Rodney was thrilled when he got the job. And again, Jonathan was a delight — even remembering how he took his tea — white, two sugars, with just the right amount of milk. Rodney was charmed, and when Jonathan kept on giving him more and more work, he accepted, even though he had promised other people that he would work for them. Rodney ended up cancelling his other jobs and working pretty much full time for Jonathan. A new patio here, a new window there, a shed — on and on it went.

Slowly Rodney found himself getting to work early, just to have bit of banter with Jonathan before he left for school, and to take any instructions for that day. He then started staying slighter later, to catch up with him when he returned. If he ever did leave on time, Jonathan would draw attention to it the next day, by making a joke. "Half day again yesterday Rodney?!" he'd quip. It was funny at first, but then Rodney started to feel criticized. Was Jonathan accusing him of slacking? *Oh, I'm just being sensitive,* he'd tell himself, when everything seemed normal the next day.

Occasionally Jonathan would ask Rodney to come in at the weekend to sort something out. But when he did, he'd make sure Rodney joined the family for a sit-down cooked breakfast. Rodney felt so special and included at these times.

But at the same time, bit by bit, Jonathan was starting to erode Rodney's self-confidence. "That window frame is definitely not straight," he would complain, although it looked alright to Rodney. "You'll have to do it again, but I won't be paying for materials or labour." "It only took you 12 hours to mend the gate, but you quoted for 14 hours…" "Have you thought about doing it like this instead?" he would say to Rodney, trying to get him to use different building methods to the ones he knew best.

Rodney, even with his 20 years of experience, was starting to doubt himself. And although he didn't want to admit it to himself, he didn't like the fact that Jonathan was suggesting ways of doing things that he wasn't comfortable with. Sometimes the things Jonathan would suggest were downright unsafe — but Rodney found it hard to argue as Jonathan was paying. *Perhaps I should do things his way after all,* he would find himself thinking. And perhaps Jonathan really did know best? He was such a clever bloke, and Rodney was just a builder, after all. But now and then Rodney started to feel like his own professional standards were being compromised. And as time went on he was never sure whether Jonathan would approve of his work or not.

One day, after nearly year had passed of continuous work, Jonathan told Rodney that he'd 'drunk his own bodyweight in tea' since he'd worked there. Even though he'd had a big smile on his face as he spoke, something made Rodney feel deeply ashamed. So much so that he started bringing his own tea with him in a flask from that day on.

And was he also being oversensitive when he heard Jonathan making a joke in a thick Scottish accent, not unlike his own, to the electrician; the new guy, who now seemed to be flavour of the month? Surely Jonathan wasn't doing impressions of *him*? And was that a guilty smirk on the electrician's face, when he caught sight of Rodney?

But every now and then things would go back to being like they were at the start — Jonathan praising Rodney's work and saying that he wouldn't trust anyone else to do it. At these times Rodney felt massive relief, and his wife would reassure him that he had indeed just been a little touchy for no good reason.

When it came to Rodney's planned week off with his kids and wife, Jonathan seemed irritated that the building work would be paused, even though Rodney had given him three months' notice. Rodney had put off taking leave for the whole time that he had been working for Jonathan, much to his wife's annoyance. But Rodney desperately needed the break, so this time he decided to stick to his guns and go on holiday anyway. He was shocked to receive an email on his return, informing him that another builder had taken over the job and would be staying on in his place.

Rodney had been well and truly discarded. He never did get the outstanding money that he was owed from Jonathan, on the grounds that the work was 'too shoddy to pay for', and it took him months to build up a list of new jobs, leaving him doubly out of pocket.

Although he didn't know it, Jonathan had been complaining about his poor work ethic and building standards for months to their mutual acquaintances at the pub, leading to a big conversation when Rodney was away on holiday. Jonathan had convincingly played the role of Mr. Nice Guy, too kind to fire Rodney for his poor work, whilst the others persuaded him that he should do just that, outraged at how Rodney was clearly taking advantage of Jonathan's good nature. It's no surprise that they were far from sympathetic when Rodney returned.

Devastated at the loss of his friends from the pub, Rodney stopped going and, having lost a big part of his social life, fell into a depression. He didn't recover his spirits for well over a year, and to this day he makes big detours to avoid driving his van past Jonathan's house, in case he should see him. And every now and then Rodney still catches himself wondering where on earth he went wrong with the man he once so revered — and even considered to be his friend.

The cycle of idealization, devaluation and discard

You may have noticed that if you catch a narcissist's eye as a potential source of supply, you are likely to be 'love bombed' at first. We will discuss this in detail in the following chapter, but it can happen in all types of relationship with a narcissist, even a casual one. Although Rodney started in Jonathan's fourth orbit (where he might have been relatively safe had he been allowed to stay there), he was pulled, completely without his knowledge, into the third orbit. It's no wonder Rodney could suddenly feel an increased gravitational pull, which he experienced as a strong attraction to Jonathan — the feeling of wanting to be his friend.

Jonathan knew how to make Rodney feel special, and even remembering how he took his tea was flattering to him. I'm sure you can see similarities to the way Jonathan treated Fiona here, as he lulled them both into a false sense of security through these 'idealizing' behaviours.

But look how subtly Jonathan then begins to devalue Rodney, when he quips about his working hours being short. And notice how Jonathan intersperses these tiny put downs, disguised as jokes, with more idealizing behaviours — inviting Rodney to eat breakfast with his family, or complimenting his work. This cycle is hardly ever obvious to a narcissist's victim. If one day Rodney is being ridiculed for his accent, but the next he is being praised, it's no wonder he would feel off-balance. Rodney, like all victims of narcissists, just tried harder to please Jonathan when he was devalued, and he allowed him to trample all over his professional boundaries (like Fiona did) by allowing him to tell him how to do his work. Can you see how these patterns are similar throughout the orbits?

When Rodney decided he would stick to a boundary and go away on holiday, Jonathan reacted badly. Incensed by the audacity of it, he discarded him. The narcissistic supply he derived from not paying Rodney what he owed him (from the conflict) would have made him feel clever and superior. He would also have derived a great deal of supply from his 'smear campaign', conducted in the pub, during which he badmouthed Rodney to others — another bog-standard narcissistic tactic.

But why did Jonathan eject Rodney from his solar system, instead of keeping him there, as a source of supply? Probably just because he could. After all, these casual acquaintances are only minor sources of supply, and are easily replaceable. It's nice to switch things up every now and then in the fourth orbit.

5

How narcissists trap their victims

If you have a narcissistic parent, grandparent or sibling, you would have been unfortunate enough to have been *born* into their trap. Furthermore, it's going to be hard for you to escape the trap, not least because *society* tells you that you must put up with your family, no matter what they do to you.

But what about those narcissists out there who are not your family members? How do *they* lure their victims into their traps? Narcissists employ a two-step procedure — first they identify their victim, and then they deploy their entrapment tactics.

STEP ONE: IDENTIFYING A VICTIM

Most narcissists need victims who will enhance their status in some way, so they will consider your social desirability when considering you as a potential victim. However, *all* narcissists need victims who are going to be compliant with their wishes, so that they stay in whichever orbit they have been placed, as a reliable source of narcissistic supply. They will glean this information from your relationships and your personality characteristics. Bear in mind that your social media is likely to be a great starting point for a narcissist who is investigating you.

Your status enhancing properties

It's not just the Closet Narcissists who are attracted to people who appear 'special', although this is a particularly pronounced feature with them, to the extent that their targets can range from minor local celebrities to A-listers. But *most* narcissists are attracted to people who have something different or special about them, that reflects well on them.

It may be that you are particularly attractive. Perhaps you are the life and soul of the party. You may be successful in your line of work. You may come from a background which will enable the narcissist to 'social climb'. You might be very young, and so seen as a 'trophy' by a middle-aged narcissist who is hunting for a partner. Perhaps you are rich. Perhaps you are impressively intellectual, or a great conversationalist. Perhaps you have an image as a leader or a public speaker, which a narcissistic business partner might want to be associated with, or a skill which they can exploit or take credit for. You might be a wonderful cook and homemaker, or be good at home renovating, allowing a narcissistic mate to be the envy of their acquaintances. You may just have great potential for the future, obvious to all who meet you.

All narcissists have hierarchical thinking, and constantly compare themselves to others. In the ideal scenario, a narcissist's victim will be someone who will be able to lift the narcissist's own status up, in their own mind. However, not all narcissists will be looking for this — those narcissists who are particularly wealthy and successful may simply not need another person to enhance their status, and will

"All narcissists have hierarchical thinking, and constantly compare themselves to others..."

just be happy with someone well below them in the food chain, who they can look down upon as they bleed them for their narcissistic supply. Tragically though, for the people who *were* targeted for their status enhancing qualities, the narcissist will inevitably become jealous of those qualities, and will try to sabotage or destroy them as the relationship progresses — often successfully.

Your relationships

A narcissist will always look at your other relationships, when assessing your suitability as a target. Some narcissists will ask a lot of deep questions when they first meet you — about your relationships with parents, family and friends, and about your career. Some may self-disclose *first*, revealing what you assume are their vulnerabilities, so that you feel as though you are safe to do the same. Others will be more subtle. If you are in the online dating arena, a narcissist might be able to glean a lot about your past relationships from your dating profile. Statements like 'no game-players' are hugely informative to a narcissist. You are at a higher risk of being targeted by a narcissist if:

- **You have been in a previous abusive relationship**. It doesn't matter what that relationship was — it may be that you were taken advantage of by a co-worker, or bullied by a boss. Perhaps you have been in a romantic relationship with an abuser, who emotionally or physically abused you (or both). Perhaps you had a narcissistic friend who destroyed your self-worth, or badmouthed you in your community. These will all tick a narcissist's boxes.

- **You are still in an abusive relationship**. It is possible that you are currently in an abusive relationship — but you do not even know it. However, you can be sure that a narcissist looking for a victim will be able to pick up on it. So perhaps you have a toxic friend or sibling, or you are having legal issues with your neighbour over a property dispute. As you now know, there are many possibilities.

- **You were brought up by a narcissist**. If you have a narcissistic parent, and have not healed from the relationship, you are the perfect victim for another narcissist. The childhood wounds that you carry will be easy for a narcissist to identify, and, better still (for them), you are likely to feel a strong chemistry with narcissists, making it even easier for one to reel you in. Humans are subconsciously drawn to people who remind them of their primary caregivers. What you may feel to be a soulmate connection, or an instant feeling of 'having known someone your whole life' may actually be a huge flashing warning light for you. If you have been brought up by a narcissist, take heed of the following: 'You find the person whose teeth fit your wounds.'

- **You have played a 'caretaker' role in previous relationships with adults**. Perhaps the person you looked after was a substance addict, or had a chronic illness. It may be that as a child you had to look after a sick parent, or one who was an alcoholic. People who come from relationships like these often need the *other person* to feel okay for *them* to feel okay. They are used to putting the other person's needs ahead of their own — making them perfect for a narcissist who sees their own needs as paramount.

Your personality characteristics

Many people find it difficult to accept that their personality characteristics might have contributed to them falling prey to a relationship with a narcissist, and incorrectly perceive this as 'victim blaming'. I want to stress here that, in fact, the blame does *not* lie with the victim, but with the narcissist, who is hunting for people who happen to have these characteristics. The narcissist will need to uncover these stealthily. Personality characteristics which make you attractive to a narcissist are:

- **Being naturally trusting.** If your default position is to trust people, until they give you a reason not to trust them, you are an ideal target for a narcissist.

- **Believing that all people are 'basically good'.** This is a great footing on which to begin a relationship with a narcissist (for them, that is).

- **Believing that 'love conquers all'.** In romantic relationships or friendships with narcissists, this mindset allows the narcissist to behave badly, knowing that they will be forgiven by you repeatedly — and that you will try to make things better by loving them even more.

- **Being 'too easy-going'.** I'm talking here about people who come across as easy-going because, in fact, they have no preferences or needs. These people may actually have come from co-dependent relationships, where they have put the needs of the other person above their own. They may have no idea what *they* actually want, and may not even realize that they are *allowed* to want anything, or to have a preference. If you don't mind which type of food you eat, where you sit in the office or bar, which movie you watch, or whether you'd prefer a tea or coffee, a narcissist may well set their sights on you as a target.

- **Having an aversion to feeling special.** How do you respond to compliments? Can you accept them graciously, or do they make you feel uncomfortable? If you are the sort of person that bats compliments away (perhaps by telling the person who is complimenting you that they are actually wrong, and that your hair is looking terrible at the moment/you've actually put on weight/you had a lot of help with the presentation), this could be very attractive to a narcissist. If you receive a lovely gift, do you ever feel that it is too good for you, so you give it away, or save it for a special occasion with others? This again can be a sign that you feel undeserving and unworthy. It means that you are the polar opposite to a narcissist, who is always looking to try to feel special — and as we all know, opposites attract.

- **Being highly empathic.** A narcissist will play on this attribute time and time again, telling tales of woe so that their poor behaviour is forgiven and made excuses for by the empathic person. If you are the sort of person who cannot watch the news because you find it too upsetting, or if you work in a caring profession, rescue animals, or are involved with charities, narcissists will be drawn to you like moths to a flame.

- **Being a people pleaser.** People pleasers are also prime targets for narcissists, because their focus will be on pleasing the narcissist, and they will be unable to see their situation objectively. Do you always need other people to like you and to positively accept you? Do you desperately avoid conflict with others, including by apologizing often, even for things that are not your fault? Do people take advantage of your giving nature? Do you find it difficult to say 'no' to doing what others ask of you? Do you struggle more than most with criticism? Do you find it difficult to disagree with other people? Do you feel as though you are 'not enough' as you are? Are other people's opinions of you more important than your own? Do you fear not being liked or accepted? If so, you might be one such people pleaser.

- **Having 'rescuing' tendencies.** Rescuers are easily taken in by a narcissist's pity plays and exploited. They may need to rescue others to feel needed and to matter, and this is a trait that has developed in their own childhoods, perhaps as a result of abandonment, or because they had a parent to rescue, perhaps from drug or alcohol misuse. If you are a rescuer, you might only feel good about yourself when you are saving others, something a narcissist will use to enable their abuse, drawing you in, exploiting your kindness and claiming dependency on you.

- **Being loyal.** If you are a loyal person, and you do not badmouth others, a narcissist will know that you will keep *their* bad behaviour towards you under wraps. Narcissists need others to see them as perfect and special, so that they can see themselves as being that way, and they know that you will be complicit in this — a highly attractive trait to a narcissist.

- **Having poor boundaries.** A boundary is where you end, and another person begins. Setting and sticking to solid boundaries enables people to protect and take care of themselves, by defining what they will and won't be responsible for. Boundaries can be physical, professional, personal, emotional, sexual, to do with time, or a combination of these. You might be good at exerting one type of boundary (professional, for example), but not so good with other types. If you have poor boundaries, you may be unable to say 'no' and mean it, and you might feel resentful for much of the time. People might repeatedly cancel you, or fail to show at agreed meetings without warning, if you are a poor boundary setter. Narcissists are flagrant boundary violators — they will not take 'no' for an answer, so those with poor, porous, weak, moveable boundaries are ideal targets for them.

The testing process

A narcissist will not be able to glean all the information that they need about the personality traits above by just asking you questions — a certain amount of testing will be required, and how you respond to their tests will determine whether or not they choose you as a victim.

Which tests they use depends on the type of relationship you have with them. For example, a narcissistic boss might test your boundaries by sending you a friend request on social media, and seeing whether you accept it, whereas a narcissist who wants to be your friend might turn up to your house unannounced, late in the evening with a bottle of wine, to see how you respond. A narcissist who wants to be your partner might see how you respond to staying out with them on a weekday night until 1 am, when you'd previously said that you needed to be home by 11. They might test the solidity of your boundaries by insisting that your first date is dinner in their home, even though you'd stated that you'd prefer to meet in a coffee shop during the day, to see whether you cave in.

A narcissist on a first date, testing how trusting you are, might tell you that you can leave your bag with them whilst you visit the restroom, whereas a narcissist who wants to go into business with you might see whether you look at the lunch bill, or just let them divide it and tell you how much you owe.

Seeing how you respond to a compliment will give a narcissist lots of information about your personality, as will seeing how you deal with them exerting a bit of control over your choices. For example, a narcissist will be keen to see how you react if they go to the bar to get you a gin and tonic, as you requested, but instead return with a very sweet tasting cocktail. If you are a people pleaser, you'll thank them politely — a dead giveaway.

Empathy is easy to test, and a simple sob story to test your reaction is all that is required. Do you actually wince when they tell you something physically painful, like about the time they chopped off the top of their finger? Do you become visibly upset when they tell you something sad?

Do you offer to help them when they tell you of the difficulties they are having (even though you don't really know them), giving away your rescuing tendencies?

Loyalty is also easy to test — if you can't be drawn into telling tales about your old place of work, or badmouthing your previous partner or your wicked stepmother, then you will be a pretty safe bet when it comes to exposing their flaws to your support network. (This is the only scenario I can think of where being a bit bitchy might actually be a good thing).

Seeing how you respond to a mild criticism or put down is also something that a narcissist will wish to test early on, perhaps disguising the criticism as a joke. If you believe that all people are basically good, or you make excuses for people's bad behaviour ('they must have been tired or stressed') a narcissist will know that you will accept such criticisms without pushing back. You may even apologize or *change* the thing that you have been criticized for, which is an even better sign that you are ripe for exploitation. Seeing how you respond to repeated lateness is another great way to test you.

STEP TWO: LURING THE VICTIM INTO THE TRAP

Once the narcissist has identified a suitable victim, who they are confident they will be able to place and keep in their orbit, they start the entrapment process, using love bombing, shapeshifting, future faking and rescuing (or being rescued).

Relationships with narcissists usually progress at a very fast pace, and this is a big red flag for narcissism being at play. If, within a month of meeting, you've signed that contract with your business partner, booked to go abroad with your new best friend, or discussed baby names with your 'soulmate' partner, you may have already fallen into the trap, and fallen prey to the highly effective tactics described below.

Love bombing

Love bombing is often known as the 'idealization' or the 'idolizing' phase. If you think back to our four different types of narcissist, they all employed love bombing in some way with their victims. The whole point of love bombing is to make you feel special. A narcissist will put you on a pedestal, and tell you how great you are. They will laugh raucously at your jokes (even the rubbish ones). They will hang upon your every word, ask you for your opinions and appear to agree with them.

Jonathan, our Exhibitionist Narcissist, the headmaster, love bombed Fiona, one of his teachers, through spending lots of time with her, and by giving her special treatment and a promotion. He love bombed the builder, Rodney, by complimenting his work, and by treating him as a friend in the initial stages of their relationship, with much banter.

Exhibitionist, Devaluing and Communal Narcissists will go on an all out charm offensive as part of their love bombing. This makes their victims feel flattered to be noticed by them (which, in turn, makes the victim feel special by association).

Closet Narcissists may be less obvious in their love bombing. Lina, our Closet Narcissist, love bombed Raj by cooking for him, and providing him with emotional support.

'Mirroring' is an essential part of love bombing. Narcissists will often mirror their target's likes and dislikes at the beginning of a relationship, so that they can appear to be the perfect person for them. Think back to how Oonagh would love listening to classical music with Geoff, and would ask him to play his violin for her at the beginning of their courtship, and how heavily this contrasted with later on.

Narcissists are adept at working out what a person needs most in order to feel valued. I like to think about this in terms of the five so-called 'love languages', but actually it doesn't just apply to romantic relationships and friendships.

Some people express their love mostly through the *words* they use. These people will compliment their loved ones, and tell them how much they value and love them.

Some show their love through *giving gifts* to others. Spending *time* with loved ones is another way to demonstrate love, and some people are very *physical* in their expressions of love, hugging, holding hands or putting their arms around their loved ones. And some people are much more *practical* in the way they show their love, through helping them with chores, tasks and projects.

A narcissist will work out, by watching how you express your love, which of the love languages is important to you, and they will love bomb you accordingly, mirroring your preferences. You might be constantly complimented on your abilities, your looks, or your personality. You might be showered with gifts or taken out for lavish meals, if that is your thing. The narcissist might spend every waking hour with you, or be in constant communication with you, if spending time with your loved ones is how you express your love. They may be very physical with you, turning into a sex kitten or love god, if they glean that that is your bag. Or they may give you practical help, by painting your garden shed for you, making you delicious meals, or helping you with your tax return.

> *"Relationships with narcissists usually progress at a very fast pace — this is a big red flag for narcissism."*

Workplace narcissists have their own ways of leveraging your love languages against you too — by making a beeline towards you every morning and clapping you on the back and shaking your hand; by insisting on buying you lunch; by choosing you as the person to accompany them on the swanky business trip; by complimenting your work publicly in team meetings; or by offering you help with your project.

Shapeshifting

I don't wish to ascribe a supernatural kind of power to narcissists, which they don't actually have, but shapeshifting is a really good word for the way that narcissists can become the exact person you are looking for.

Because they often grew up having to tiptoe around a difficult parent, narcissists learned how to become hyper-aware of other people's moods and sensitivities, so that they could stay safe. You already know that narcissists have limited 'emotional empathy' (which means that they are unable to step into someone else's shoes and *actually* feel what they are feeling, rendering them unable to really care about them). However, many narcissists have excellent 'cognitive empathy' and are able to intellectually pick up on a person's emotions. So narcissists can be very well attuned to other people's desires, and can deliver upon them, as part of the entrapment process. Remember that a narcissist's false persona is an invented outer shell, and is basically a lie — it's not hard to make some temporary tweaks when required.

You can be sure that your narcissistic business partner will be organized, motivated and great at delivering whatever is needed at the beginning of your partnership, lulling you into a false sense of security. Your new narcissistic bandmate will have practised the songs, and printed them out for you. If you have come out of a difficult intimate relationship, your narcissistic date will be patient and appear to be empathic and a good listener, as they construct an identity which is the exact opposite of your awful ex. Your new super-empathic narcissistic friend will help with your deceased spouse's funeral arrangements, and will make the vol-au-vents for the reception. And your new neighbour will insist on sewing 150 name labels into your child's new school uniform to lighten your load. None of this seems like suspicious behaviour on the surface — so you can see why it's easy to be fooled. Whoever you need a narcissist to be, they will become — until you are safely in their trap.

Future faking

Future faking is often used by narcissists as part of the lure. They will offer or promise things that simply won't materialize. A promotion, a raise, or an invitation to next year's annual conference in the Maldives. Recommending your business to all of their contacts, if you do this one big project for them for free. A wish to get married, have a white picket fence, and have children with you. Remember Geoff's bitterness when, after several years of marriage, Oonagh went back on her proclamations of wanting to have children? The options for future faking are endless, and the narcissist will uncover your future wants and offer them to you. Maybe don't post your bucket list on Facebook?

Rescuing you

This is a terribly common way for a narcissist to trap their victim, by riding in on a big white horse, and scooping them up. If you are having a tricky time in life, a narcissist *will* take advantage of it, if you let them. Thinking back to Lina, our Closet Narcissist, she even told Raj that she believed that Parvati, the Goddess of Love had sent her to save Raj from his grief. Our Communal Narcissist, Marcus, saved single mother Irina and her young son Janis from poverty, by moving them into his sizeable London home. Workplace narcissists will swoop in with a job offer when you lose yours, the narcissistic person who wants to be your friend will lend you your rent money, and the narcissistic village vicar will start inviting you to Sunday lunch at the vicarage, and rope you into becoming a regular churchgoer, as soon he finds out about your bereavement.

The result is that you feel indebted to your rescuer and so, eventually, you go along with their requests or demands. If you've been rescued, you've been disempowered — and narcissists seem to know this instinctively.

Being rescued by you

Another oft-employed entrapment tactic is constructing a scenario where the narcissist gets *you* to rescue *them* (if you happen to have the rescuing personality trait). They *need* you, and they trap you through your own empathy, and keep you there through guilt. Think back to Oonagh's meltdown in the university park, in reaction to her sister getting engaged before her. Geoff fell for it, and got down on one knee and proposed there and then.

Why is it so easy to fall into the trap?

Narcissists look 'normal'. The very nature of narcissism means that most narcissists superficially appear to be not much different to 'ordinary' people — people like us — which is just one of the reasons why they fly under our radars so very effectively. The exception is the subtype of narcissist who appears to be much *better* than average. They are better looking, funnier, cleverer and more successful than everyone around them, and often fall into the exhibitionist category.

But regardless of subtype, narcissists don't have two heads, or come with warning symbols tattooed on their foreheads, and nor do they speak in an alien tongue. And we assume that, just because they *appear* to be like us, they must *think* like us, and their values, beliefs and motivations must be like ours. We believe that they hold the same moral principles. That they are guided by the same star. But, whilst still being human, those with Narcissistic Personality Disorder do *not* think like us, behave like us, or feel like us, *because underneath they are completely different from us, no matter how similar they may superficially appear to be.*

Do narcissists *know* that they are narcissists?

I think we have reached a good point to tackle this important question, because I recognize that, reading the above section, the implication is that narcissists 'know exactly what they are doing'. But in fact, the vast majority of narcissists do not actually know that they are narcissists. The occasional chest thumping braggart of an Exhibitionist Narcissist, may know that they are a narcissist (because they have repeatedly been told that they are) but, to them, this is actually something to be *proud of*, as it works to their advantage.

Whilst narcissists may know *what* they are doing to some extent, the vast majority don't know *why* they are doing it — they are unaware of the subconscious programming that is driving their behaviours. Contrary to popular belief, most narcissists do not plot and scheme late into the dead of night — their manipulations are effortless. However, a minority most certainly do consciously manipulate — and these are the really frightening ones.

"Most narcissists do not plot and scheme late into the dead of night — their manipulations are effortless"

So, most narcissists just naturally follow the two-step procedure above, without knowing that that is what they are doing. The behaviours described in this book are merely a description of the narcissist's operating manual — which most narcissists don't know even exists.

THE NARCISSIST TRAP

Could *you* be a narcissist's enabler?

An enabler is someone who allows and even enables the narcissist to carry out their abuse, usually unwittingly.

The narcissist's enablers are the people who have absolutely no idea that they have been sucked into the trap. They are orbiting the narcissist, but the narcissist is not subjecting them to any abusive behaviours (at least, not to a noticeable degree). So how have they escaped the abuse? Because the narcissist's enablers are fuelling the narcissist with huge amounts of narcissistic supply, by lavishing them with attention, admiration and adoration. They don't need to be abused to do their job — they are excellent sources of supply anyway. Most partners of narcissists find themselves in this role, but only at the very beginning of their relationship. Enablers may occupy any orbit — but what is common to all is that, however far away they are from the narcissist's sun, they are completely dazzled and blinded by it.

Essentially, enablers are the narcissist's fan club, who are colloquially known as their 'flying monkeys.' The term originated from *The Wizard of Oz*, where the flying monkeys were the creatures who would do the evil bidding of the Wicked Witch for her. These people are so invested in the narcissist's false persona, so utterly charmed by it, that they will carry out abusive behaviours on their behalf, in order to remain in their good books, or to be promoted to Very Special Person To Them, by being pulled into a closer orbit. They may even be 'waiting in the wings' for the narcissist's primary relationship to fail.

They might spread rumours (that they probably believe are true) about someone who has fallen out of favour with the narcissist. They might relay gossip about someone to the narcissist. They might even help them in immoral ways — hiding money or property for them during a divorce, or worse.

Flying monkeys will vehemently deny any wrongdoing on the narcissist's part, no matter how compelling the evidence is against them, and they will be completely taken in by the narcissist's stories of victimhood. They'll deny the narcissist's true character and stand up for them. We see these flying monkeys every day in the world of politics, where narcissistic leaders are hailed as heroes by their political subordinates, usually to the ridicule of the press.

These are the people who are always pleased to see the narcissist, and make a big fanfare when they show up. These are the people who are flattered to be in the narcissist's orbit, and who feel special to be seen and heard by them. These are the people who always invite the narcissist to important occasions in their life. The type that mentions them in their wedding or birthday speeches, because they think that they are one of their best friends (even though the narcissist might only consider them to be a passing acquaintance). The narcissist's enablers are the people that always fall for their pity plays and drive over with meals for them when they say they are having a bad time. The people who take them out to parties to cheer them up when they have been abandoned by their latest 'awful, crazy ex'.

So, if you happen to be such a flying monkey, it is likely that you think very highly of the narcissist in your life. If you ever hear anything unfavourable about them you will probably refute it, or stand up for them. "But he's a lovely chap!" "But she's always very pleasant to *me*," or "They've never done anything horrible to *me*!" are common refrains from the narcissist's enablers.

Be honest now. Could this be (or have ever been) *you*? Have you ever found yourself doing something you shouldn't as a result of falling for a fake sob story, only questioning your judgment years down the line? Are you cringing, red-faced as you read? Have you ever noticed a narcissist's bad behaviour, but chosen to deny it, minimize it, or justify it, because it felt better that way? Because you wanted to be in their social sphere? Ah well. Don't beat yourself up about it — we've probably all been there.

6

Why is it so hard to escape?

To use a physics metaphor, if you want to overcome a narcissist's gravitational pull you have to build up enough speed to reach your 'escape velocity.' Only once you reach this can you break free of your orbit. But to reach this critical speed, you need to have enough *fuel* on board to burn — and fuel is the very thing that narcissists deplete you of. Your fuel is made up of your self-confidence, your self-esteem, your self-worth, your self-belief and your healthy self-love. Without it, you are too weak to leave.

A narcissist will keep you trapped not just by stealing your fuel, but by making you *dependent* on them. And narcissists will also use your own *brain systems* against you, to prevent you from seeing what is really going on, and to make you *addicted* to them. In this chapter we examine all of these,

> *"Being in any type of relationship with a narcissist is exactly like being in a cult."*

and we also have a look at what happens to those who try to eject themselves from the narcissist's orbit.

Being in any type of relationship with a narcissist is exactly like being in a cult (cult leaders are known to be pathologically narcissistic). I was first struck by this some years ago, having chanced upon a documentary in which three victims, who had been ensnared by different cults, told their stories, upon escaping. They sounded *exactly* like the partners of narcissists I'd come across in my work, who had managed to exit their orbits.

But your everyday narcissist will use exactly the same tactics to keep their victims trapped as their cult leader cousins do. These methods are extremely effective, and they start *small*. Because they are then turned up in volume, little by little, their victims stay put. The analogy of the frog in the pot of boiling water is a good one here. Frog A starts out in a pot of cold water on the stove, but the temperature is turned up so slowly that the he accepts more and more of the heat, and doesn't even jump out when the pot is boiling. But frog B, who is thrown into a pot of water which is already boiling, jumps out immediately. The victim of narcissistic abuse is, of course, frog A.

Once again, those with NPD do these things completely naturally and effortlessly, because this is what they have become programmed to do, with little conscious awareness. Let's take a deeper look at exactly how stealing their victims' fuel, creating dependency upon them and using their victims' brain systems against them keeps victims stuck in their orbits.

STEALING THE VICTIM'S FUEL

Narcissists steal their victims' fuel (made up of their self-confidence, self-esteem, self-worth, self-belief and healthy self-love) in two major ways — by 'devaluing' them and by 'gaslighting' them. Let's look at devaluing behaviours first.

DEVALUATION TACTICS

You already know how the so-called 'Devaluing Narcissists', such as Oonagh, put their victims down to keep them in their place. These devaluations are virtually unmissable in this type of narcissist, but in fact, *all* types of narcissist employ this tactic, to some degree. If you've been lured into the Narcissist Trap you might be able to identify tiny devaluations *early on* in your relationship. Even back then, the narcissist would have been noting your reactions to these putdowns, to assess your suitability as prey.

If a narcissist devalues you and puts you down enough, eventually you are likely to feel less important than the narcissist, and therefore *less powerful.* Devaluation tactics can be non-verbal or verbal.

Imagine that you walk into your office and your, usually pleasant, co-worker completely blanks you. The first time, you make an excuse for them, thinking that they were too engrossed in a task to notice you. Perhaps another time they look bored when you are speaking, and yawn, or check their phone. Again, not great, but hardly a crime. Perhaps you are eating your sandwiches at your desk, and you get a bit of mayo on your chin, which you wipe off. You may catch them wincing slightly, so you feel embarrassed, and decide not to eat in the office again.

"Narcissists steal their victims' fuel (made up of their self-confidence, self-esteem, self-worth, self-belief and healthy self-love) in two major ways — by 'devaluing' them and by 'gaslighting' them."

As the devaluations increase, you might find them pulling faces at another co-worker or rolling their eyes, when you are speaking. They might completely refuse to talk to you for a whole day, resulting in you wondering what you have done wrong. You might fawn to try to get back in their good books, perhaps by buying them a coffee or persistently trying to engage with them. They might actually start to walk away when you try to speak to them, and if you ask them a work-related question by email, they might just ignore it completely, stonewalling you. They are likely to start being late for you, and to keep you waiting when you have arranged to meet to discuss a project, making you feel unimportant. They may begin to leave your meetings early, making you feel that they have more important things to attend to than working with you.

You can see how all of these non-verbal devaluations can be ramped up over time, to the point where they look openly disgusted or repulsed when you walk into the office, they give you the silent treatment for days on end, and your work 'mysteriously disappears' from your computer when you leave your desk to go to the water cooler.

But what will throw you off balance, is that they will *intersperse these devaluations with times when they act completely normally towards you.* You will, most likely start to question whether they really happened at all, or make excuses for them during these reprises. ('They must have been stressed/tired/ill…'). I like to call this alternating game 'Nice Narcissist, Nasty Narcissist'.

The same will be true for verbal devaluations, which will also start small. Think back to Jonathan, and Rodney, his builder. His jokey assertions that Rodney must be on a 'half day' when he left work on time was the classic criticism disguised as joke. Telling him that he had 'drunk his own bodyweight in tea' whilst working for him was another little put down, resulting in shamed Rodney bringing his own tea to work in a flask. On Jonathan and Brigitte's wedding day, Jonathan told the wedding guests in his speech, with a broad smile, that 'Brigitte had indeed scrubbed up well for the day'. The guests had chuckled good-naturedly, but Brigitte had felt humiliated.

If the target accepts these put downs, the narcissist will slowly ramp up the insults, testing how far they can go. Eventually, frank name-calling and insults can become the norm. "You are boring," "You speak too fast/slowly/quietly/loudly," "You are a social embarrassment," "You are hard to get along with", "You can't dance/sing/cook/write/do your work properly/deliver what is required of you…" It's only when it gets this extreme that people might recognize it as frank bullying — but by this point they may already be well and truly trapped.

Your taste in clothes, furnishing, houses, art, music, or anything else can be used to devalue you, as can your choice of career or parenting methods. The way you stand, the way you speak, the way you blow your nose; the list is literally endless, no matter what your relationship is to the narcissist. Even a narcissist's children will be demeaned and criticized behind closed doors, to keep them in their place.

Over time it's not hard to see how a narcissist's victim could eventually come to believe that they are 'not enough' in any way. After all, their self-esteem, self-belief, self-confidence, self-worth and self-love has been pilfered by the narcissist — and their fuel tank is practically empty.

Triangulation

Another great way to devalue someone is by 'triangulating' them with other people. Triangulation is where a third person is brought into the dynamic with the purpose of making you feel threatened and inadequate — so draining away your self-belief and self-confidence.

Remember how Oonagh started to openly ogle the muscular men on their beach honeymoon, making lanky Geoff feel insecure? She knew his vulnerabilities, and she deployed them against him. You can be sure that your narcissistic co-worker, whilst completely ignoring you, will be engaging loudly and enthusiastically with the other people in the office, whilst you look on, perplexed and upset. When Jonathan met new teacher, Fiona Jones, he made sure he would recount his conversations with her to his wife, Brigitte, ad nauseam, so that she felt boring and stupid by comparison. And Lina would wax lyrical to Raj about 'Jenni's husband', the George Clooney lookalike, which had the effect of making him try harder to please her — putting her needs above his own, and so shifting the power dynamic in her favour.

"Silent treatments are a classic example of passive aggression, as is persistent lateness."

Passive aggression

You might have noticed that many of these examples have an element of 'passive aggression' to them, which enables the narcissist to *covertly* devalue others, in subtle ways. These passive aggressive manoeuvres also allow the narcissist to believe in their own image of 'niceness' so they can avoid having to feel any shame for their actions — highly important to a narcissist who has to believe in their carefully constructed image of perfection, to feel emotionally safe.

Silent treatments are a classic example of passive aggression, as is persistent lateness. Blaming a third person for the insults they are using against their victim ("My sister says you've put on weight. *I* think you look fine though...") also falls into this category, as does putting someone down 'out of concern' for them. ("Don't be too disappointed when it doesn't work out/you don't get the job.").

Pretending that you are putting someone down for 'their own good' is another form of passive aggression. I remember, as a junior doctor, working on a hospital ward where another doctor (at the same level as me) was slowly and deliberately explaining something to the nursing staff, in a deeply patronizing tone. He always used to come into work wearing a cravat (yes, seriously) and a matching handmade waistcoat, even though he was only in his early twenties. When he spotted them exchanging glances with one another, I remember him declaring, at full volume, in plummy tones, "I am only telling you this because I know you want to *better* yourselves." I believe he went on to be very successful, as so many of these types do, but I doubt he won many long-term friends along the way.

Making other people do their tasks for them

If a narcissist can get you to do more and more things for them, it automatically devalues your worth and makes you feel less important than them. Over time, you will start to actually *believe* that you are less important, as your levels of self-worth are depleted.

Procrastinating when it comes to tasks (or doing them ineffectively or deliberately badly, so that the victim takes over) are common narcissistic acts (which also overlap with passive aggression). Could it be that the wife who seems to be 'unable' to load the dishwasher effectively may actually be actually asserting her dominance and importance, relative to her husband?

Closet Narcissists might be particularly subtle here, using pity plays to get you to take over their tasks. Remember how Lina's mystery aches and pains rendered her completely unable to do the housework, but she wouldn't let Raj employ a cleaner? Oonagh also managed to assert her dominance over husband Geoff by expecting to be waited on hand and foot by him, on the dubious grounds that her job was 'intellectually more demanding' than his.

And just think back — have you ever had a narcissistic co-worker who always 'panics' at the eleventh hour, because the 'hours of work' they assure you they did on your joint project 'just wouldn't save'? These 'dog ate my homework' type of excuses are often employed by narcissists at work. They know that if their victim repeatedly takes up the slack and does the work for them, they will unknowingly slide down the food chain relative to them — so losing the fuel (and the power) they need to escape.

Now that we've looked at devaluation, let's have a look at the other big way that narcissists raid their victims' fuel stores — by 'gaslighting' them.

GASLIGHTING

Gaslighting is a key feature of narcissistic behaviour, and it's quite a frightening method of draining you of your self-confidence and self-belief, so lowering the fuel reserves you need to escape your orbit.

The narcissist actually alters their victim's *reality*, so that they are unable to see things as they really are. Confused, they lose confidence and trust in themselves, *and they come to trust the narcissist instead*, which gives them even more power.

So what exactly is gaslighting? To give its proper definition, it's the 'act of undermining someone's reality, by denying facts, denying the environment around them, or denying their feelings.'

But let me simplify that. Basically, if someone is lying to you in a way that makes you question or stop trusting your own perceptions, memories or beliefs, they are gaslighting you. Make no mistake — this really is a very dangerous form of psychological abuse.

Gaslighting versus lying

You may be wondering what the difference is between gaslighting and 'normal' lying, so here's an example to illustrate.

If we'd agreed to meet for dinner at 7 pm, but I'd left the house late because I just couldn't get my act together, I could lie to you and tell you that the traffic had been awful, and that that was why I didn't arrive until 8 pm. Here I'm not making you question or doubt yourself — I'm just telling you a lie.

But, if I was gaslighting you, I could tell you with absolute conviction that *you* had got the time wrong, and that we had agreed to meet at 8 pm. I might then embellish that further by telling you that I'd noticed that you seemed to be forgetting small things, and 'losing your thread' in conversations. I could even then ask you whether you'd considered talking to a doctor about it.

It's gaslighting *because it would make you question yourself,* and make you doubt whether you had got the time right, or whether you are, in fact, making mistakes and forgetting things. Gaslighting is itself a two-step procedure — first you are made to think that your thinking or feelings are distorted, and then the gaslighter tries to persuade you that *their* ideas are the true and right ones.

> *"If someone is lying to you in a way that makes you question or stop trusting your own perceptions, memories or beliefs, they are gaslighting you."*

The term gaslighting originated from a 1938 thriller in which a husband makes his wife think she is 'going mad' by dimming the gas lamps in their home to just a flicker, and then denying that they are flickering when she questions him.

As it happens, narcissists do both things — straight lying and gaslighting, and they do them both utterly convincingly, because *the truth, to a narcissist, is what they say it is, at the time that they are saying it.* They completely believe their own lies, which is how they get others to doubt themselves. And if you think about it, lying and gaslighting actually come very easily to narcissists, because it's essentially what they do all the time anyway — if you look at the essence of narcissism, the narcissist hides their low self-esteem behind a false persona, which they need other people to believe in so that they can believe in it themselves. This false persona is basically a lie — it's not a true representation of who they are. So you can see why it is so easy for them to effortlessly lie about other, smaller things too.

Gaslighting your memories

One of the most common forms of gaslighting is when a narcissist denies a person's *memory* of events, by saying something along the lines of 'That didn't happen'. This is incredibly common, and narcissists are known for rewriting history, completely denying that things have happened. They might say "I never said that — actually what I said was this…" Or "I never did that — actually what I did was this…" If you work with a narcissist, you may well find yourself poring of the minutes of the meetings to check that you are not losing your mind. You can even find yourself wanting to record every conversation, to prove that what you heard was true.

A client of mine told me that her narcissistic ex would make himself a cup of tea in front of her, and then tell her, with absolute conviction, that it was actually coffee he was drinking, and that she had remembered it wrong. After years of this, she began to doubt herself — although, after she eventually left, she came to understand how bizarre this behaviour had been.

Gaslighting your feelings

So how can gaslighting be applied to a person's *feelings?* Anyone who has had a relationship with a narcissist will be familiar with expressing their emotions to them, only to have them trivialized, minimized or invalidated.

Imagine the scenario where a male narcissist has been caught in a compromising position, perhaps with a prostitute, perhaps on an office night out.

Quite justly, their partner will feel betrayed and upset — but a narcissist might tell them that *all* the men who work in his office regularly do this, and that it is normal. They might tell their partner that they are 'thinking about it incorrectly', and that they are *not* actually being unfaithful, because they are paying for the service. They might assert that, in truth, they are helping someone in need (the prostitute) to pay their bills and make their way in life, and that this should be seen as a 'good thing'. They may tell their partner that using prostitutes has no bearing at all on how they feel about *their* relationship, and the two things are completely separate. They may even try to make their partner feel guilty, perhaps suggesting that *they* are a bad person for not allowing the narcissist to help the prostitute to do her job, to keep her family in food. They may accuse their partner of intruding on their private life, or they may blame them for needing to visit prostitutes in the first place, because they always seem too tired to service their needs themselves. A narcissist might even demand an *apology* — and if the victim has been gaslit enough, for long enough, they may actually *feel guilty* and do just this — apologize, even though, in their heart of hearts, they know they have done nothing wrong.

Do you remember how, when Geoff's dog was put to sleep, Oonagh tried to tell him that his feelings of grief were wrong, because 'you can't love a dog'? Classic gaslighting.

Do you recall how Marcus invalidated Irina's distress about how he had made Janis wait in the car for an hour, with a broken leg, without painkillers? "The body is a miracle of God," he had gaslit her "It produces *natural* painkillers, and heals itself…"

And what about when Fiona tried to voice her upset about how the staff in her department were treating her, as a result of her promotion? Jonathan simply told her that she was 'thinking about it all wrong' and that, as she had received a small pay rise, she 'didn't really have the right to complain'.

Other forms of gaslighting

Projection

Gaslighting often happens in conjunction with other narcissistic behaviours as well, such as 'projection'. I remember a client of mine telling me that her husband, in a narcissistic rage, was repeatedly punching the wall, whilst screaming at her and telling her that it was *her* who was 'breaking his hand'. Here he was trying to project the blame onto her.

Essentially, in projection, the narcissist accuses you of doing or being what *they* are doing or being, but they do it *unconsciously* — it's an unconscious form of gaslighting.

So when your narcissist business partner tells you that you are lazy and incompetent, they may actually be talking about themselves. They cannot bear to feel the shame of their own behaviours, and so they just ascribe it to someone else.

If you are in an intimate relationship with a narcissist, and they accuse you of having an affair, you may wish to examine *their* behaviours. But if you have been in that relationship for a long time, and have been gaslit enough, you may actually start to believe that the narcissist is right, and that you must be having an affair, just like they say. This is known as 'projective identification' — you actually come to believe the thing that is projected on to you. You can see why people in narcissistic relationships often feel as if they are 'crazy'.

Toxic positivity

I also think it's important to mention 'toxic positivity' at this point, a subtle form of gaslighting. This is a fascinating behaviour that many Exhibitionist Narcissists, in particular, employ. Here the narcissist tells everyone that their life is perfect – that their job is great, their children are amazing and that their partner is wonderful. On the surface this may sound as if it is a good thing, focusing on the positives in this way, but actually it is a method of invalidation, denial and punishment.

The narcissist, who can only feel emotions on a very shallow level, believes that no one has the right to feel sad, deflated, upset, tired, stressed or annoyed, and that absolutely no one has the right to 'kill their vibe'. This makes anyone in a relationship with a narcissist feel as if they are being ungrateful or churlish, just for having a normal, appropriate range of human emotions. They then try to suppress these emotions, feeling that they don't have the right to them, especially when the narcissist seems so positive.

If they do ask for empathy or comfort, the narcissist will turn on them for their ingratitude, and gaslighting will ensue. They are likely to be told their feelings are 'wrong', and a diatribe about how *they* never complain may follow. The 'correct' feelings that they should be feeling may be offered.

This leads to guilt in the victim, who comes to believe that there is something wrong with their normal, negative emotions — and that their feelings are indeed wrong. They find themselves trying to 'be happy' around the narcissist, and push unwanted emotions away, in order to keep the peace. Even as a very little boy, Janis, who was crying when he hurt his finger, instantly stopped, as soon as he heard Marcus coming through the front door. Hurriedly wiping away his tears, he said to Irina, "Quick Mummy — act happy — Daddy's home."

Narcissistic pseudo-logic and word salad

The majority of effective communication is non-verbal, and this is where many narcissists have a big advantage, particularly when it comes to gaslighting. Their tone of voice, speed of delivery and body language convey great conviction, deep understanding and intelligence. But if you look at the *actual words* they are using, you may gain a very different impression. This is particularly obvious in their written communication. Here it is easy to see the multiple contradictions, irrational conclusions, and loose associations between ideas that is the hallmark of the narcissist. This is what I call 'narcissistic pseudo-logic'.

Think back to Irina's concerns about Marcus's spending, and the size of his ever-expanding designer trainer collection. Remember how Marcus justified it with great conviction? "They are an important part of my cultural identity as a black man," he had told her. She came away confused, and feeling as though she was somehow being racist. This gaslighting was delivered using narcissistic pseudo-logic. Marcus's assertions, if you examine them, made no sense, but they did what they were supposed to do — cause Irina to question herself.

This pseudo-logic goes a step further when the narcissist experiences 'narcissistic injury' from being slighted, rejected, ignored or humiliated. Once the narcissist's defensive armour of superiority is punctured, narcissistic rage ensues, and their style of communication nosedives into full 'narcissistic word salad'.

Here the narcissist loses all sense of logic. They deny that things happened; blame the injured party; re-write history; use senseless reasoning; project onto the other party things that they themselves have done, or have felt; make accusations; go round and round in circular discussions, which descend into a downward spiral; and say something one minute, and deny having said it the next. They introduce new topics frequently or reintroduce old ones, and try to logicalize events using nonsensical explanations. They might make intimidating threats, but then profess undying love, or offer you a promotion, in the very next sentence.

The recipient of this ranting, raging, nonsensical, accusatory word salad will be left reeling, breathless and utterly confused, as they question their own reality.

If you are receiving emails and texts from a narcissist in full meltdown, the contradictory word salad will be obvious. One of my female clients, upon leaving her narcissistic husband, received a barrage of such nonsensical texts. He accused her of 'not letting him into the

124

marital home' — but he was actually sending the texts from the comfort of the marital bed, which he was occupying at the time. You can see how, if you don't know that you are simply dealing with word salad, you could start to question your reality.

What effect does gaslighting have on the victim?

As with other abusive behaviours, the narcissist turns up the volume on their gaslighting so slowly that the victim barely notices. It's not hard to understand why, in a relationship that has gone on for years, the victim actually *believes* what the narcissist is telling them — even though anyone looking in from the outside would find the narcissist's assertions utterly ludicrous.

I'm reminded at this point of the true story of the famous opera singer, whose narcissistic partner eroded her beliefs and thinking about herself and the world so much, that she actually came to believe that she couldn't sing. Even though the whole world celebrated her ability, the narcissist had managed to get her to question herself. The years of gaslighting had led her to accept what he was telling her as reality.

And that is actually one of the major points of gaslighting — it enables the narcissist to get you to doubt yourself so much that you start to rely on them — *they become your 'voice of reason'.* That means that you might start wearing what *they* tell you to, rather than what *you* think looks good. It means you might not be able to make decisions, even little ones, without their input. It means that you might become quiet in work meetings, because you have been

> *"Effective gaslighting has the effect of making the victim dependent on the narcissist's opinions, memories and versions of the truth."*

gaslit into believing that people find you irritating or boring, or that you talk too much. The ramifications are really quite varied but, ultimately, if the narcissist can undermine you and deplete your reserves of self-confidence and self-belief, you will be too weak to leave your orbit — and so will remain a ready source of narcissistic supply, just as they want.

Some red flags of gaslighting to look out for

The more of the following that resonate with you, the more likely it is that you have been gaslit.

- If a person tries to persuade you to doubt the evidence of your senses, or your thoughts, or your feelings.

- If they never accept that you have a different opinion to them — and won't stop trying to persuade you that you are wrong.

- If, when they are called out on something, they use flawed logic to turn the tables on you, making out that you are at fault and that *they* are actually the victim, or the hero.

- If you find yourself relying on a person to make decisions for you, micromanage you, or to tell you how to behave, or what to wear.

- If you find yourself apologizing and feeling guilty for things that you have been accused of, that you know, deep down, you haven't done.

- If you feel more and more confused, to the point where you feel as though you might be going crazy.

- If you stop expressing your emotions to a person because you know that your feelings will always be 'wrong', according to them.

- If there is a big imbalance of power between you and a person.

So, once the narcissist has weakened their prey, by stealing their self-confidence, self-esteem, self-worth, self-belief and healthy self-love, thus depleting them of their fuel, they deliver the second part of their strategy to keep them stuck in the trap. They make their victim dependent on them.

MAKING THE VICTIM DEPENDENT ON THEM

Narcissists can make their victims emotionally, psychologically, socially and financially dependent on them.

Emotional and psychological dependence

Now that you understand how a narcissist devalues their victims, you can probably see how these devaluing behaviours can make the victim *emotionally* dependent on them, jumping through hoops to try to please them, so that, eventually, they only feel okay themselves when they have the narcissist's approval.

You will also realize that effective gaslighting has the effect of making the victim dependent on the narcissist's opinions, memories and versions of the truth. If this happens, they are now *psychologically* dependent on them.

Financial dependence

Making a victim financially dependent on them is another important way that some narcissists exert control over their victims, making it hard for them to leave. High earning narcissists (as many are) often trap their partners in this way. They tell them that they 'shouldn't have to work', and that they should enjoy lunches out with their friends, or be stay-at-home parents. Dressing up their control as 'generosity', by providing for them, is what I call the 'bird in the gilded cage phenomenon'.

Narcissists may tightly control their partner's spending, or do the exact opposite, and they themselves are often not financially transparent. It's not uncommon for the partners of such narcissists to discover that the family finances are in a much worse position than they thought, or that the business is heavily in debt. During devaluation phases the narcissist may use this financial situation (that *they* created) against their partner, accusing them of being spoiled, ungrateful and materialistic, and of being 'gold-diggers'.

If the narcissist owns their house, and isn't actually married to their partner (at least here in the UK), the partner who is financially dependent on the narcissist actually has no financial rights to any of the narcissist's money, if they leave them. High earning narcissists love to cohabit for this reason — so that their cohabitee is well and truly financially stuck in their orbit.

Narcissists often sabotage their partner's career plans too, in order to remove their financial ability to leave. Think back to Irina, whose cleaning business was struggling. She was keen to train to become a psychotherapist, but Marcus derailed this plan by undermining her confidence in her own abilities and by spending excessively, so that she couldn't afford the training. She also felt dependent on him for a place to live, as he had inherited his grandmother's sizeable London house (she'd probably been gaslit into believing that, if she divorced him, she wouldn't be entitled to a proportion of the money from this house).

This financial dependence can easily be created in the workplace too. I remember once working with an Exhibitionist Narcissist surgeon (who I'll call 'Greg'), who targeted a single female anaesthetist, 'Anna'. She worked within a consortium of anaesthetists, who would equally distribute their work between all the surgeons. This meant that each surgeon would be randomly allocated an anaesthetist for the day, to put their patients to sleep for their surgeries. But this system did not work for the narcissistic surgeon, because he only wanted an attractive female anaesthetist, and preferably one who would make eyes at him and fawn over him whilst he worked. To this end, he persuaded Anna, through flattery and attention, to leave the consortium, and work exclusively with him.

But because Greg was a particularly busy surgeon, and a high earner, Anna ended up earning way more than the other anaesthetists. Predictably, her resentful colleagues stopped speaking to her, angry that she had taken a big slice of the work for herself, instead of leaving it in the pool of work to be shared out. This wasn't the only way in which she paid the price for being the narcissist's 'favourite', however.

Anna, drawn in by Greg's love bombing, started to harbour romantic fantasies about him. You can imagine how utterly humiliated she felt when she found out, from the other theatre staff (after a whole year had elapsed) about his long-term girlfriend. When she tearfully confronted him, and asked him why he'd never mentioned her, he looked at her as if she had crawled out from under a rock, and coldly replied "Why would I tell *you*? My private life is none of your business." She was, by this time, completely dependent on him for her entire income, and she knew that there would be no way that her former colleagues would let her back into the consortium.

Think back to Fiona Jones, and how Jonathan threatened to badmouth her to all the local schools, when she finally handed in her resignation. Spurned narcissistic bosses give very poor references, and their employees are often far too scared to resign because of this — fear of future financial difficulty is another tool that a narcissist can leverage very effectively, to make a victim financially dependent on them.

Social dependence

Another bog-standard tool in the narcissist's kitbag is isolating their victims from their support networks, to make them socially dependent on them. This also removes people from the equation who could give the victim a frame of reference about the narcissist's behaviours.

In intimate relationships, the narcissist will often initially use romantic assertions to do this, such as "We don't need anybody else!" "It's just you and me against the world, babe!" If you *do* try to see your friends and family, the narcissist may, at first, play along, making sure that they are always invited too. This gives them the opportunity to win the people concerned over, and assess *their* potential flaws and vulnerabilities.

But, little by little, the narcissist will start to pull you away, using covert methods. Perhaps they will tell you that the people in question don't treat with with the respect you deserve, making you doubt the strength of these relationships, whilst being grateful to the narcissist for having your back. Perhaps they will invent a disturbing rumour about them, or tell you that the people in question treat *them* badly, so that, hurt, you disengage from them.

Remember — narcissists are extraordinarily good at lying, because they do it twenty-four hours a day when holding up their false persona, so you are very likely to believe the lies you are told — even about the people you know best, who really do love you.

You will also be *trained to respond* in the way the narcissist wants, in the same way that dogs are trained by their owners. When you turn down an invitation, or pull out of a meet-up at the last minute, the narcissist will reward you, throwing you a metaphorical bone, which you gnaw at delightedly, enthusiastically wagging your tail. 'Not seeing support networks = Good' your reward-based brain will note down, for future reference.

Narcissists also know that *punishments* for unwanted behaviours are incredibly effective too. Again, we meet the silent treatment — a stealthy way of getting you to behave. Remember how Lina would retreat to the spare room for days on end to punish Raj, and how Oonagh managed to stop Geoff from seeing his parents, using a combination of complaints about them and silent treatments towards him, if he ever had the audacity to visit them?

Directly behaving badly towards your support network is usually a reserve tactic, but it may be used early on by a Devaluing Narcissist. Causing fights, being openly bitchy, or just being plain embarrassing, will eventually cause all but your most loyal friends to fade away, especially if they perceive that this relationship of yours is here to stay. Of course, you'll be so taken in by the narcissist's charms at this stage that you will let these friendships go, finding whatever justifications work, such as 'they are just jealous of what we have'.

Your narcissistic boss can easily isolate you from your co-workers too. Think about how effectively French teacher Fiona Jones was isolated from hers, when Jonathan openly made her his favourite, and then promoted her to head of department. Eventually, Fiona had no one to talk to at work except Jonathan.

'Divide and conquer' strategies enable narcissists to keep people away from each other, who might, if they talked, work out what was really going on. If your new business partner badmouths their old business partner to you, you'll be unlikely to wish to interact with them when you come across them. You could easily misinterpret their behaviour towards you too — their glances might be perceived by you as suspicion or jealousy, when in fact they could be shooting you looks of pity, and wondering whether they should warn you about what is to come. And feeding lies about former victims into the rumour mill is a great way to isolate them, so others keep them at arm's length.

USING VICTIMS' BRAIN SYSTEMS AGAINST THEM

It's quite remarkable how a narcissist can manipulate a person's neurochemistry, brain mechanisms and psychology to their advantage, but this is exactly what they do, in various ways. Let's start with the most shocking one — how a narcissist makes their victims addicted to them, which is also known as 'trauma bonding'.

Addiction and Trauma Bonding

If you have been in any type of relationship with a narcissist, you will usually have been 'love bombed' at the beginning, as described in the previous chapter. You may have been showered with attention, with over-the-top professions of admiration and with grand gestures, or been in constant communication. But what you might not realize, is that this love bombing actually has an effect on the levels of neurotransmitters in your brain — because, in this phase, your 'feel-good' brain chemicals are produced in huge quantities, and they flood your brain. At this point in your relationship, you feel great. This is known as the 'idealization phase'.

We've already talked about the next phase, the 'devaluation phase' in some detail, and how the 'perfect' relationship turns ever so slightly sour with subtle abuse. At this point the victim's brain chemicals come crashing down, and their heart sinks. They feel desperate to get those initial feelings back — but they don't realize that what they are actually craving is the neuro-chemical high that they were previously experiencing.

They find themselves jumping through hoops to placate or win over the narcissist, and every now and then they will be rewarded by the narcissist, leading to a gratifying boost in their brain chemicals. But what is really interesting is *how* exactly a narcissist will do this, and how their precise method, which has two components, leads to the victim becoming addicted to them.

Firstly, a narcissist will use 'intermittent reinforcement' — a highly effective way to cause an addiction. So what this means is that they will reward their victim *randomly*. So, after a while, they'll stop responding favourably to their victim's fawning every single time, but just respond *occasionally,* and in an unpredictable pattern. Secondly, they will reward their victim with wins of *varying sizes*. Sometimes they will be rewarded handsomely for their efforts (perhaps with a lavish meal or through public praise). But, at other times, the rewards will be small (perhaps just a tiny bit of attention, or the termination of a silent treatment). The same is true for their punishments — they can vary from mild humiliation all the way up to even physical abuse.

It's crucial to understand that this is a *cycle* — the so-called 'cycle of idealization and devaluation' (or 'Nice Narcissist, Nasty Narcissist', as I like to call it), and it's the cyclical nature of it that causes the addiction, as the brain chemicals alternately soar and then plummet. But the fact that the cycles are of *unpredictable lengths* means that the victim can't even tell when the next devaluation is coming — and this adds to the addictiveness even more.

I remember a quiz game that my friends and I used to play back in the 1990s, in the pub, and it's a great analogy for how people become addicted to narcissists. We'd put our money into the machine, answer the questions, and celebrate when the coins came tumbling out, as our neuro-chemicals rocketed at this medium sized win. Of course, we'd then put more money into the machine, but become increasingly disappointed as we failed to win. However, just as we were about to walk away from the machine, with our brain chemicals on the floor, we'd get a tiny win, reigniting our interest in the game.

This little boost of neurotransmitters was enough to keep us sinking more and more money into the machine, and the unpredictability of the sizes of our wins (and the timing of them) got us seriously hooked. I'm sure you can see the similarities with narcissism here, and how victims become addicted to (and invested in) the narcissist. Did we ever leave the pub with more money than we put in? Of course not — because gambling machines like this are designed to be *profitable*, and they use your neurochemistry against you — in exactly the same way that a narcissist does.

These days we are all familiar with how addicted we can get to a pinging phone, notifying us of social media likes and comments, and most people are aware that every ping causes a little boost in our brain chemicals (dopamine being the most commonly cited one). But narcissists have been doing this since time began, without truly knowing how their victims become addicted to them, to the point of being so hooked that they become grateful for any crumbs of attention the narcissist throws their way.

Euphoric recall

A bit like looking back on things with the proverbial 'rose tinted spectacles', euphoric recall is 'the act of remembering events positively'. The victims of narcissists have a tendency to remember past events in a positive light, and to forget the negative things associated with those events. The interesting thing about this is that this also happens to people with substance addictions. It is thought that addictions cause changes to an area of the brain, known as the hippocampus, which is responsible for the formation of memories, and how they are stored and retrieved. It also processes the *context* in which things happened. Addicts with euphoric recall seem to remember these contexts incorrectly, and in an overly positive light. This result in addicts being more likely to return to the contexts and environments that they remember incorrectly — and, of course, once they are there, they are likely to relapse.

How big a part does euphoric recall play in keeping victims stuck in their orbits with narcissists, I wonder? I don't know the answer, but it's certainly an interesting question.

We see what our brains think we want to see

Our brains have systems to filter out incoming information that they do not consider to be relevant to us. However, when it comes to narcissists, these brain filters can often inadvertently filter out the very things the victim *needs* to be aware of, preventing them from reaching their *conscious* awareness.

If you noticed every single thing that was happening around you, you'd be pretty overwhelmed. Imagine if you were aware of every single bit of incoming sensory information, such as the feeling of the inside seams of your jeans on your legs. It's not just sensory information like this that the brain filters out — but information that is not in line with your beliefs and your view of the world, as well as stuff that just isn't relevant to you. You probably won't clock the political headline on the front page of the papers, as you walk past the newspaper stand, if you aren't interested in politics, for example. The brain simply deletes this information — a so-called 'deletion', so you never even become aware of it.

Our brains also *distort* how we see reality, magnifying or diminishing our conscious perceptions of things, and these are known as 'distortions'. And finally, the brain's mental filters lead to 'generalisations', where we make automatic assumptions, based on our past experiences, such as 'all nurses are kind'. Some of these filters are formed by our life experiences and the beliefs we have formed as a result of them, and they produce unconscious (or conscious) biases.

It's not hard to see how your brain could be inadvertently stopping you from seeing things as they really are, when it comes a narcissist's behaviours (especially if you believe that people are 'basically good', and you brain is filtering out anything that it not in line with this belief). *We literally see what we want to see* (and believe what we want to believe), but with no idea that this seriously limited view of the world is what we are actually experiencing.

'Cognitive dissonance'

Our brains also work against us when it comes to the narcissist's bad behaviours that it *has* let in. The brain feels uncomfortable holding two opposing beliefs at the same time ('Nice Narcissist' and 'Nasty Narcissist'), so it tends to choose just one. It does this by denying that bad behaviours ever happened, by minimizing how bad they were, by justifying them as being reasonable under the circumstances, or by making excuses for them ('they were just having a bad week').

In practical terms, this means that the brain of a victim of a narcissist does a very good job of convincing itself that *nothing is wrong.*

Complex PTSD, Depression and Anxiety

It's no wonder that those stuck in relationships with narcissists can develop anxiety and depression, but something you may not have heard of is 'complex PTSD'.

Complex post-traumatic stress disorder is fairly common in the victims of narcissists, and it is caused by the abusive tactics that a narcissist uses to keep their victims in their orbits. It differs from PTSD (which most people have heard of) in a few ways.

When we think of PTSD we usually think of the sufferer having experienced one very big traumatic incident — a serious car crash, or a horrific episode when fighting on the front line in a war zone, for example. They wake in the night, or are sideswiped at various times by the incident, which they re-experience as if they were actually back there. Visual flashbacks are a very common part of PTSD.

In complex PTSD, the person has experienced a series of much smaller traumatic incidents, which accumulate to give them this different type of PTSD. The way that this shows up is different to the other form of PTSD, in that the flashbacks they experience tend to be *emotional*, rather than visual. They are similarly sideswiped by them, and they can be debilitating. Complex PTSD can be triggered by all sorts of things, including memories, and most people don't even realize what they are experiencing.

Their 'sympathetic nervous system' is thrown into overdrive, and the high levels of stress hormones (adrenaline and cortisol) have various effects on their body during these episodes, including feelings of panic, sweaty palms, a racing heart and breathlessness, and even pains or tightness in areas such as their throat or chest. Crucially, blood is diverted away from the thinking and logical areas of their brains to their muscles during these episodes (an evolutionary mechanism, designed to help them run away or fight). Of course, this leads to fuzzy thinking, and their 'inner critic' might make an appearance here too. These hardly help a victim of narcissistic abuse to see things objectively.

Victims of narcissists who suffer from anxiety, depression or PTSD may also turn to alcohol or other substances to help them cope. Of course, this can further reduce clarity about their relationship with their narcissist, making escape even harder to contemplate.

Let's now take a look the tactics narcissists use to pull their victims back into the relationship, should they summon up the courage to try to make a break for it.

WHAT HAPPENS IF YOU TRY TO ESCAPE?

It is widely quoted that it takes an average of seven attempts to finally (successfully) leave an abusive relationship. I always like to ask my clients, after they make their final escape, how many previous attempts they had made. Unscientific though my conclusions may be, around six attempts (of varying intent) does seem to be about the norm. This number is around the same regardless of what type of relationship the victim was in with the narcissist — whether they were their partner, adult child, work colleague, friend or sibling.

Let's just look at that number again. Six failed attempts. That's a lot of times to make a decision to leave, build up the courage to try, actually instigate the attempt and then be roped back in again.

Are the escapees just pathetic and weak, or are there good reasons why escaping is so hard, even for 'mentally tough' people?

Many of my divorcing clients find themselves in court because of the behaviours of the narcissist during their marriage and divorce. Often they make (true) allegations of abuse against the narcissist, especially when they are concerned at how much time their narcissistic ex will spend with the children, and give details of that abuse. You already know that *all* narcissistic abuse is made up of various types of covert psychological abuse, but physical abuse may also be present in relationships with narcissists.

Sadly, if physical abuse isn't present or provable, they may have little chance of being taken seriously. The lack of understanding around why it's so hard to escape the Narcissist Trap means that I commonly hear of judges dismissing the non-narcissistic spouse's allegations as being exaggerated, because "if it was that bad you would have left earlier." I have held my head in my hands, upon hearing this, far too many times. They fail to appreciate that this isn't about *leaving* — it's about *escaping*.

So what tactics does a narcissist use, once they sense that their victim is about to attempt an escape (or if they actually go ahead and try)?

Let's look at Fiona Jones's first attempt to hand in her resignation to Jonathan. If you remember, his first response was to beg her to stay, with tears in his eyes. He told her that her support was the only reason he could keep going. He told her that he was depressed, and that his son had shut him out of his life. "You are my *best friend*" he had proclaimed, "please don't desert me now".

'Hoovering' is the colloquial name, in narcissistic abuse circles, given to the tactics a narcissist uses to suck a victim back into the relationship. It is made up of various components. In the example above we can see:

- Begging
- Guilt-tripping
- Playing the victim (Jonathan pretended to be ill with depression, due his poor relationship with his son, to excuse his behaviour)
- Flattery and renewed love bombing

Jonathan also promised that he would take some of the additional responsibilities away from Fiona and speak to her departmental staff about co-operating with her. He also suggested that they could deliver their LGBTQ inclusivity talks jointly. Here he was employing the standard hoovering tactics of making false promises and 'future faking'. A narcissist may actually deliver on some promises for a short time, but inevitably they will go back on them when they feel safe again. In contrast, in future faking, the promised thing *never* materializes; for example, Jonathan had no intention of ever delivering his inclusivity talks with Fiona, but he knew that promising to do so would be a big draw for her.

"'Hoovering' is the colloquial name, in narcissistic abuse circles, given to the tactics a narcissist uses to suck a victim back into the relationship."

The narcissist plays on the victim's sympathy, hope that things can get better and guilt, for the first few hoovers, and the victim falls for it, feeling huge relief.

Hoovering is similar for the partner of a narcissist, but worse, as they are feeling an even stronger gravitational pull in the first orbit. Usually, after a big, dramatic showdown with the narcissist, during which they bare their soul, they too will find themselves back in the love bombing phase, when the narcissist will appear to turn back into the perfect partner. They will become seductive and charming. They will seem caring and helpful. They will put the bins out, load the dishwasher and stop texting their young attractive subordinates in front of their partner. They will stop all devaluing behaviours, and will apologize for the error of their ways, claiming stress or any other suitable excuse.

But what happens during subsequent escape attempts? Now you can expect the narcissist to really up their game, begging harder, guilt tripping more, making even grander promises, and playing the victim with even greater aplomb.

Let's look at Jonathan and Fiona, once again. When Fiona finally resigned, Jonathan went into full-on threat mode. All charm left the building. He hissed angrily at her that if she left he would make sure that she never got a decent teaching job again. He declared that he would give her the worst reference imaginable, and told her that he would contact every school to warn them about her incompetence. He threatened to lie and suggest that she had embezzled from the school. His narcissistic rage was terrifying.

I've seen narcissists feign all sorts of illnesses to try to guilt trip their partner into staying — strokes, chest pain, depression — nothing is off-limits. If they are married, they very often pull out the 'in sickness and in health' card, claiming that their 'illness' means that their partner can't leave. If there are children involved, they will be used as part of the guilt tripping — "You will be ruining the children's lives if you leave…" Threatening suicide is also an absolutely standard tactic. Promises to buy a new house, to work less (or more), to emigrate back home with the family — the narcissist will say whatever is necessary to prevent their biggest source of supply from leaving.

Partners of narcissists nearing their final escape attempt will also be *threatened* by their narcissist. They might endure threats to burn the house down, financial threats, threats to call the police and have them arrested. They will threaten to hurt the pets or give them away. They will threaten to make sure the partner never sees the children again. They will threaten to blackmail them, to tell all their secrets to everyone, including work colleagues and family members. They will tell them that they will never let them go, even if they do leave them. They will threaten to ruin their partner's life in every possible way, emotionally, financially and socially. They may actually *carry out* their threats, engage in physical abuse for the first time, or even lock their partner in a room.

If you are in this close orbit, it's no wonder threats and behaviours like these leave you too weak to do anything other than capitulate, and stay with the narcissist — they've successfully depleted the fuel reserves you need to reach your 'escape velocity', once again, in spectacular fashion.

But what does a narcissist do, once you've capitulated? They will behave as if *absolutely nothing happened*, and expect you to accompany them to the dinner party, the business conference, the weekend away, or whatever else was in the diary, where they will behave completely normally towards you, replete from the bounty of overflowing narcissistic supply.

It is not easy to leave the Narcissist Trap — but you've probably got that message by now.

7

The limitations of being a narcissist

I t's important to realize that those with NPD are severely *limited* by their brain wiring. There are so many things that they just aren't able to do or feel to the degree that 'normal' people can. Without wishing to pull on your heart strings, especially if you have fallen prey to a narcissist, I wonder if you might imagine, as you read this chapter, how dreadful it would be to live life constrained like this.

They can't truly care about others

As you know, narcissists have low empathy, but *they* don't realize this, because they haven't ever actually experienced empathy in a 'normal' way. Because of this, a narcissist might even tell you how very empathic they are, but their behaviours will not match up. Marcus, our Communal Narcissist openly describes his empathy levels as being 'off the scale', and yet was able to leave his stepson, Janis, in pain for an hour with a broken leg, whilst he watched the rest of a football match — an impossible thing for a person with empathy to do.

There are two types of empathy — emotional and cognitive. Emotional empathy is the ability to step into someone else's shoes and *actually feel* how they are feeling. This is the type of empathy that is lacking in narcissists, because, due their upbringings, the developmental foundations needed to develop emotional empathy were never laid. They cannot feel your pain, or joy, or anything else, and so they can't really care about your feelings. Extrapolate this a bit further and you can see why they cannot really care about others, other than in the context of what that person can do for them.

However, the waters may be muddied by the fact that that narcissists *do* develop 'cognitive' empathy, with life experience, and from watching others. So, if someone's relative dies, a narcissist will be able to look sympathetic and utter condolences, because they know that this is the socially accepted norm.

However, very often narcissists will give themselves away here, even when it comes to cognitive empathy. They will very often overplay it, and behave in inappropriately over-the-top ways. Remember how Lina would tearfully throw herself into helping people she barely knew with the funeral arrangements for their loved ones, and yet was completely disinterested in caring for her own family when they were ill?

I recall a story of a man whose former secretary was dying of lung cancer on a

> *"Emotional empathy is the ability to step into someone else's shoes and actually feel how they are feeling. This is the type of empathy that is lacking in narcissists."*

hospital ward. He would make a big show of frequently visiting this secretary, turning up with bouquets of flowers and chocolates, and he would sit by the bed, holding her hand, pushing her close family members out of the way. He would usually also bring his nine-year-old son with him, even though this lady was struggling to breathe and had tubes coming out of her, and an oxygen mask.

The narcissistic man in question genuinely thought that he was demonstrating empathy, and was totally unable to pick up on his own son's feelings about being forced to be in this scary environment. He also gave no consideration to how his secretary might feel about being seen at her lowest point by him, her former boss, nor to how her family might be feeling about him taking away their precious final moments with her, through his insistence on visiting.

Narcissists can go to surprising lengths to demonstrate their empathy. A client of mine was flummoxed by her partner, who had no empathy at home, but who went as far as donating his kidney to a stranger. The coverage in the local press hailed him a hero, and he dined out on the story for years — here was incontrovertible proof that he was a 'nice' guy — all part of his false persona.

Another client told me about an occasion when her narcissistic boss and the team were abroad at a conference. One of their team members became ill, but no one knew what exactly was wrong. She stayed in her room for most of the conference, so her colleagues made sure to check up on her by messaging her and taking her food, water and painkillers. The narcissistic boss seemed to only remember to pretend to care if reminded by other people's conversations, when he would say "Ah yes, poor Sarah. What shame she is missing the conference…" He would also occasionally suggest that it was "probably just a hangover". Whilst the team couldn't stop worrying, the boss couldn't even *start* to care. The lady in question ended up in hospital with a ruptured appendix — and the narcissist remained completely unaware that he had not been the very model of empathy.

So, when looking for this inability to care, watch for the discrepancy between their assertions and their actions. If no one is around to witness their demonstrations of empathy, they can't tell people about it later, or they can't use it to point out what a good person they are, they are unlikely to bother to even feign empathy.

They might even turn the attention onto themselves or try to outdo the person who needs their support. Stories about their own experiences often surface here, under the guise of 'I know just how you feel', or 'I had it much worse'.

THE NARCISSIST TRAP

No narcissist can really hide their callousness for long, if you look beneath the thin veneer of their cognitive empathy.

They can't truly love

Ouch, you might be thinking here, and with good cause. All love to a narcissist is transactional and conditional, including their love for their children. Of course, at the start of an intimate relationship, the love bombing phase is an extremely convincing portrayal of love, but the narcissist's rapt gazes at their victim are merely them holding up a mirror to their victim, to reflect their *own* adoration back at them. Because, later on, they pull this trick out of the bag intermittently, throughout the relationship, their victims remain confused. This inability to love is extremely hard to take on board, even after decades of behaviours that clearly show that the narcissist couldn't really have ever loved them.

So your narcissistic boss, who shows off his glamorous wife, and has pictures of her and the kids on his desk, doesn't actually love them, no matter how convincingly he plays the role. You can be sure that underneath her smiles, if she's been with him for long enough, she will be feeling uncherished and unloved, just like Irina in her relationship with Marcus.

Some narcissists will even openly admit to their partner, as time wears on, that they 'can't love', or that they 'don't know how to love.' Inevitably their partner believes that this can't possibly be true. Oonagh gave her own limitations (regarding her capacity to love) away when she told Geoff that "you can't love a dog." I am reminded here of the sage advice of the late great Maya Angelou — "When a person shows you who they are, believe them."

Of course, those with NPD can feign love, or even actually feel their shallow version of it when they are getting enough narcissistic supply back from their victim. In contrast to Oonagh, I commonly hear about narcissists who seem to love their dogs, for example. But if you think about it, a tail wagging Labrador who is always pleased to see you is the epitome of unconditionally given narcissistic supply. Adoring small children can also be excellent sources of supply for their narcissistic parent, as long as they toe the line. Remember Lina as a child, and how she revered her shopkeeper Exhibitionist Narcissist dad, who appeared to love her (as long as she didn't take the spotlight off him)?

Related to this, is the fact that relationships with narcissists lack emotional intimacy. Narcissists simply *cannot* genuinely emotionally connect to other people in a vulnerable way. I've already explained how narcissists see others simply as objects; 'its.' There's a good chance that if you ask your narcissistic partner why they love you, they won't be able to come out with any deep and meaningful reasons that demonstrate any level of emotional connection with you. The answer you get is likely to be very telling indeed, and may range from superficial reasons, such as "You are sexy," "You make people laugh," or "You make a good lemon drizzle cake," all the up way to a slightly confused "I don't know — I just do."

They can't maintain deep, long-term friendships

The inability to be emotionally intimate with other people means that, although many narcissists might know a large number of people, their friendships tend to be superficial, and limited to mere acquaintances. They rarely have deep, long-term friendships, which are on an equal footing, because friends tend to drop away over time, as a result of the narcissist's emotional limitations, lack of empathy and tendency to view other people as two-dimensional objects.

They can't cope with imperfection

Narcissists need the world to see them as perfect (and unique and special), so that *they* can see *themselves* that way. They might also need their environment to be perfect, their work to be perfect, their outward appearance to be perfect, their children to be perfect and their colleagues to be perfect. Lina's fancy tea parties were a testimony to how, if she did anything public, she had to do it perfectly. Oonagh learned early on how to dress and do her make-up to present herself as flawless, and never had a hair out of place. Carefully curated images on social media are also often used by narcissists to present an image of the perfect life.

And narcissists also demand perfection from their partners and their children, who cannot help but disappoint them at times. To add to this, because narcissists don't see their children as being separate from them, their 'flaws' are felt deeply, as being flaws in *themselves*. Remember how Marcus couldn't deal with Janis having asthma? How Jonathan couldn't accept that Max had ADHD and was gay? And how deeply disgusted Lina was with her daughter Laila's anorexia nervosa? These imperfections were utterly unacceptable to them.

You already know that narcissists make difficult bosses, but this need for perfection can make things even more difficult, with 'substandard' work being ripped up and tossed in the bin, or completely unrealistic expectations being the norm. Note that narcissists themselves don't need to actually *be* perfect; they just need other people to *believe* they are, so that they can believe it too — which is why they are very happy to take credit for other people's good work.

Because narcissists can't see people as a simultaneous blend of good and bad (what psychologists refer to as having a 'lack of whole object relations'), they are only able to see people as either 'all good' or 'all bad' at any one time. It's important to say here that

*"Narcissists need the world to see them as perfect (and unique and special), so that they can see **themselves** that way."*

147

narcissists also feel the same way about *themselves*. They are either defective and worthless, or superior and unique — but never a blend of these. Remember how Marcus sunk into a deep depression after he was thrown out of the church band because he was not the accomplished guitarist that he had claimed to be? He was suffering from a 'narcissistic collapse' at this point, where he could only see himself as useless and 'all bad'. Here his narcissistic defences, the armour of his false persona, had been shattered temporarily, and could no longer protect him.

Healthy people start to develop whole object relations at around the age of two, which is why, if you've ever been out shopping with a young toddler, you are likely to have experienced the following scenario. When you agree to buy the toddler the toy they want, they see you as the best person in the whole world. But five minutes later, when you deny them an ice cream, you become the object of hate, and have to endure an embarrassing public meltdown.

This is because the toddler hasn't yet developed whole object relations. You can't be good Mummy and bad Mummy at the same time. You can only be one or the other — loved or loathed, but not both. They cannot integrate the liked and disliked parts of you into one picture, so they carry out what is also known as 'splitting'. Eventually, if they are brought up in a healthy enough environment, they will start to be able to love you even if you don't get them the ice cream.

But not so for the narcissist, who will continue, even as an adult, to vilify you when you are less than perfect (when you disappoint them, hurt them or deprive them of narcissistic supply), and then put you on a pedestal when you do comply with their expectations of you. This is why you can expect to lurch from hero to zero in your narcissistic relationships, and be treated accordingly.

They can't genuinely feel happy for other people

Narcissists exist in a very hierarchical world, meaning that they compare themselves to other people constantly. If someone else has more of something they want (looks, power, status, money, success, a perfect marriage, clever children, to name a few) they are unable to be genuinely happy for that person, *because they feel that it detracts from their own success.* That is part of the reason why they devalue others by shaming them, criticizing them and putting them down — so that they can feel better about themselves by comparison.

You can see why 'schadenfreude' (taking pleasure in other people's misfortunes) is a feature of narcissism — because if someone else *fails*, the narcissist automatically *succeeds*, boosting their own self-image, which, as you know, they so badly need to believe in.

Jealousy is a huge feature of narcissism as a result of this hierarchical thinking, and incredibly, narcissistic parents can even be jealous of their children. I recall a middle-aged narcissistic mother who was wildly jealous of her sixteen-year-old daughter for her youth, slim figure and her talents as a singer-songwriter. The irony was that *she* had pushed her child relentlessly to achieve musically, because she had never been able to gain fame in this area herself.

She would outwardly bask in the glory of her daughter's successes, taking the credit for them to gain narcissistic supply. But in truth, she actually *resented* her daughter because her own position in the hierarchy was pushed down by her daughter's achievements. At times, she tried desperately hard to compete with her, getting plastic surgery, dieting obsessively and making repeated attempts to find fame herself. At other times, she would resort to putting her daughter down, telling her that she was fat, ugly and of 'average musical ability'.

As you know, narcissists are often attracted to victims who are 'special' themselves in some way, so that they can gain admiration and narcissistic supply by associating with the extraordinary person. But the 'little green monster' will commonly surface later in the relationship, as they become jealous of the very attributes that they were initially so drawn to. Your narcissistic business partner, who was once so enthusiastic and complimentary about the skills you brought to the table, will inevitably start to badmouth you behind your back when their jealousy gets the better of them (as it did with the business partner before you).

Causing much confusion, narcissists will also be jealous of their *partner's* successes — or at the very least, will downplay them, so that they don't have to actually *feel* their jealousy at being comparatively inferior. Remember how Oonagh reacted when Geoff was promoted, sabotaging the celebratory meal he had prepared by deliberately not turning up for it? You can't expect a narcissist to cheerlead you, unless there is an outside audience, or you are in a love bombing phase.

A narcissist's jealousy can seem quite bizarre at times. Do you recall how Oonagh was jealous of Geoff's relationship with their dog, because it seemed to favour him by always greeting him at the door, when he came home? Narcissistic parents are commonly even jealous of the other parent's relationships with their *own children*, and may even try to sabotage them.

Even narcissists who have achieved great things, who are rich, well regarded in their field and powerful, will be jealous of seemingly the strangest things, and this so commonly plays out in adult sibling relationships. It doesn't matter how much the narcissist earns or how lavish their lifestyle is in comparison to their non-narcissist sibling — they will still resent even minor wins in their sibling's life, and may try to compete with them.

When it comes to intimate relationships, a narcissist will *always* baselessly accuse their partner of having affairs, and will be intensely jealous of anyone who they feel might be able to remove their primary fuel source from their orbit. Partners might incorrectly perceive this jealousy to be 'love', and even feel flattered by it, but as you now know, nothing could be further from the truth.

Most narcissists also need to believe that other people are envious of *them*, as this bolsters their sense of superiority. You may recall how our Closet Narcissist, Lina, took pleasure in her belief that everyone attending her lavish children's parties was secretly jealous of her. And what about Jonathan, who was envious of another headmaster who regularly discussed education on the TV and radio? In order to cope with his jealousy, he convinced himself that this headmaster was actually jealous of *him* — projecting his own feelings onto another person so *he* didn't have to feel them.

They can't admit defeat

Narcissists need to see themselves as 'winners' to maintain their feelings of specialness and superiority. They can be openly competitive with others, even needing to beat their toddler children in games. They are usually terrible losers, and will often blame their failure on someone, or something, that is out of their control. Narcissists may also rewrite history if they lose, and even deny that it actually happened. I remember a client once telling me that her narcissistic brother had always been completely unable to accept that he had lost at anything. "Even when he loses, he wins," she told me.

This plays out horribly in the divorce process, where a narcissist will feel the need to annihilate their spouse in order to come out on top.

If you are trying to negotiate with a narcissist, and they don't get what they want, it is always best to at least *let them have the last word*. This way they can leave with their defensive shield partially intact. Otherwise, their lasting resentment is likely to cause episodes of rage, which will be directed at you, for *years* to come. You have been warned.

They can't feel most emotions deeply

A narcissist's emotions are often only superficial, and as a result they may come across as 'insincere'. Because they are shallowly held and not deeply felt, some narcissists also seem able to switch between their emotions disconcertingly quickly.

A narcissist who is upset with someone, for a perceived misdemeanour, is likely to act in a cruelly cold way towards them, to show their displeasure and punish them. But upon receiving a text message, or seeing something on TV, that same narcissist might quickly switch emotions and laugh heartily, as their victim, who is still suffering, looks on, confused as to how they were able to recover their spirits so quickly.

Your narcissistic work colleague might go from a huge row with you, straight into a meeting, where they are able to banter with your colleagues, as if nothing untoward had happened with you, just moments before.

In the early stages of divorce, narcissists ramp up their abusive behaviours towards their spouse, in order to scare them into not leaving them, and this may even escalate to physical abuse. You can be sure that when the police arrive, the narcissist, who has just been snarling at you, with their hands around your neck, will instantly be able to turn into a completely calm and rational-looking person, whilst you, shaken by the incident, look like the crazy one. This is a story that I have heard far too many times.

Of course, this works in reverse too — positive emotions can turn into negative ones, at the drop of a hat.

It's probably the case that different narcissists actually feel their emotions to different degrees, some more than others. But with many, particularly the ones who aren't particularly theatrically gifted, it can seem as though they are just 'play-acting' their emotions, without feeling them at all. They may even over-act, making extreme facial gestures, such as inappropriately giant smiles, or sob loudly with suspiciously dry eyes.

Narcissists may also claim to be feeling a certain way which isn't congruent with how they actually outwardly appear. It's not uncommon for a narcissist to tell you that they are depressed, suicidal, grieving or stressed, whilst only momentarily appearing to look sad, if at all.

They can't say 'sorry' and mean it

I don't think I have ever come across a narcissist who has apologized for their behaviours and actually meant it.

Narcissists *can't* accept blame, because that goes against the very point of what their narcissism is *for* — to protect them from feeling shame, worthlessness and inadequacy. If they accept the blame for something, they risk feeling shame — the intensely painful feeling of believing that one is flawed and unworthy of love.

Because narcissists rarely accept blame, they also rarely feel guilt, which often leads to them showing a distinct lack of remorse for their behaviours.

So how do narcissists *avoid* accepting blame for their behaviours and feeling shame? Firstly, they often *fool themselves* by denying, justifying or minimizing their behaviours. 'It didn't happen', 'it wasn't that bad' and 'they deserved it' are common narcissistic mantras.

It's also particularly interesting to watch a narcissist engage in the techniques of 'blame-shifting' and 'shame-dumping'. Here, with lightning speed, a narcissist will shift the blame onto someone else, or, in the case of shame-dumping, try to shame the other person for behaviours that *they themselves* have perpetrated. When Marcus suffered the humiliation of being asked to leave the church band (because of his poor guitar skills) he blamed the luthier, who had handmade his expensive guitar for him, for 'making it wrong' — a classic case of blame-shifting.

Narcissists will blame others for everything, from the biggest disasters to the most inconsequential of events. When Oonagh spilt her wine by knocking it with her elbow, she was incensed with Geoff, who she blamed for it without even a moment's hesitation, even though he'd been careful to put it in its usual place. In reality, it really didn't matter whose fault it was — Oonagh simply couldn't accept any culpability, even for this small mishap.

When your narcissistic co-worker fails to do their work on a joint project on time, they will blame *you* for not reminding them about their deadline. When your narcissistic subordinate doesn't deliver work of a high enough standard to you, they will blame you, as their superior, for not supporting them enough, or for not being clear about what you wanted. They'll blame things ('my computer wouldn't save it'), systems ('my email must have been erased from the server'), external events ('my granddaughter's divorce has put me in a really dark place') and other people ('I wasn't even told about it by the team until this morning'). It doesn't take long for the pattern of blame-shifting to emerge in the workplace with people like this.

Shame-dumping and blame-shifting also fall into the category of 'projection', which I mentioned earlier. Projection is a psychological defence mechanism that *all* people use. It's completely unconscious, and it enables the person to 'give away' their shame and guilt to someone else, for the behaviours, inadequacies and feelings which they can't accept as their own.

Although everyone projects to some degree, to protect themselves, narcissists do it astoundingly commonly, also with no idea that this is what they are doing. The classic projection is the false accusation from a partner that you are having an affair. They are handing the guilt and shame of their own affair, or fantasies about it, on to you, so that they don't have to feel it.

When your narcissistic co-worker tells you, for no good reason, that your presentation is rambling and incomprehensible, have a look at their presentation — it is likely that they are describing their own work.

When your narcissistic mother calls you 'selfish' and 'uncaring', as you unload and put away the groceries that you have bought for her, take a step back, and recognize that she is actually describing herself.

When your narcissistic wife tells you, petulantly, "You don't love me" they may actually be telling you that *they* don't love *you*. When they tell you that 'no one else would ever be able to love you', they are giving away their shame at the fact that they believe, deep down, that no one else would ever be able to love *them*.

When your narcissistic sibling hisses at you at your mother's deathbed that 'you always wanted to be the favourite,' you can be pretty sure that they are telling you that *they* wanted to be the favourite. When they accuse you of 'elder abuse', don't be surprised if *they* have been emptying out your aging parent's bank account behind your back.

Narcissists will often accuse their victims of being bullies and abusers and, stunningly, they will also accuse them of *actually being narcissists*. I estimate that around ten percent of the people who consult with me are actually the narcissist themselves, projecting their own narcissism onto another person.

"Projection enables the person to 'give away' their shame and guilt to someone else, for the behaviours, inadequacies and feelings which they can't accept as their own."

And if you leave a relationship with a narcissist, you can expect the projections to increase. "You are mentally unravelling," "You need serious help," "You can't cope," "You are stealing from me," "You want to abduct the children". All of these are projections, and are highly informative as to what the narcissist is up to, or how they are feeling.

They can't be alone

This goes back to the fact that narcissists need to be continually receiving narcissistic supply. Remember that a narcissist stores their narcissistic supply in a metaphorical bucket with a hole in it — which means it *constantly* needs topping up.

Narcissists can only get their narcissistic supply from *other people's* attention or adoration, from their emotional reactions to drama and conflict, and from their fear.

Of course, narcissistic supply can, these days, be easily gained from social media at any time of the day or night, so narcissists don't ever really need to be alone. Twitter, Facebook, Instagram, Snapchat, TikTok and the others serve as extensions to the narcissist's false persona. Carefully taken photographs, and accounts of their lifestyle and opinions can be shared with thousands of followers with minimal effort and, when comments and likes come flooding in, narcissistic supply is boosted nicely. Marcus, our Communal Narcissist, posts daily videos of himself sharing 'his insights', precisely for this reason.

Trolling people on social media is another great way to get supply from the comfort of your armchair, and I often wonder what proportion of trolls would actually qualify for a diagnosis of NPD. Propagating conspiracy theories is also a favoured narcissistic pastime, with all the debate and attention that it generates.

Instant messaging and forwarding memes to others are also great ways to secure supply from people who aren't in the room, and dating apps are even better.

But even with these various methods, narcissists still tend to need *actual people* for the really premium grade supply. They are rarely out of intimate relationships for long because of this, which is disconcerting to a grieving ex, who can't even contemplate finding another partner so soon after a breakup.

Narcissists often can't even do journeys alone, and often phone people to interact with when driving, or on the train. Like Marcus, many don't even want to watch TV on their own. Remember how he would make Irina feel obliged to sit with him, to watch programmes she didn't even like, just to get narcissistic supply from her being there?

The better a source of supply you are to a narcissist, the less extra sources they will need. But you would be very hard pushed indeed to find a narcissist living a completely isolated life, with no social media, and no opportunity to gain supply from even work colleagues.

8

Narcissistic Super-skills

J ust as there are 'normal' things that narcissists *can't* do, there are other things that they do supremely *easily*. I call these their 'super-skills'. Let's take a look.

Putting people down

It stands to reason that it's pretty difficult to put a person down to their face, if you care about their feelings. But, of course, narcissists don't — which is why they excel in this area.

We've already talked about the ways in which narcissists will devalue others, to weaken them so that they cannot escape their orbits, and how they put people down in order to elevate themselves within their own hierarchy of importance, to feel better about themselves. You also know about how they intersperse these devaluations with idealizations to cause trauma bonding, which make their victims addicted to them.

Even children are subjected to these devaluations, with criticisms, ridicule, and name calling. They can expect to be body-shamed by their narcissistic parent and called too weedy, or too fat. The Closet Narcissist might be less obvious about this, but may come across as the ever-giving parent, whose child disappoints them over and over, no matter how hard they try. This is simply a more covert way of making the child feel 'not good enough', and a failure.

Narcissists always devalue people behind their backs too — a very big warning sign. I recall meeting a vicar at a party, who, drunk, didn't hold back with his criticisms of people he disliked at all. He already had a reputation in the parish for being attention seeking and for hogging the limelight — he'd deliver sermons that went on forever, with anecdote after anecdote, and sing solos during hymns. He was also known for being a bit of a control freak in his role on the parish council. It is thought that there is a relatively high proportion of Communal Narcissists in the clergy, and I suspect that this chap, with his rather ungodly bitchiness, may well fit the bill.

Lying

You now know that the truth to a narcissist is what they say it is, at the time they are saying it. They completely believe their own lies, and do not see truth as a fixed entity. They are especially good at it because they are so practised at it — their whole false persona, which they hide behind and use as a shield, is an invention — a lie which they need to maintain 24/7.

When people eventually leave a narcissist's orbit, they often find themselves questioning everything the narcissist ever said to them (with good cause) — and the real truth about the lies that they fell for can keep surfacing for years to come.

It is really important to mention smear campaigns here too. If a narcissist gets wind that you are about to exit their orbit, they will begin this campaign against you, telling lies about you to important people. Your family, friends, work colleagues and potential employers will be told that you are an alcoholic, a stalker, a prostitute, an embezzler, an abuser, a plagiarizer and more, in utterly convincing tones.

Interestingly, neither lying nor gaslighting are mentioned as diagnostic features in the DSM-5 — a glaring omission, in my view.

The ability to ignore rules and laws

Narcissists are perfectly *capable* of following rules and being law abiding citizens when it suits them, but, in reality, they don't believe that the rules and laws apply to them, and so find them supremely easy to ignore. This comes in part from their sense of entitlement, and from their need to be special. Rules are for other people, people who are less important than them.

So how does this play out? The most bizarre ways seem to relate to the laws of nature. Some really extreme narcissists behave as if they can defy the laws of physics, for example. These are the narcissists that drive at high speeds around blind corners, or literally take off in cars or on motorbikes, terrifying their passengers. They even drive through rivers — the wife of a particularly grandiose narcissist once told me how her husband had done this, with a car full of pleading passengers, just to prove that he could. She said that he seemed utterly perplexed when the car did not make it through the river and had to be towed out, as if he had expected the waters to part for him.

The laws of biology also seem to be commonly disregarded by narcissists. It's a known fact that a person who has had to undergo multiple abortions whilst in a relationship might actually be a victim of abuse. Male narcissists often refuse to use contraception, with no regard for the biological consequences on their victim, violating boundaries and showing a distinct lack of empathy, in one fell swoop.

Relatively minor rules are often disregarded too, such as 'no entry' or 'private' signs. I recall a client whose first date with the narcissist she eventually married (and then divorced) involved him climbing the wall of a beautiful private garden, and letting her into it. It had seemed fun and romantic at the time, but actually, it was a big red flag.

It is also surprisingly common for a narcissist to coerce their spouse into taking the blame for their speeding tickets, so that they do not lose their driver's license — which is illegal here in the UK. Illegal drug use is also common in narcissists, with cocaine as a particular favourite, on account of its ability to boost feelings of omnipotence and grandiosity.

Self-employed narcissists, and those who run small companies, are often tax evaders. They may flout employment law when it comes to their employees, sacking them if they get pregnant, for example. In divorce, they ignore court orders, and fail to give a true picture of their finances. Narcissists lie under oath because the oath is completely meaningless to them, and they sign statements of truth which they know are untrue, because of their lack of respect for the law.

Narcissists also have fluctuating morals — after all, these are just another type of 'rule' that they can bend to their own advantage.

Narcissists have a big advantage when it comes to being able to disregard rules and laws — they don't feel guilt or shame, and have limited capacity for remorse — no wonder it's easy for them to construct their own, ever-shifting, rulebook.

Behaving in an entitled way

Most people would cringe just at the *thought* of behaving as flagrantly as narcissists do in this regard. Narcissists feel absolutely *entitled* to use and manipulate other people. They feel entitled to be late for people. They feel entitled to special treatment. They feel entitled to take the credit for other people's work. They feel entitled to not have to pull their weight, at work, at home or anywhere else, if they don't feel like it, or if it doesn't bring in narcissistic supply. They feel entitled to violate other people's boundaries (more on that later). They feel entitled to spend other people's money, to be rude to them and to upset them. They feel entitled to lie, cheat and steal if they feel like it. They feel entitled to your undivided attention and your lifelong loyalty. They feel entitled to complete transparency from you, but total privacy for themselves. They feel entitled to be hypocritical. They feel entitled to be utterly selfish in the way they approach everything.

However, the Closet Narcissists can hide their sense of entitlement under a veneer of 'niceness' and shyness. They get what they feel they are entitled to in sneakier ways than the other types of narcissist. They may believe they are entitled to the best table in the restaurant, but use quiet flattery and charm with the waiter to secure this, rather than by loudly demanding it. They may believe that they should be first to board the airplane, and so feign a disability, so that they are driven in an airport buggy to the boarding gate, and made a fuss of on the plane.

In divorce, narcissists believe that they are entitled to all the money, and that their spouse is entitled to nothing. This classically wreaks havoc in the divorce process, as they hide and spend the marital pot of money. They also feel that they are entitled to punish their former spouse to the point of near annihilation, in any way they so choose, nicely topping them up with premium narcissistic supply in the process.

Another big area where this shows up is in wills. Narcissists may challenge wills that they didn't benefit from, or try to convince elderly parents to change their wills to favour them. It's also really common for adult narcissists to extort money from their aging parents for years before their deaths, without their other siblings' knowledge.

Exploitation

It's a doddle for narcissists to shamelessly exploit others, partially because they don't view them as actual three-dimensional people. They see others merely as objects — 'its' — over whom they have a permanent sense of ownership — and this is particularly noticeable for those residing in their closer orbits. The people who revolve around them are there to be used in whatever way best suits the narcissist — it doesn't really occur to them that other people think differently. It's a sort of vampiric relationship in this way, and it doesn't matter which orbit you are in — in some way you will be serving them.

So, if you are the barman in the pub, who sees the narcissist every week and has a bit of a joke and laugh with them, they are probably not exploiting you in any big way. It's perfectly possible for you to have a mutually satisfying relationship with them on a purely superficial level, if you respond to them by giving them good narcissistic supply. Perhaps the only way in which they are mildly exploiting you is by using you for your little fuel top-ups. Maybe you always remember their usual drink and let them stay after-hours — it hardly matters, if no harm is being done.

But what if they view you, as the barman, as being inferior to them, and you occasionally get the sense that they treat you with contempt? Or what if you start to wonder why it is, given that you get on so raucously well, that you never seem to strike up a proper friendship? Most likely, at some stage, you will be left feeling confused and mildly disappointed by them.

Narcissists, particularly of the exhibitionist variety, can be experts at making you think that you are their best friend, when actually they have no genuine feelings for you at all. You may eventually feel resentment if, after five years of them coming to your pub, where you treat them like royalty, they haven't even bothered to remember your name, or have no idea who you are if you bump into them in another context. You definitely might feel a bit exploited then.

So narcissists exploit everyone to some degree, regardless of their orbit, with the ultimate aim of securing narcissistic supply, whether directly, or indirectly. For example, you might have been chosen to be their friend because you are particularly attractive looking, and so are good to be seen with, leading to indirect supply from the admiring glances of others. Perhaps you have been chosen because of your social network or contacts, which can get them into the best restaurants — so making them feel special and important. Perhaps you gaze at them adoringly, or hang upon their every word and so give them narcissistic supply in this direct form. There are a myriad reasons why you may have been singled out to be their special friend. But at

*"Narcissists exploit **everyone** to some degree, regardless of their orbit, with the ultimate aim of securing narcissistic supply."*

the end of the day, you are just an 'it'. The deep feelings you may have for them are not mutual, and never will be.

In the workplace, exploitation is rife — taking credit for other people's work being a big one here. Remember how Jonathan never gave Fiona credit for the work she did for him about inclusivity, which he used in his talks up and down the country, passing them off as his own? And how Marcus pretended his pastor's sermons and obscure poems were original content, in his videos?

Partners will be exploited and taken advantage of in all manner of ways too, from financial exploitation to emotional exploitation. Even children will be used as a way to secure narcissistic supply — Jonathan delighted in openly applauding his son Max at concerts, outwardly basking in his talent, whilst secretly putting him down for playing an instrument he didn't approve of. Lina's children were a way for her to gain narcissistic supply from others by throwing spectacular birthday parties for them, which were the envy of the other mothers. And Janis was simply a tool for Communal Narcissist Marcus to publicly play the role of doting stepdad to the outside world, securing praise and admiration from everyone around.

But try to take from this, if you are realizing that you are being exploited in some way by a narcissist, that it is not personal. *It's not about you as a person* — just your usefulness to them. And that is not a reflection on your worth — really.

Boundary trampling

I described in Chapter 5 how narcissists test their potential victims' suitability for entrapment by pushing and violating their boundaries, to see how they react, but I mention it again here because boundary violations continue *throughout* any relationship with a narcissist, and they are able to do this with unparalleled ease.

Think back to the story of the narcissistic boss, who insisted on visiting his terminally ill former secretary in hospital, as she lay dying, with no regard for her or her family's wish for private time together. Narcissists often behave in ways which appear wildly inappropriate to non-narcissists as they blur the lines between professional and personal boundaries. Inappropriate relationships with subordinates are a common feature of this.

Narcissists don't like the word 'no' and will tend to bulldoze over anyone who tries to exert a boundary, either by completely ignoring it or trying to persuade the person that what they want is 'wrong'. They may ignore physical boundaries, by encroaching on your space or taking food off your plate, or waking you up in the middle of the night because they can't sleep and want to chat. They might borrow your things without asking, or use them even when you have requested that they don't. Snooping on other people's computers is another common violation of privacy.

Social boundaries can be violated in many ways, such through making excessive eye contact with victims, or not leaving your dinner party until 3 am, in spite of your yawns and hints. They may also make socially inappropriate comments in social settings, or be excessively nosey about your life. Sexual boundaries are also commonly overstepped, as are boundaries to do with time. Narcissistic bosses will often expect their subordinates to answer their emails at the weekend, or work late without warning.

I recall the story of a narcissistic ex-wife who was caught on webcam, letting herself into his apartment, using the key he had given his daughter. He was shocked to see her rifling through his new partner's wardrobe and underwear drawer, and going through his desk papers, particularly as they had been divorced for four years. I've even heard of a narcissist who, when his neighbour went on holiday, climbed a ladder and prised open an upstairs window, which had been left open just a crack, just to have a look around the house.

Narcissists are inherently selfish — only *their* needs and wants matter, and they will scale any boundary you put up if they want to get to the other side, irrespective of your feelings.

Narcissists find it even easier to violate their children's boundaries, which can become problematic as they get older. They might read their diaries, go through their phones, and barge into their rooms without knocking, and they often subject any boyfriends and girlfriends to inappropriate and embarrassing questioning.

Manipulation

It's probably pretty obvious from everything you have read so far that narcissists are excellent manipulators. They have learned to manipulate at an early age, and so do it completely unconsciously and effortlessly, because it is second nature to them. Even these narcissists are likely to be at least five steps ahead of any non-narcissist. However, some narcissists are also able to *consciously* manipulate, making them all the more difficult to manage. Trying to out-manipulate a narcissist can be like trying to play three-dimensional chess wearing a blindfold, with heavy metal music blaring straight into your brain, so you can't think straight.

Projecting a convincing outward image

By now you know that narcissists are highly practised at projecting an outward image to the world, to act as an armour to hide behind, to stay feeling emotionally safe. You understand that how they appear to other people desperately matters — because those people's belief in this image keeps it strong enough to shield them from their own low self-esteem. They are therefore proficient at acquiring *things* that feed into that image, whether it's expensive things to show their wealth, things that make them look powerful, things that make them look clever or sexy — or whatever else they need to prove that they are who they are claiming to be.

Many narcissists are also adept at superficially appearing *cleverer* than they actually are, and so many people are fooled into believing that they are particularly intelligent as a result.

However, just like with all different groups of people, in narcissists IQ is distributed on a bell-shaped curve — a so-called 'normal distribution curve', meaning that there are a few intelligent ones, lots of ones of average intelligence and a few less intelligent ones. In other words, contrary to appearance, the narcissist you know might not be as brainy as you think.

Firstly, the narcissist's wired-in ability to manipulate can mistakenly look like cleverness, at first glance. The conviction with which narcissists speak (a big contributor to their gaslighting ability) can also feed into this — but if you examine what they are *actually saying*, and the words they are using, you are likely to find that it makes little sense. I describe this use of 'pseudo-logic', on page 123.

It's a well known fact that tall men reach higher positions of power than shorter men, and earn more than them, because of the positive biases people apply to them — but I wonder if this is also true for narcissists? Do some narcissists achieve greatness, which is out of proportion to their abilities, because of how they are perceived? Political beliefs aside, if we examine certain narcissistic world leaders, who can barely string a sensible sentence together, it certainly does appear that way.

Triangulation

I mentioned triangulation earlier, as one of the narcissist's devaluation tactics which is designed to weaken their victims, so that they cannot leave their orbit. To recap, triangulation is where the narcissist brings a third person into the dynamic, either to make their victim feel jealous or insecure, or to fulfil some other function. Narcissists naturally triangulate without shame, guilt or remorse, with impressive skill.

"Triangulation is where the narcissist brings a third person into the dynamic, either to make their victim feel jealous or insecure, or to fulfil some other function."

If you happen to have been brought up by a narcissist, you may recognize triangulation from your upbringing, because if a narcissist has more than one child, they will triangulate them against each other. One child will be the golden child (who can do no wrong), one will be the scapegoat (who can do no right) and, if there is a third child, they will be the invisible child, who is completely ignored. All the children will want the approval and love of the narcissistic parent, and will jump through hoops to get it, sometimes even turning on each other. This is a wonderful way for the narcissist to gain narcissistic supply, and they can be warm and loving towards the golden child, whilst at the same time being cold, critical and demeaning towards the other children.

Do you remember how Oonagh, growing up on the dairy farm in Ireland, would complain to her sisters about how her narcissistic father treated her? She was the scapegoat in her family, but it was very telling when one of her sisters (presumably an invisible child) retorted, with "Well, at least he knows your name"). You may also recall how Arun was Lina's golden child, praised for everything he did, whilst daughter Laila was constantly shamed, put down and criticized.

Narcissists often like to switch things up in this family dynamic, by reassigning the roles to different children, without warning. The golden child suddenly becomes invisible, and so on. This is the ultimate in control and power, and the instability of the children's roles is an excellent way to keep them on their toes.

Narcissists can triangulate anyone with anyone else. You can be triangulated with a narcissist's family members, work colleagues, or even with their favourite movie star.

Even at work they will have favourites for a while, who will then be discarded and replaced with others. Remember how devastated the builder Rodney was, when he caught Jonathan laughing with the electrician about him? How Jonathan would talk endlessly about Fiona with his teacher wife Brigitte, and then even promoted her into a role that Brigitte should have been offered? And how Oonagh greatly enjoyed flirting with Geoff's boss at his work Christmas dinner in front of him, as he watched on, ashamed and embarrassed?

This brings me on to another variation of triangulation, The Drama Triangle. There are three players — The Victim, The Persecutor, and the Rescuer, but their roles are not static (the victim or rescuer may become the perpetrator, for example), but at all times the three roles have to be filled. This means that if one person changes role, the others are forced to change too, usually with no idea of what is happening.

Narcissists love the drama triangle. They use it in couples' therapy, casting themselves as the victim, so the couples' therapist tries to rescue them, unwittingly actually becoming the persecutor of the true victim — the narcissist's spouse. They use it at work, in friendships and in family dynamics, playing people off against each other. The sense of control and power they gain, together with the conflict and drama it creates, are wonderful sources of narcissistic supply.

Playing the victim

This key narcissistic behaviour, disappointingly, is another one that is not mentioned in the DSM-5. Narcissists deploy this form of manipulation with pinpoint accuracy, whenever required.

The Closet Narcissists, like Lina, play the victim all the time, but the other types of narcissist will wheel out this tactic when required too, often if they are called out on their bad behaviours, or if someone threatens to leave them.

Again, look at how Jonathan responded when Fiona tried to resign. He broke down in tears and told her that he was depressed, and that his son had shut him out of his life. He was also able to manipulate young Mollie, who he was having an affair with, by claiming that he was the victim of a loveless marriage.

Marcus, who was of mixed race, constantly used this fact to his advantage, implying that others (even his wife, Irina) were being racist, when things didn't go his way. Racism will also commonly be alleged by a narcissist who has been reprimanded or sacked in the workplace, as will accusations of bullying. Narcissists will also frequently allege that they had physical or mental health issues which were unsupported by their employers, and they'll happily make formal complaints (which can escalate all the way to court).

Issues with physical health will be exaggerated, or completely made up by narcissists when required, with claims of incapacitating pain, immobility, or any other health condition that works to secure them what they need.

In divorce, narcissists often claim to be victims of domestic violence, and the police may even be duped into arresting their partner. The 'DARVO' acronym is relevant here — if you've ever accused a narcissist of anything, you will have noticed that they will Deny, Attack and Reverse the true Victim with the true Offender. In short, narcissists play the victim with aplomb, and are highly convincing.

Giving unsolicited advice

Narcissists are highly skilled at giving advice, especially if you haven't asked for it. You can expect to be told to your face what you should want, what you should have, what you should be, how you should do things and what you are doing wrong. Narcissists usually do not feel that they need experience of a situation to be able to advise on it. It can present a bit like 'mansplaining,' but female narcissists are equally prone to it.

Narcissists who are not parents will tell you where you are going wrong with your children, and narcissists who have never worked a day in their lives will tell you how to manage your boss. A giveaway is that no consideration will be given to people's feelings when advice is being doled out — when your narcissistic sibling is arguing with you as to what is best for your octogenarian parents, they will have conspicuously failed to ask them what *they* want.

Do you recall how Jonathan would tell Rodney, an experienced builder, exactly what building methods he should use when he was working on his house, to the point where Rodney started to question his own professional judgment?

Closet Narcissists may do things slightly differently. They may hide their opinions about how you are living your life from you, but instead criticize you to other people, behind your back (often under the guise of 'worrying about you'). They often enlist other people to pass on their opinions to you, sneakily triangulating them with you.

Controlling others

This is a big feature in many narcissists, which is also conspicuously missing from the DSM-5 diagnostic criteria for NPD. There are various areas in which different narcissists excel at being in control.

Many control the *people* around them, dictating how they spend their time, where they go, who they see, even what they eat. They can also be overly controlling when it comes to money, and demand receipts or check bank statements.

Narcissistic parents often control what activities their children do, what subjects they take at school, and even what career they choose. They might refuse to let them see certain friends, or not allow them to come to their home. One narcissistic mother I knew of wanted to know exactly what her teenage son was up to at all times, and insisted that he always kept the door to his room open, even whilst he slept. Marcus, our Communal Narcissist insisted that his stepson Janis play football, because it was *his* interest as a football coach, and Lina controlled what everyone in her family wore, even putting their clothes out ready for them the night before. She even felt she had the right to dictate how her fifteen-year-old daughter wore her hair, and was incensed when she sneakily went to the hairdresser, to have it chopped into a crop.

Remember how Jonathan insisted that Brigitte drove a hybrid car, but wouldn't let her turn the radio or heating on, because it would start using petrol, instead of electricity? Things got so bad that she stopped driving it completely, and just took the bus, which limited her freedom significantly. And what about how Oonagh refused to take her house keys out with her, so that Geoff would always have to be home before her, to let her into the house?

Narcissistic siblings can be particularly controlling too — and often order even their adult siblings around. Of course, control occurs in workplace relationships too, with micromanagement and workplace bullying being huge features of NPD — all adding to a narcissist's sense of power and omnipotence.

Narcissists also shine at putting their own stamp on special occasions, to subtly wield control. If not actually organising the occasion, at the very least you can expect a degree of sabotage. Remember how Lina loved to organize other people's funerals, even if she barely knew them, but when she didn't organize Raj's 40th birthday party, she made him late for it, and hogged the attention by feigning being in pain? To spoil things further, she then refused to speak to him for days afterwards, accusing him of dancing inappropriately with a work colleague.

Birthdays, Christmases, weddings and any special occasion can be ruined by any narcissist who needs to be in control. And if, heavens forbid, you divorce a narcissist, you can be sure that they will control the whole process — and not in a good way.

Interestingly, some narcissists need to be in control so badly that they actually develop genuine fears (and even phobias) of things they can't control, such as a fear of heights, or of flying. Some are scared of driving, because they don't feel completely in control of the other motorists around them. They may try to stop driving altogether and make their partner do all the driving instead, as Lina did.

9

Take the Narcissist Test

Are you worried that *you* are a narcissist?

When people (who are not narcissists) first learn about narcissism, they usually start to worry that *they* might be a narcissist, because they recognize some of the traits in themselves — so if this is what is happening to you, let's tackle it head on.

Personality disorders are actually extreme manifestations of *normal* traits. In other words, all narcissistic traits exist on a 'spectrum'. It's where you *are* on that spectrum that determines whether you have narcissistic personality disorder or not.

Of course, this idea can muddy the waters a bit, until you really understand the spectrum. So you might be worried that you have a sense of entitlement because you don't like waiting in queues, or always take cabs, rather than the underground. Or you might suspect that you have low empathy because of that time your child was ill, and you were impatient with them, after you'd been up for three nights straight with their teething baby sister. Or you might think you are a control freak, because you really don't like it when your flatmates don't put their plates in the dishwasher. Or that you have a false persona, because you rarely leave the house without make-up on.

The Spectrum of Narcissism

So let's take a look at the spectrum, which lies on a scale of zero to ten. Now, where you want to be, in order to be a healthy person, is slap bang in the middle of the spectrum, at four, five or six. Here you know what your needs are and are able to get them met by yourself and others, but without exploiting anyone. You know what your boundaries are — what you are prepared to do for other people, and what you are not prepared to do, as well as where you draw the line as to what behaviours you are prepared to accept from others. You have a good sense of where you end and others begin. You are able to stand up for yourself, because you know that you are worth standing up for, but you also have empathy for other people, and see them as real, three-dimensional entities, with wants, needs and lives, who you can genuinely care about. You do like to enhance your outward image to a degree, but it's not all-encompassing. Your sense of self-worth mostly (around 70%) comes from an intrinsic self-belief that you are worthy and enough, with a lot less (around 20%) coming from what other people think of you, and even less (around 10%) coming from how you feel you measure up to other people. People in the middle of the scale like this have what is known as 'healthy narcissism'.

Now let's look at the people lower down the scale — at zero, one, two and three. These people actually don't have *enough* healthy narcissism to be living optimally — and they are actually very attractive to narcissists.

They have a real aversion to feeling special, and try to bat off any feelings of specialness, often finding it difficult to accept compliments. They feel undeserving of gifts or offers of help. They may avoid self-enhancing activities to do with image. They put their needs below other people's needs, and don't actually feel entitled *enough,* perhaps even feeling that they shouldn't take up space in the world. They may be people pleasers and rescuers, with a tendency to prioritize endlessly giving to others. They may have poor boundaries, and find it difficult to say no and mean it, and they may be almost overly empathic, caring 'too much' about others at the expense of being cared for and caring for themselves. These people are unofficially termed 'Echoists' after Echo, from the ancient Greek myth of Echo and Narcissus.

Those with pathological narcissism have traits on which the volume has been turned up too high. They are the people who would qualify for a diagnosis of NPD, and they lie at seven, eight, nine and ten on the scale, with increasing amounts of pathological narcissism the higher up the scale they are.

Moving up the scale from seven through ten, they are increasingly concerned with getting their own needs met, even at the expense of others. They have less and less empathy for others, and feel more and more entitled to the best of everything, and to special treatment. This increasing entitlement and selfishness means they exploit people increasingly, the higher up the scale they sit, and have a greater capacity to actually abuse others for their own ends. Image enhancement, and how they are seen by others, also becomes increasingly important. They don't see themselves as separate from other people, and so violate their boundaries, but at the same time, they do not view people as fully real equals, but rather as mere objects, about whom they cannot really care.

"Personality disorders are actually extreme manifestations of normal traits."

Their sense of self-worth comes mostly from what other people think of them, and how they feel they compare to others, with only a very small amount coming from their own intrinsic sense of self-belief and 'enoughness'. They chase feelings of specialness more and more, the higher up the scale they are, to compensate for their intrinsic lack of self-worth.

THE NARCISSIST TRAP

Narcissists can be attracted to people at any point on the scale of narcissism, but the people at the lower end are particularly attractive to them as long-term prospects — a case of 'opposites attract'.

Testing for narcissism

Taking the following tests might give you an indication of how narcissistic you are. Note that these tests are not diagnostic, but just for your own interest — only a specially trained clinician can make a formal diagnosis of Narcissistic Personality Disorder.

There are five tests below. The first one (the Narcissism Screening Test) will give you an overview. If you score highly in this, you may wish to take the others too. The relative scores you get in these further tests will give you an idea which type (or types) of narcissist you predominately might be.

If you suspect that you have a narcissist in your life, you might find it useful to try to consider the questions from *their* perspective, thinking about how they might answer them (if they were being completely honest). If you do not know an answer, score 3, for neutral.

The Narcissism Screening Test

To what extent do you agree with the statements that follow?

    Strongly agree — 5
    Agree — 4
    Neutral — 3
    Disagree — 2
    Strongly disagree — 1

Write the relevant score next to each statement and add them up to get a total.

THE NARCISSISM SCREENING TEST	Score 1-5
Deep down I resent others who have what I lack	
I believe that other people often exaggerate their successes	
When other people achieve, I feel annoyed, threatened or envious	
I know best in the vast majority of situations	
I have a different temperament to most people	
I am not 'ordinary' or 'average'	
Everybody should respect me	
I sometimes feel only special people can fully understand my uniqueness	
I value high status people and people who are 'going places'	
It is only right that I should expect a great deal from other people	

THE NARCISSISM SCREENING TEST	Score 1-5
People should automatically comply with what I expect from them	
I accomplish far more than others tend to give me credit for	
I'm not genuinely interested in other people's feelings, but can pretend to be	
Other people's feelings are often completely incorrect	
I don't genuinely care about what other people want	
What other people want is often completely wrong	
I think people are jealous of me	
It's hard to feel positive emotions for someone close to me when they have disappointed me	
I tend to see people as being either great or terrible at any one time	
It's hard to feel good about myself when I am alone	
I feel entitled to take credit for other people's work	
I feel humiliated, offended, angry or hurt by even mild criticism	
I am willing to take advantage of others to get what I want	
I often manipulate people	
I am a snob at heart	
I am better at a lot more things than most people are	

THE NARCISSISM SCREENING TEST	Score 1-5
I am extremely driven to obtain unlimited amounts of one or more of the following: power, success, brilliance, ideal love or beauty	
People close to me do not have the right to abandon me	
The truth is what I say it is	
I get incensed with people who think they can take me for a fool	
It irritates me when people don't appreciate how good I am at things/mistake me for an average person	
I have hardly any deep friendships	
It's hard to admit to the weakness I feel inside	
I have never apologized and really meant it	
I often take pleasure in people's misfortunes	
If I do things for other people, it's usually because I stand to gain in some way	
TOTAL SCORE	/180

If you scored 60 or less, you may not be narcissistic *enough* to be emotionally healthy, and might be a 'narcissist magnet'. Between 60 and 120, you fall into the 'healthy' narcissism range. And if you have scored above 120 in this test, you may be at a high overall risk of having NPD, and you may wish to do the following tests, for further clarity. Each test has 21 questions. Bear in mind that, although most people are predominantly *one* subtype of narcissist, many do exhibit features from more than one category, which these tests will highlight.

And remember — these tests are not diagnostic, but just indicators for your own interest.

I also think, if you are starting to worry that you *are* a narcissist, that it's important to understand this one basic discriminating factor - *you cannot be a narcissist if you can genuinely feel a normal amount of empathy for others.* So, if you know in your heart of hearts that you can step into another person's shoes and truly *feel* how *they* are feeling, you can breathe a sigh of relief.

The Exhibitionist Narcissist Test

To what extent do you agree with the following statements?

Strongly agree — 5
Agree — 4
Neutral — 3
Disagree — 2
Strongly disagree — 1

Write the relevant score next to each statement and add them up to get a total.

EXHIBITIONIST NARCISSIST TEST	Score 1-5
I have a natural talent for influencing people	
I can make anyone believe anything I want them to	
I can usually talk my way out of anything	
I can read people like a book	
I always know what I am doing/have everything figured out	
I am special and important in a unique way	
I have outstanding qualities that few others possess	
I have a different temperament to most people	
I will usually show off if I get the chance	
I like to talk about my relationships with high status people	
I like to be the centre of attention	
I like it when people suck up to me	

EXHIBITIONIST NARCISSIST TEST	Score 1-5
I am highly motivated to do things that gain me the admiration, validation and compliments of others	
I am often preoccupied with thoughts of success, power and status	
I often reflect on my accomplishments and fantasize about my future endeavors.	
I like to have authority over other people/be in charge	
I insist upon getting the respect that is due to me	
I can't bear to feel weak eg. by admitting to imperfections/ vulnerabilities/illnesses or asking strangers for help	
Everybody likes to hear my stories	
I can live my life in any way I want to — rules don't apply to people like me	
I have good reason to be arrogant	
TOTAL SCORE	

The Devaluing Narcissist Test

To what extent do you agree/disagree with the following statements?

Strongly agree — 5
Agree — 4
Neutral — 3
Disagree — 2
Strongly disagree — 1

Write the relevant score next to each statement and add them up to get a total.

DEVALUING NARCISSIST TEST	Score 1-5
People tell me that I am hard to please	
I often fall out with work colleagues	
Nobody I know is truly good enough for me	
I will find fault with people, no matter how hard they try	
I often badmouth people behind their backs	
I am always spoiling for a fight	
I often call people unflattering names	
I often ridicule people	
I deliberately rain on people's parades	
I feel powerful when I hurt people's feelings	
I do not feel remorse when I hurt people	
People should behave as if nothing has happened after a fight with me	

DEVALUING NARCISSIST TEST	Score 1-5
Show-offs need to be brought down a peg or two	
Deep down I know that other people's successes/talents/ attributes make me feel bad about myself	
Even if I congratulate someone for a success, I do not really feel happy for them	
I rarely compliment people and mean it	
I think that most people are beneath me	
I am a morally and intellectually superior person compared to most others	
If I get to know someone I admire, I usually eventually realize that they are actually defective, worthless losers	
I ridicule and shame people if they tell me their feelings	
I feel incensed if someone dares to disrespect me	
TOTAL SCORE	

The Closet Narcissist Test

To what extent do you agree/disagree with the following statements?

Strongly agree — 5
Agree — 4
Neutral — 3
Disagree — 2
Strongly disagree — 1

Write the relevant score next to each statement and add them up to get a total.

CLOSET NARCISSIST TEST	Score 1-5
I secretly feel resentful when people tell me their troubles, wanting my sympathy and time	
I have enough on my plate without having to worry about other people's problems	
I am often absorbed by thoughts about my woes relationships, personal affairs or health	
Nobody fully understands my problems	
People would be shocked if they knew my real thoughts and feelings	
I sometimes secretly fantasize about being violent	
I feel self-conscious in the limelight and try to shy away from it	
I generally feel under-appreciated by people	
I often feel resentment towards others	

CLOSET NARCISSIST TEST	Score 1-5
I often fantasize about accomplishing things that are probably beyond my means	
When others disappoint me, I often get angry at myself	
When I am with a group of friends, I often feel alone	
My feelings are easily hurt, even by comments made in jest	
I often take things personally	
I feel deeply ashamed or angry if things do not go my way but I try not to show it	
I often feel irritated/angry/hurt because people don't see what a good person I am	
I often feel irritated/angry/hurt because people do not notice all that I do for them	
My self-esteem tends to fluctuate a lot	
I often resent sharing the credit of an achievement with others	
I wouldn't disclose all my intimate thoughts and feelings to someone I didn't admire	
Associating with high status people makes me feel special	
TOTAL SCORE	

The Communal Narcissist Test

To what extent do you agree/disagree with the following statements?

Strongly agree — 5
Agree — 4
Neutral — 3
Disagree — 2
Strongly disagree — 1

Write the relevant score next to each statement and add them up to get a total.

COMMUNAL NARCISSIST TEST	Score 1-5
I am one of the most caring people you could ever meet	
My empathy levels are off the chart	
I am one of the most generous people I know	
I am one of the kindest people you will ever meet	
I am one of the most helpful people I know	
I am incredibly understanding	
I am completely trustworthy	
I am a fantastic listener	
I am the best friend anyone could ever have	
I know I enrich people's lives hugely	
I know I am a really good influence on people	
The sacrifices I make demonstrate what a good person I am	

COMMUNAL NARCISSIST TEST	Score 1-5
Helping others proves what a good person I am	
I am changing (or will change) the world for the better	
I am (or will be) an amazing parent	
It irritates me when people don't seem to notice how good a person I am	
I am entitled to, and deserve recognition for, my good deeds	
Having people rely on me shows how important I am	
I often fantasize about becoming world renowned/winning awards for my important contributions	
I know better than anybody in my field the best way to help others/improve things	
Deep down, I resent other people being lauded/achieving recognition instead of me	
TOTAL SCORE	

Write your results for each test below. Comparing the scores will give you an idea of the relative proportions of the four subtypes within you.

Type	Exhibitionist	Devaluing	Closet	Communal
Score				

Summary Table of Narcissistic Traits and Behaviours
Low empathy
Inability to truly care about others
Sense of entitlement
Exploiting others
Love bombing in initial stage
Cycles of devaluations and idealizations ('nice/nasty narcissist')
Need for attention/adoration/drama/conflict/to scare others
Invalidating other people's feelings, beliefs, successes
Inability to take the blame/blame-shifting
Shame-dumping
Projection
Inability to see people as a blend of good and bad ('hero to zero')
Selfishness
Gaslighting and lying
Jealousy
A preoccupation with outward image
Manipulativeness
Triangulation
A need to be in control
Playing the victim
'DARVO' (Deny, Attack and Reverse the Victim with the Offender)
A need for perfection
Violating boundaries

Summary Table of Narcissistic Traits and Behaviours
Flouting rules and laws
Moral hypocrisy
Highly sensitive to criticism
Tantrums
Rage
Aggression (and passive aggression)
Silent treatments
Stonewalling (completely ignoring you or your communications)
Narcissistic pseudo-logic and word salad
Schadenfreude (taking pleasure in others' misfortunes)
Need to win/have the last word
Needing to appear clever
'Knowing best'
Superficial, easily changeable emotions
Only conditional/transactional love
Difficulty being alone
Lack of deep, long term friendships
Seeing their children as extensions of themselves
Future faking

10

Help — I'm in the Narcissist Trap!

arcissists, Narcissists everywhere…

It's quite possible, as you have been reading this book, that you have had a series of lightbulb moments regarding the people you know, because various scenarios and characteristics have resonated with you. And very often, as people learn more, they start to realize that they don't just know *one* potential narcissist, but *a few* — often including people they had never even previously suspected as being narcissistic.

And, once you are attuned to narcissism (once your 'narcissist radar' is turned on), you cannot stop seeing narcissists all around you — to an almost disconcerting degree. I still remember when this first happened to me, and how confused I felt about it. You start to wonder if you are seeing narcissists where none exist. You ask yourself whether you are making it all up. You start to question yourself. It feels uncomfortable, and strange.

I remember being at a legal event, and being approached by a lawyer who had read the book I co-authored for lawyers, *Narcissism and Family Law: a Practitioner's Guide*. In reading the book, and learning about the characteristics of narcissists, he found that he was continually being sideswiped by unwanted realizations.

He confided in me, in hushed tones, that he was always finding himself in conversations about narcissists, in the most random of locations. He told me how disconcerted he felt to find himself recognising narcissists in interactions all over the place. Even his mother, his paternal grandfather, his brother and his sister's husband had become suspects, he told me, with quite some measure of distress. Surely, he asked me, he was making everything fit with a preconceived narrative in his head? Surely his mind was playing tricks on him? Surely this was just some strange type of 'confirmation bias' — after all, there couldn't possibly be *this* many narcissists in the world, could there?

I reassured him that this was the normal response that pretty much everyone goes through, and explained that it is largely down to an area of our brains called the 'reticular activating system' (the RAS). The RAS has an important function — it protects us from being overwhelmed by all the sensory stimuli that continually come our way.

Imagine if you were to be completely aware of everything around you — every noise, for example, such as the ticking of the clock in your bedroom, or the birds constantly singing throughout the day. Now extend that to noticing everything that crosses your field of vision, or every sensation, such as the feel of your slightly scrunched up sock on your big toe. It would all be far too intrusive to cope with.

In Chapter 6 I briefly mentioned brain filters, and how they often work against us in preventing us from recognizing that someone is narcissistic. Well, the RAS is one such culprit. Its job is to filter out incoming information from the outside that doesn't seem relevant to us. But when the brain tells us that something *is* relevant, the RAS dutifully removes that particular filter, to make sure that it *does* reach our conscious awareness.

Consider this, as an example I'm sure you can relate to. Imagine that one day you decide that you want to buy a yellow convertible sports car. Suddenly, everywhere you go, you will notice yellow sports cars, and mostly likely you will be struck by how many there are. You may even wonder why you hadn't ever noticed them before. Well, the reason is because your reticular activating system has suddenly stopped

"In family systems, if you know one narcissist, you genuinely are likely to know many — because narcissists exist in clusters."

filtering them out, now that it knows that they are relevant to you.

The same is true for *all* the things that our brains deem as relevant to us — and narcissists are no exception. Once you see narcissism as relevant to you, and you recognize the behaviours, the relevant filter is removed — and the veil lifts.

But when you keep noticing narcissists, it doesn't feel good. People don't *want* to label other people. It makes us feel unkind, unforgiving and judgmental. We want to give our fellow humans the benefit of the doubt. We want to believe that people are like *us* — basically kind, fundamentally empathic and caring. We tell ourselves that we don't have the *right* to label others — that it should be left to the experts — the psychiatrists and psychologists perhaps.

So, even once your radar *has* learnt to pick up the narcissists around you, don't be surprised if, in between your 'ah ha' moments, you also experience a smattering of self-judgment and guilt.

But there is another important point to make here, and it relates to what the distressed barrister said to me about his new-found suspicions regarding his mother, uncle and his brother-in-law. In family systems, if you know one narcissist, *you genuinely are likely to know many* — because narcissists exist in clusters.

We've already discussed how narcissism mostly comes into being as a result of how a child reacts to a difficult upbringing. So, looking at the barrister's example, his narcissistic mother is likely to have had a difficult childhood. He was also convinced that his paternal grandfather was a narcissist — a man likely to have made things quite traumatic for his own father, growing up. You can see how his father

194

could have become a narcissist himself as a result of this, or, as many do, have become unconsciously attracted to narcissists as an adult instead, because of the subconscious pull of the familiar. This would explain quite nicely why his father was attracted to his narcissistic mother.

His mother's difficult parenting would explain why his brother became a narcissist, but also why his sister (who was not a narcissist), like his father, ended up *marrying* a narcissist — she too was drawn to the toxicity she felt comfortable with.

So, if you were brought up by a narcissist, but didn't become one, it is highly likely that, as an adult, you will have relationships with narcissists, because you are so powerfully drawn to them — and this can include friends, as well as intimate partners. If this sounds like you, you may well be shocked at how many narcissists you find, when you examine your inner circle. Of course, none of this is easy to take on board — and you have my sympathy. You may well have quite a journey ahead.

What to do if you are in The Narcissist Trap

The problem with being caught in a narcissist's trap is that there is no 'one size fits all' solution. What you can do largely depends on which orbit you are in, what your relationship is to the narcissist, and whether escape is even an option (or something you even want to do). I tackle the possibilities in detail later.

Having said that, there are definitely a few things to be aware of before you pick up the phone, send that email, or go banging on the narcissist's door to angrily confront them with your suspicions. So hold your horses if you can, whilst we break down the important considerations, starting with the question 'should you tell the narcissist that you think they are a narcissist?'

To tell or not to tell...

The short answer to whether you should enlighten the narcissist regarding your suspicions about them is 'no' — although this advice can be really hard to follow. In all interactions with narcissists, it's worth trying to step back before you actually do or say anything, to ask yourself the following question: *What good can come of it?*

If you tell a narcissist your suspicions, you may be hoping that they will see the error of their ways, and commit to getting a proper diagnosis and having therapy. Perhaps then they will get better, and their relationship with you, and others, will improve. It could be 'win win', you might imagine. I will have done them a favour in telling them, you may believe. At least it will give them a *chance* to try to change. If *I* were a narcissist, I would want someone to tell *me*, you may surmise, quite reasonably. Perhaps you just want see their reaction, because you are so fed up with their toxic behaviours. Or maybe you are genuinely thinking 'what harm could it possibly do?'

Well, to answer that last one, in terms of harm, it could do quite a lot, depending on who the narcissist is to you. If you are married to the narcissist, and considering divorce, then telling them your suspicions is an absolute 'no no' as the narcissist may claim that *you* are the actual narcissist and not them. This could have ramifications in the divorce, and even on where your children end up living. If you are the narcissist's adult child, you can expect to be written out of their will. If you are the narcissist's sibling, similar financial shenanigans are likely to ensue, as they manipulate the rest of your family of origin against you, causing immense emotional fallout.

But telling *any* narcissist that you think they are a narcissist is likely to backfire on you, as they are likely to react with narcissistic rage — because you will have punctured their shield and caused a narcissistic injury, forcing them to face the truth about themselves.

Even if the narcissist you tell is already aware of their narcissism, and happily considers it to be a testimony to their superiority, you will still be left with the problem that little good will come out of the conversation. It is actually likely that you will have handed the narcissist a way to manipulate you further, perhaps by claiming that they will commit to therapy and to 'getting better' — all part of the 'hoovering' tactics that narcissists employ to suck you back into the relationship, so that you can remain as a source of narcissistic supply.

Labelling someone as a narcissist to their face can also give them a great excuse for all their behaviours — "Well I can't help it. I have low empathy, because I am a narcissist. What do you expect? You just need to accept it/love me more/get over it..."

Narcissists just don't behave like non-narcissists, and it's important to realize this early on, and *stop expecting them to*. You have a whole new rulebook to get to grips with.

Getting the narcissist diagnosed and treated

You already know that NPD is a diagnosable condition, so you may be feeling relief that a diagnosis is possible. But I'm afraid there is some bad news — because the fact is that most narcissists will never be formally diagnosed.

Firstly, psychotherapists, counsellors, psychiatrists or other doctors who have a deep understanding of narcissism are few and far between, because these specialists aren't actually routinely trained in Narcissistic Personality Disorder. When looking at narcissistic behaviour earlier on, we looked the DSM-5's (Diagnostic and Statistical Manual of Mental Disorders) diagnostic criteria for NPD, but what I didn't tell you is that that is an American manual, and although it can be used in other parts of the world, it often isn't. In most other parts of the world, the diagnostic manual used is the 'International Classification of Disease', the latest being 'ICD-11.' In this manual there is no formal category for NPD, just a 'Personality Disorder' category. And although NPD fits into this category, no *detail* about the specifics of the disorder are given. Even in the USA, there is a very long way to go in training psychologists and doctors in NPD. Sadly, this lack of education seems to be very much a global phenomenon.

That's not to say that there are *no* professionals trained and experienced in diagnosing NPD — there are. Some clinical forensic psychologists and psychiatrists are able to make this diagnosis, as are some clinical psychologists. However, a narcissist would actually have to *agree* to being diagnosed (unless a court orders an assessment, or they are incarcerated). Getting a diagnosis outside of this latter scenario also costs a lot of money — this is not something that is available on the National Health Service in the UK, for example. But the thing about narcissism is that it works to the narcissist's

"In practical terms, pathological narcissism is not a 'curable' condition. There's no drug treatment and 'normal' psychotherapy won't help."

advantage. It allows them to manipulate and exploit people for their own gain, so that they can feel good about themselves. To a narcissist, there is nothing to fix — so you can see why they would be unlikely to agree to getting a diagnosis.

And, even if you *were* able to get a diagnosis for the narcissist in your life, there's likely to be little point. In practical terms, pathological narcissism is not a 'curable' condition. There's no drug treatment and 'normal' psychotherapy won't help. Some psychotherapists who specialize in working with narcissists say that you can make a difference in a tiny minority, and you can improve empathy levels in those who aren't too high up the spectrum of narcissism. But they also say that it can take years of this super-specialized psychotherapy to have an effect. This only has a chance of working in those narcissists who are of the very intelligent, high functioning variety, who are aware that they have an issue in the first place. And the vast majority of narcissists, even if you could get them to this special therapy, would drop out. A key problem is that, in order to make any type of change, a narcissist would have to take a deep, honest look within. And that is exactly the *opposite* of what their narcissism is for — to shield them from how they really feel deep down.

And finally, in those cases where a narcissist *does* agree to being diagnosed and to have therapy, their motivation is unlikely to be so that they can become less narcissistic. The sad truth is that it is more likely to be so that they can talk about themselves, manipulate the therapist (who they will see as another source of narcissistic supply) and manipulate *you*, by pretending that they are trying to 'get better', to give you false hope that things can improve.

Managing your expectations

So now you know that your narcissist isn't going to change, and can't really be cured. Even in an intimate relationship, you cannot love a narcissist better (no matter how much they tell you that you can). You already know from Chapter 7 that they will never take responsibility for their bad behaviour or even acknowledge it (unless there is something in it for them). They also cannot apologize and mean it, because they must not allow themselves to feel shame. They are extremely limited emotionally, and there's nothing you can do about it — they cannot truly love, and all people are merely fuel sources to them. It is incredibly scant consolation, but I do want to repeat here that *it was never personal* — it was never about you. *No one* could have done enough, given enough, or been enough for a narcissist.

You also need to be aware that, even if you successfully exit your narcissist's orbit and solar system completely, there will be no sense of closure forthcoming from them, and there are likely to be adverse consequences for you. And don't expect justice or fairness — narcissists need to feel that they have won, and you might have to swallow your pride and let them, purely in the interests of self-preservation.

It may be that you decide that you can't (or don't want to) just 'up sticks' and leave the narcissist in your life, but you still need strategies to help you to cope. I tackle these in Chapters 12 and 13. The next chapter, Chapter 11, is for those of you who *are* considering making a break for it. But regardless of whether you choose to stay or go, you are likely to have to replenish your fuel, which will have been depleted by the narcissist to some degree. Let's have a look at how you might do that.

How to replenish your fuel

If you remember, I described in Chapter 6 how one of the major ways that narcissists keep you trapped in their orbits is by stealing your fuel, so that you don't have enough of it to reach your escape velocity. This fuel is made up of your self-confidence, your self-esteem, your self-worth, your self-belief and your healthy self-love — and narcissists deplete it by devaluing you and gaslighting you.

How effectively they do this, and how low your fuel levels go, is mostly dependent on how closely you are orbiting the narcissist and how long you have been in their orbit for — but it's likely that the narcissist you know, even if they are not in a close orbit, will have at least tried to undermine your self-confidence and self-belief. Your boss might have told you that you are incompetent, your co-worker might have suggested that other people don't like you and your mother may make you believe that no matter how hard you try, you will always be a disappointment to her.

You need to be sure of your own reality so that you can no longer be devalued and gaslit in this way, and so that you can start to rebuild your fuel reserves, in preparation for either leaving your narcissist, or keeping them your life. This starts with taking a good look at yourself, to remind yourself of who *you* are, so that you can be secure in that knowledge.

There are few things you may want to consider here. For victims of narcissistic abuse, it can often feel indulgent to spend time in this way but, take it from me — you are totally worth it. So, with pen and paper handy, in a place where you cannot be disturbed for an hour or so, try asking yourself the following questions:

- What have I achieved?
- What are my strengths?
- What are my core values?
- What sort of personality do I have?
- What do I want from my life?

If you have been in a very close orbit to a narcissist for a long time, perhaps as the partner or child of a narcissist, you may have no idea how to answer these questions, and have little idea of who you actually are. If this sounds like you, I've included a few tips to help you get started, together with a few exercises which can be enormously powerful.

What have I achieved?

Close your eyes and think back to your earliest memory. The aim is to replay your life from there onwards, *all the way to the present*, calling to mind all the things that have made you feel proud of yourself. Don't let your brain distract you from your task by pulling you down a chain of irrelevant or sad memories — if this happens, just notice it, and gently bring your mind back to the task in hand.

Every time you remember something, write it down quickly. Then go back to the memory, and take a few moments to really engage with the feeling of pride you had at that time. Remember what it was about the event that made you feel proud of yourself.

Bear in mind that I'm not just talking about huge events, like childbirth and getting your PhD here. I mean *everything* that you can think of that made you feel proud, no matter how seemingly small it might appear now. The time your painting was put up on the school art board when you were five-years-old. The tiny solo you played on the xylophone at the Christmas recital, when you were seven. The time you helped the old lady who had fallen in the street when you were twelve, and how grateful she was.

You are likely to come out of this rather lovely exercise with a renewed sense of who you are, and what matters to you. You might remember a whole host of talents that you forgot you had, and you'll certainly be reminded of just how much you have actually achieved in your life so far.

Keep the list you have made, and refer to it whenever you need to top up your own fuel, to combat a narcissist's devaluations.

What are my strengths?

The VIA Institute on Character has a free ten-minute online test, which ranks your strengths in order. It can be found here: https://www.viacharacter.org/character-strengths. The 24 character strengths which they identify and explain are:

- Creativity
- Curiosity
- Judgment
- Love of Learning
- Perspective
- Bravery
- Perseverance
- Honesty
- Zest (approaching life and situations with excitement and energy, rather than halfheartedly)
- Love
- Kindness

- Social intelligence (being aware of and understanding your own feelings and thoughts, as well as the feelings of those around you)
- Teamwork
- Fairness
- Leadership
- Forgiveness
- Humility
- Prudence (being careful about your choices, stopping and thinking before acting — a strength of restraint)
- Self-regulation
- Appreciation of Beauty & Excellence
- Gratitude
- Hope
- Humour
- Spirituality (feeling spiritual, believing in a sense of purpose or meaning in life, and seeing your place in the grand scheme of the universe)

What are my core values?

It's important to differentiate 'core values' from 'things you value'.
For example, you might value money, because it allows you to have a decent lifestyle, but it can't be a core value — if it can be taken away from you, then it can't be a value.

There is a lot of overlap between your strengths and your values, and you may want to take another look at the strengths list above to see which of those are also values by which you want to live. Other values that might be important for you to live in accordance with include:

- Loyalty
- Compassion
- Integrity

- Selflessness
- Generosity
- Tolerance
- Trustworthiness
- Equanimity (the ability to stay emotionally and mentally calm, even when under stress)
- Altruism
- Appreciation
- Empathy
- Toughness
- Self-reliance
- Attentiveness

What sort of personality do I have?

Not only can narcissists leave their victims not really *knowing* who they are, but they can also make them believe that they have personality traits that they *don't* really have. As you already know, they often project their own personality traits onto others — "You are so selfish", "You are so unreasonable" etc. This nonsense needs to be culled, pronto, if you are to manage the narcissist in your life without being diminished, or to build up enough fuel to leave. There are a variety of great personality tests to research and try out, including:

- The Big Five
- Myers-Briggs
- Enneagram Personality Test
- DISC
- Colour Code Personality Profile

What do I want from my life?

This exercise, 'the rocking chair test', is a powerful way of helping you to determine what you really want from life, which can be enormously helpful if you are dealing with a narcissist. Very often, people who have been orbiting a narcissist forget what *they* really want and need, because they have put the requirements of the narcissist first. They may even come to believe that the narcissist's desires are actually *their own,* and so find themselves striving to achieve things that they don't actually even want, which are not in line with their values.

It may also be quite useful to understand what you really want for other reasons. For example, you might discover that you don't actually *want* the high-powered job in finance that you are waiting to be promoted to by your narcissistic boss — and you could actually just quit after all. Perhaps you only believed you did want that job because you unconsciously took on the values of other people (your parents, or ex perhaps). Or you may discover that you don't actually want to live in the city, and that the ugly dispute over parking with your narcissistic neighbour would just go away if you followed your own heart, and moved to the country.

You'll need a quiet, calm space for half an hour or so, and a pen and paper, to carry out this wonderfully life-affirming exercise.

Close your eyes, and focus for a few moments on your body. Notice the way your body makes contact with the chair or bed you are on. Notice the way your abdomen moves in and out as you breathe for a few moments. Notice any tension in your face — in the muscles of your forehead, in your cheeks, in your jaw and around your eyes, and allow that tension to soften, if you can.

And now imagine that you are 100 years old, and that you have lived the happiest, most fulfilled life imaginable. You are sitting in a rocking chair, perhaps on a verandah, perhaps on a warm summer evening. (Perhaps instead, you are sitting out on a cool evening, next to a fire or under a blanket — whatever works for you). Look around you for a moment. What do you see? Great grandchildren playing in the garden? The sea? Your partner?

What do you hear? The birds singing? The sound of laughter? Silence? What sensations do you feel? The cool glass in your hand, or the hot mug? The fresh breeze on your face? The warm sun?

And now think back, as this wise old person, over the life that you have lived, with a smile. Think back to all the things that happened, for which you are grateful, and what made you happy. You may wish to think in categories, such as:

- Love
- Family
- Health
- Social life
- Finances
- Work
- Home

Once you have done this, you may wish to open your eyes and write a letter, perhaps to your grandchild or to a friend, explaining to them all the things that made you happy in your life — all the things that really mattered to you. Or perhaps you'd find it easier to list the points. However you do this, writing it down will be enormously helpful, as once you have finished, you really will have a clear idea of how *you* wish to live your life, unburdened by the demands or needs of other people or society.

Hopefully, by now you have built up your fuel reserves enough to be able to move on with the next part of your life. And if you are considering escaping your narcissist's orbit, the next chapter is for you.

11

How to escape

You may decide, now that you've worked out the true nature of the toxic person in your life, that the best thing to do is to leave them — to exit their solar system, and never look back. The gold standard is to leave without warning, and cut off all contact with them, permanently.

It sounds so incredibly simple, when I put it like that, but you will know by now, having read Chapter 6, that leaving is never easy, and it's mindbogglingly difficult if you are in a close orbit. It's hard to leave a narcissist because of the very *nature* of their trap — starting with the addiction you may feel to them, because of the trauma bonding. The confusion you may feel as to whether they really are a narcissist, because of the good times that they interspersed with the bad. The fact that they have weakened you, precisely to prevent your escape, through devaluing you and gaslighting you. The 'hoovering' tactics they employ to suck you back into the trap every time you try to leave. And, when you do eventually break free, the rage and the 'smear campaign' that will be waged against you, during which everyone you know, from every facet of your life, will be told lies about you, as the narcissist slips effortlessly into the role of the poor victim,

"There are two major escape strategies to consider—getting them to leave you, or leaving them yourself."

who suffered wordlessly for so long — and all because of you.

But even with all of that, if you *can* leave the narcissist, then do, when you feel you are strong enough. If you can quit the job, or move out, or stop taking their calls and block them — do it, and deal with the backlash. The only way out is *through*.

But if you are married to a narcissist, or have children with them, there are a whole host of escalating abuse behaviours you can expect to be subjected to when you leave, which could even continue for years. I've tackled these issues in detail in *Divorcing a Narcissist — the Lure, the Loss and the Law* — a book which became a bestseller as result of just how common this problem is. Narcissists do not like to be left by anyone, but certainly not by those in their closest orbit, who they feel they have an even greater sense of ownership over. Be warned — they will not let go of you easily, and you are likely to be taken all the way to the very edge of your sanity in leaving them.

If you are looking for ways to get out of your narcissistic relationship, there are two major escape strategies to consider — getting them to leave you, or leaving them yourself.

HOW TO GET A NARCISSIST TO LEAVE YOU

It's important that I put the caveat here that if you are married to (or have children with) the narcissist, even these tactics won't make them behave any better towards you during the divorce. But for those of you in more peripheral orbits, these can be excellent options, if used with caution. Whilst some narcissists will quickly abandon you, others might react with rage instead. And, if this becomes a continuing theme, or you feel unsafe, abandon these strategies. So, with that said, how exactly might you get them to leave you?

THE NARCISSIST TRAP

The Grey Rock Technique

Although this technique does not actually involve throwing rocks at the narcissist, it is still a highly effective way to encourage a narcissist to discard you. The aim of it is to reduce the narcissistic supply that the narcissist can get from you, if you have to see them face-to-face.

What you are trying to do is be as boring to them as a grey rock. You need to be lifeless, inanimate and dull. If you are a 'trekkie' you may remember Mr. Spock, played by the actor Leonard Nimoy, who had a very limited ability to show or feel any emotions, because he was half Vulcan. This is exactly what you need to go for here — you need to channel your inner Mr. Spock.

When you are in the presence of the narcissist, no matter what inflammatory provocation they are throwing at you, you need to give them *nothing* — no reaction at all that could give them supply. Firstly, you have to completely avoid eye contact, actually turning your head to look away. Secondly, no facial expression at all should cross your features — no eye rolling, no raising of the eyebrows, no clenching of the jaw and certainly no open-mouthed incredulity. Even a tiny, benign smile is too much.

If you do have to speak to them, your voice should be low and monotonous, with no variation of tone or speed. Speak unnaturally slowly, and limit the number of words you use to the absolute bare minimum. If you have to say much more than 'yes' or 'no' then you've probably said too much.

I am completely aware of how bizarre this concept sounds, but I can tell you that it really does work, and it works incredibly quickly. Of course, anyone watching will think you have lost the plot, or will criticize you for your rudeness, but even with that it is still worth doing. What is odd is how *unlikely* it will be for the narcissist to call you out on these behaviours.

It's also really important to understand that consistency is key here. You cannot do this for a bit, but then later allow yourself to be drawn

209

back into the drama. Every single time you slip up and give them a reaction, you have essentially gone right back to square one.

A narcissist who is being grey rocked is also likely to ramp up their behaviours for a short time to try to get a rise out of you — but will quickly slink off to find a better source of supply, if you can just ride it out.

I remember being contacted by the chairperson of a sports club, who had realized, after two years of utter toxicity, that the president of the club was a narcissist. He was impossible to deal with, and refused to agree with anything that the other committee members wanted. He would send ranting, nonsensical emails out to them, attacking many of them personally, and the entire committee had been losing sleep as a result of his behaviour. The club had been offered a huge amount of money from a charity for a revamp, as part of an initiative to encourage more local young people into the sport. But the bullying president of the club kept stalling the charity, whilst coming up with bizarre excuses as to why it would not be a good idea to accept the money. In reality, he didn't have the interests of the club at heart at all, of course. He just wanted power, control and the ability to cause drama, as a means to getting his quota of narcissistic supply. The chairperson was desperate, and told me that the narcissist would never go quietly, and that everyone was scared of him.

Upon my advice, a committee meeting was arranged, against the will of the narcissist. The agenda was a final discussion about whether to accept the money from the charity (who were about to offer it elsewhere), and a vote. The narcissist was furious, and sent numerous emails and text messages to the committee members, and tried calling them individually, to get them to agree to vote with him. But the entire committee were grey rocking him. No one picked up or returned his calls, nor responded to any of his inflammatory messages, on my strict instructions.

On the day of the meeting, the chairperson emailed a picture of a grey rock to all the committee members, except the president, to remind them of the plan. They all arrived twenty minutes early and took their seats, leaving one chair (which was slightly smaller than everyone else's) for the president, which notably was not in its usual place at the head of the table.

When he arrived, they managed to hold it together. Not a single person made eye contact with him for the whole meeting and responded only monosyllabically to him, in robotic tones. The vote hadn't even taken place when the narcissist stood up to make an announcement, with no one looking directly at him. He grandiosely proclaimed that he had some incredibly important work coming up in London, meaning that he no longer had any time for the club, and that he was going to have to resign, with immediate effect. His announcement was met with no emotion, and so he got up and left.

The chairperson was staggered. Two years of conflict had been terminated in less than 30 minutes. Such is the power of the grey rock technique.

'Be more narcissist'

I often tell my clients to make this their mantra, whether they are trying to get out of a narcissistic relationship, or trying to cope whilst remaining in one. Write it on your mirror in lipstick. Use it as the password to your computer or phone. Perhaps even have it tattooed onto your palm (if you have a masochistic streak), so that you can frequently remind yourself of it. It can be oddly empowering, let me tell you.

Remember that narcissists want to feed off victims who they can exploit — people who are givers, rescuers, forgivers, endless cheerleaders and those who put their needs behind the needs of others. As explained in Chapter 9, it's very often the case that victims are *not narcissistic enough*, so if you think this applies to you, you may wish to give this a go.

So, to change the power dynamic, how could you increase your sense of entitlement with the narcissist? How could you ignore society's rules, when it comes to them?

When your narcissistic flatmate helps themselves to your food from the fridge, could you start eating *their* food, with the same lack of respect? When they let their dishes pile up in the sink, until you can stand it no more, and you wash them up, could you do the same to them (accepting that you'll be living in a pigsty for a while)? If they repeatedly have friends over until the small hours on week nights, so that you can't sleep, could you find a way of keeping them up when *they* have an important day the next day? Perhaps by playing loud music or having the TV on on full blast? When they ask you how they look, before a night out, could you do what they do to you, and fail to compliment them, or even be critical of their outfit?

"If you are trying to get a narcissist to discard you, a change of tactic to behaving towards them as they behave towards others, might be exactly the thing to try."

Could you deliberately start cancelling meetings with your narcissistic business partner at short notice, or start turning up late, as they do? Could you start ordering your narcissistic sister around, as she does you? Could you feign concern, and tell your narcissistic co-worker that they are looking really pale and tired these days, as they do to you? When your narcissistic boyfriend expects you 'ooh and aah' appreciatively at the dessert he has made for your dinner party, could you push it around on your plate instead, looking unimpressed, even if it's actually quite tasty?

And how about when they play the victim, or want your sympathy? Could you bring yourself to just yawn and check your texts, when they turn on the waterworks? Could you even stretch to gaslighting them back, by telling them that they are 'thinking about it all wrong', and explain that actually they have it easy, because there is poverty, famine and war in the world, so they don't really have the right to complain?

It's initially deeply uncomfortable for decent, conflict avoidant people to act in more narcissistic ways, even towards those who have been abusing and exploiting them — but desperate times call for desperate measures. I'm not saying that you have to behave in ways which are against your moral principles, but I do think it's worth asking yourself this — 'What would the narcissist I'm trying to get rid of do, in this situation?'

So many people who remain stuck in narcissistic relationships tell me, with pride, that at least they are 'taking the moral high ground', 'playing with a straight bat', or 'refusing to sink to the narcissist's level'. Whilst this is admirable, and absolutely the way to be with people who are not toxic, it's misguided when it comes to narcissists — because *different rules* apply to narcissists, due to their abnormal wiring.

"Make 'Be more narcissist' your mantra."

So, if you are trying to get a narcissist to discard you, a change of tactic to behaving towards them as *they* behave towards others, might be exactly the thing to try. As Einstein is believed to have said, "The definition of insanity is doing the same thing over and over and expecting a different result."

Note that, if you are going to employ these tactics, you wouldn't ever explain *why* you are doing them when confronted by the narcissist, as this would give you away. You'd just nonchalantly shrug, and walk away, without giving them a hint of supply. Like the grey rock technique, this can be very quick to work, so take moral comfort from the fact that you won't have to do it for long. If you give it a try, that narcissistic flatmate of yours might pack up and leave within just a few weeks. But please — squash the urge to offer to help them with the packing when they do.

Make them feel jealous of you

Narcissists constantly compare themselves to other people, and need to feel superior to them. Putting people down (or failing to celebrate their successes with them) helps them to feel as though they are better than them, and this is why, over time, many victims of narcissistic relationships learn to hide their light under a bushel. So, it stands to reason that doing the *opposite* will make the narcissist feel comparatively inferior — which they just won't be able to stand.

Again, this tactic can feel underhand and uncomfortable, and it might feel as if it goes against your natural inclination for modesty — but, with the right narcissist, it can be very effective. Note that some narcissists will initially want to associate even *more* with you if they see you as being successful, but inevitably the jealousy and resentment will eventually kick in.

So, if you've got a university degree, and they haven't, start talking about your uni days, and dig out your certificates to hang on the wall (you can always take them down once they've left). Talk grandiosely about your future plans, and big up your talents and achievements. If you are earning more than them, or get a pay rise, make sure they know about it. You need to act as if you are on the up.

If you are stuck for things to brag about, take your cues from the narcissist. What do *they* like to 'flex' about? What do they see as being important? Wealth? Intellect? Appearance? If associating with 'special' people seems important to them, you could tell anecdotes about the funny, clever, important people you know, for example.

It may also help to think about what specific jealousies drive them to badmouth others. You may have to be inventive with your boasting (and you may have to exaggerate wildly, or even make things up).

Be warned that the narcissist is likely, at first, to ramp up their efforts to put you in your place, by devaluing you. But if you can keep it up, especially in conjunction with some of these other tactics, you may well be quickly discarded for being 'too big for your boots'.

Look unimpressed by them

Conversely, when the narcissist brags to you, be sure to look unimpressed or bored. Resist the urge to praise them effusively, as you usually might. When they message you about their latest success, or to boast about their children, either ignore the message completely, or try responding with just a single careless 'thumbs up' emoji. (Emoji's can be a fantastic way to respond to a narcissist's validation-seeking messages — but only if you use really boring ones, and singly. A single heart or thumbs up emoji is like a knife in the heart to a narcissist who is fishing for supply).

When they turn up to an event looking amazing, or have a fantastic new look, or radical haircut, pretend you haven't noticed — and if they press you for a compliment, simply tell them that they look 'absolutely fine'.

When they tell an amusing anecdote, resist the urge to laugh, even if it is hilarious. To double the impact, be sure to laugh raucously at everyone else's jokes, and compliment them wildly in front of the narcissist.

It's hard, it's horrible and you won't like yourself for it, but if you can imply that you think they are 'average' or 'ordinary', or even give the impression that you look down on them, they are likely to spit you out of your orbit faster than the speed of light.

Become needy

Narcissists do not give of themselves, and they have no tolerance for those who need support or empathy (unless they stand to benefit from being *seen* to be a kind, supportive person, in narcissistic supply terms).

There are a variety of strategies to try here, and once again you might have to make something up, or exaggerate a real problem. If you are looking for inspiration, and the narcissist you know has a tendency to play the victim, you can simply look at what strategies they use, and mirror them.

You could be physically needy, emotionally needy or even financially needy. What works best will depend on your particular narcissist.

In terms of emotional neediness, feigning a low mood, anxiety or grief could be a good start. Being 'unable to cope' with problems, or with external circumstances, like world events, can also work well. The point here is that you need to be *asking the narcissist for support*, and to talk through your feelings with them. This will not go down well, particularly if you give the impression that this is likely to be a long-term problem. Narcissists are initially likely to react by telling you to snap out of it, or by trying to outdo you when it comes to your emotional neediness. They may tell you to talk to a professional instead of them. If you can use something that the narcissist themselves has accused you of being or having, so much the better.

A client of mine very effectively got herself ejected from her orbit by telling her narcissistic boyfriend that she suspected that his assertions that she was autistic were correct. She planned her delivery meticulously, and printed out the symptoms in advance to show him. She informed him by text that she had something really important to tell him, and arranged a time for them to meet. She broke the news to him with the air of someone announcing that they had a terminal illness, saying that she believed she had severe autism, and that nothing could be done about it.

Predictably, the narcissist immediately responded with "What does this mean for me?" She explained to him that he would just need to be understanding of the way that she behaved, support her, not judge her and make up for any of her embarrassing social faux pas.

Over the next few weeks, she kept mentioning her 'symptoms' to him, relating them to everyday occurrences. The final straw was when he became ill, with a mild cold, and took to his bed. Instead of mopping his brow as she would have previously done, she told him that the low empathy that she had, as a result of her autism, meant that she couldn't really care about how he was feeling. Just a few days later he left to move in with another woman — and that was the end of that.

Becoming physically needy might also need some Oscar-winning acting skills. Feigning something that can fluctuate but that has the potential to go on for months or years is likely to be your best bet — incapacitating back pain, mystery joint pain or inexplicable tiredness all work well.

Remember — the more you need *them*, the faster they will distance themselves.

Act as though you find them ridiculous or laughable

Yes, it's mean. Yes, it requires acting ability, and yes, you'll hate yourself for doing it, but shaking your head and walking away, looking amused, when the narcissist talks to you can be highly effective. It is a fantastic way to push them down the hierarchical scale they have in their heads, so that they are below you — and if you can do this consistently, they might quickly start to avoid you. This is particularly effective if you are in one of the narcissist's peripheral orbits.

HOW TO LEAVE A NARCISSIST YOURSELF

Preparation

In Chapter 10, I describe methods to build up your fuel reserves, so that you can reach the escape velocity required to leave your orbit.

These will have been depleted, to some extent, during your relationship. But you also need to be aware that the closer you are to the narcissist, the bigger their reaction will be to being left, as result of their need to make up for your lost narcissistic supply. There are several things to mentally prepare for, before you make a break for it.

The smear campaign

If you leave a narcissist, you will inevitably find yourself becoming the victim of a smear campaign. Your narcissistic boss will badmouth you to others in the industry, possibly affecting your chances of getting another job. Your narcissistic co-worker will start rumours about you which might affect the reference you get from your boss when you leave your job. Your narcissistic family member might ensure that other family members start to give you the cold shoulder. Your narcissistic neighbour might convince other people in your community that you are a bad person, so that you are slowly ousted from social events.

Your narcissistic ex will also badmouth you to your children, and may even persuade the children to refuse to see you.

The big problem here is that narcissists are very convincing, and people who have not yet worked out how toxic they are *will believe them*. If you leave a narcissist, you have to be prepared for this, and the fact that they are likely (at least for a time) to be believed over you.

You will be painted as the perpetrator

Playing the victim is the stock response of a narcissist who has been abandoned, which means that *you* must be the 'perpetrator'.

Your narcissistic partner will be particularly venomous if you leave them, and will tell everyone you know that you are an addict, an abuser, mentally ill, a serial adulterer, and whatever else they can think of. They will report you to your professional work body for things you haven't done, and even contact your boss. If you have children with them, they might report you to social services with allegations of child abuse, and make false allegations about you to the police. Be warned that, in this scenario, particularly if you happen to be male, you have quite a high chance of ending up spending a night in a police cell, or finding yourself in court as a result of an application for a restraining order.

If you were working for a narcissistic client, and decided to terminate your contract with them, you may well find yourself on the receiving end of a formal complaint. It is highly unlikely that they will pay your bill without a big fight and, even then, you are unlikely to receive all the money you are owed. If you sacked a narcissist, there is a good chance that they will assert that they were unfairly dismissed and make allegations of bullying or discrimination, which may well end up at a tribunal.

If you pull out of a business with a narcissist, they are likely to assert that you exploited them, and didn't do your fair share of the work (when in reality, the opposite is likely to be true). They will do their best to make you leave with a lot less money than you are owed, and could quite easily involve the courts.

> *"Ironically, you may also be labelled as a narcissist yourself, as the real narcissist projects their narcissism on to you."*

If you decide that you can't continue to see your controlling, manipulative narcissistic sibling or parent, you can be sure that you will be portrayed as the bad guy, and most of your family will rally around them, disgusted by your cruelty.

Ironically, you may also be labelled as a narcissist *yourself*, as the real narcissist projects their narcissism on to you.

Other people won't believe you

When the penny drops, and you realize that the difficult person in your life is a narcissist, the temptation may be to warn as many people as you can. But there really is little point to this, and you are likely to be labelled as 'bitter' or even 'crazy'. Tell only the very closest members of your inner circle, and no one else.

Even your closest friends may disappoint you when you tell them about the true nature of the narcissist, even if they initially seemed to believe you. The fact is this — you will lose friends, at the very least, when you leave a narcissist, and there will be nothing that you will be able to do about it.

If your narcissist is an Exhibitionist Narcissist, who is wealthy and powerful, your mutual friends will likely side with them, not least because of the social cachet they gain from the relationship. Co-workers will side with your narcissistic boss rather than with you, because it will be in their interests to and, if you make a formal complaint about your boss, it is likely to go nowhere (or even backfire on you).

Frankly, trying to maintain mutual friends with a narcissist is going to be a non-starter — just the very fact that they *are* friends with the narcissist means that they do not see them for who they are, and do not believe your version of events. Those people that say "I only judge people on what I see" are essentially invalidating your experiences. You'll probably have to let them go, painful though this might be. Leaving a narcissist will inevitably show you the worst side of people — but it will also show you who your real friends are.

Flying monkeys

These are the people (named after the characters in *The Wizard of Oz*) who the narcissist will enlist to do their bidding for them. They might badmouth you on behalf of the narcissist. They might be recruited to try to hoover you back in ('Your stepdad loves you very much really —

he just finds it difficult to show'). They might be roped in as secret agents, pretending to support you with your divorce, or your complaint about your boss, for example, but actually be reporting back to the narcissist.

These folk are usually members of the narcissist's 'fan club', and want to be special to the narcissist, so that they can feel special by association. However, they might also be narcissists themselves, thriving on the drama and manipulations (especially in family systems, where there are usually many narcissists in a cluster). Beware the Closet Narcissist family member who 'gets on with everyone in the family' — they might not be the ally you think they are. You will need to be on high alert for these flying monkeys when you leave your narcissist.

Hoovering

We've already talked about how a narcissist will try to suck you back into the relationship, through guilt tripping, flattery, making false promises, future faking, playing the victim and making threats, but you really will have to become immune to these tactics, if you are to escape your orbit. Be aware that a narcissist will pull out all the stops to get you back as a fuel source and, if you are in a close orbit, they will even commonly go as far as to threaten to commit suicide unless you stay with them.

Boundary violations

If you leave a narcissist, the ways in which they will trample over your boundaries will ramp up, at least for a time. They might keep instigating unwanted contact with you, by calling or messaging you excessively (the most extreme case I saw was a client receiving 93 texts in one day from the narcissistic boyfriend she was leaving — but receiving around 30 emails or texts per day from a narcissist spurned is fairly standard).

They might appear at your house and insist on speaking to you, or turn up to public places where they know you will be (the school gates, the gym, your lunchtime sandwich place, for example). A client of mine, who was divorcing a narcissist, would have to endure him rollerblading up and down the road, past her house, whenever he knew she would be returning home with the children. Another used to walk his dog in the woods opposite his ex-wife's house, conspicuously parking his car so she knew he was there, even though he lived miles away. Just knowing that he was making her feel uncomfortable was a way to partially make up for the loss of her narcissistic supply.

A narcissist who has been left will frequently record your conversations, or even film you, and will try to goad you into reacting angrily to them whilst you are being recorded. They may stalk you on social media to try to have some indirect contact with you, and may even post recordings of you online, taken when you have lost your temper.

They may try to contact your family members or friends, harassing them, or triangulating them with you, perhaps asking them to pass on messages to you, or to 'talk some sense into you' on their behalf.

Narcissists believe they own you forever

It's crucial to remember that narcissists keep coming back to their former victims, even years down the line, whenever they are low on narcissistic supply from other sources. Once you've extricated yourself, you will have to make a commitment to never allow yourself to be lured back in by a friendly message or apology, no matter how many decades have passed. Your narcissist will not have changed, and you do not want to find yourself back in the trap, believe me.

Choosing an escape plan

So now you know what might be coming your way when you leave a narcissist — but how do you actually leave, and is there anything you can do to limit the fallout, and make it a bit easier? The following four escape plans can be tried sequentially (in whatever order works best for you) or on their own.

Tell them that you are not good enough for them

This sneaky trick is definitely worth a try in the right situation. A client of mine was stuck in a small amateur theatre group. The woman who ran the group (and who seemed to get all the lead roles) was a flaming Exhibitionist Narcissist, who was desperate for fame and fortune. She believed herself to be an incredible actress, when in fact she was merely average. She was a tyrant, and forced everyone into constant rehearsals, late into the night, regardless of whether they had families to get back to. She would criticize their performances, and throw hissy fits when things weren't exactly as she wanted them, but be charming and sweet as anything when they were complying with her demands.

My client was terrified of how she would respond if she left the group, having seen how she reacted when another member left to go fully professional. She had conducted a nasty smear campaign, and had been sure to post all the most unflattering photos of the former member on her social media, where she had been caught at the wrong angles. She had accused her of 'using her', and of learning all the tricks of the trade from her, only to 'spit her out'. She told her she was untalented, ugly and fat, and that no one would ever want to watch her act, and that she was making a fool of herself.

We decided to capitalize on her narcissist's need to feel superior, and hatched a plan. My client arranged to take her out to lunch, at a place of the narcissist's choosing. Of course, it turned out to be eye-wateringly expensive, but she went along with it, because she knew that it would demonstrate to the narcissist that she believed her to be special.

Pulling out all her acting ability, my client tearfully told the narcissist, whilst she was eating her lobster, that she couldn't stay in the group, because she felt so inferior. She told her that, every time she watched the narcissist on the stage, she was struck by the realization that she would never be as good a performer as her, and that she was wasting her time, as she simply didn't have the incredible talent that the narcissist had. The narcissist immediately agreed that she could never be as good as her, but said that nobody expected her to be, as that would be impossible. Slurping her champagne, she told her that she should stay in the group, regardless.

My client, expecting this, hammed up her act even more. She told her that it was obvious to everyone that her staying in the group was actually pulling the group down, and therefore also pulling the narcissist's reputation down, by association. Wringing her hands, she said that she just couldn't, in good conscience, be the person who held the narcissist back from achieving the fame she so clearly deserved, and that it wouldn't be right. She told her that, if she stayed, she knew she would be responsible for preventing the narcissist from becoming a worldwide, household name.

She sadly explained how sorry she was that she had not come up to scratch, and how she knew that she wasn't worthy of being in the group. The narcissist graciously accepted this, and said that she could understand why my client felt that way. The narcissist was happy to tell everyone, for years, why my client left the group and, save for the odd like on my client's Instagram posts over the next few years, she didn't try to make contact. (In case you are wondering what became of the narcissist, she never did make it as an actress, but went on to OnlyFans, in her sixties, to get her narcissistic supply instead).

If you are leaving a narcissist, no matter what your relationship is to them, this tactic, modified as necessary, can work like a charm.

The gradual exit

If you are in an outer orbit, perhaps where the narcissist is your friend, or a sibling you don't see all that much, you can try to do a phased exit, gently fading away, and reducing contact gradually. Of course, it's much harder to do this in a relationship where you are living with the narcissist, and if you are their partner it will be virtually impossible, unless you don't live with them all the time.

Essentially, what you are doing here is gradually phasing in the 'grey rock technique', described on page 209.

So, in an office environment, for example, you could start by reducing the eye contact you make with your narcissistic co-worker. You could slowly speak to them less and less, stop greeting them in the morning, and start wearing headphones as you work, so they can't talk to you. You could stop going to the staff canteen for lunch, so that you don't have to be in a group with them. You could slowly turn into Mr. Spock, limiting your facial expressions and slowly introducing monosyllabic, boring, monotonous speech.

Ideally, you want to see the narcissist less and less in person, and stop taking their phone calls, so that they are forced to communicate with you via messaging and email. Once you've got to this stage, you can delay responding to their messages, and then gradually increase the time you take to respond. You can simultaneously reduce the number of words you use in your messages over time, eventually just answering with a single emoji and no words, before you completely go off the radar.

Phasing in the grey rock technique like this can be very effective in the right situation, and gives the narcissist plenty of time to find another person to be their source of narcissistic supply instead of you (so that they don't experience a sharp drop in narcissistic supply). This could very well limit the problems described earlier.

The 'three strikes' approach

This could be a method to choose if you are not living with the narcissist, have already limited your face-to-face interactions with them, and have mostly reduced your communications with them to indirect methods such as messages and email, perhaps by employing the gradual exit strategies above.

Essentially, this is a way to cut dead all contact, but in a way that *lays the blame on the narcissist*. Note that the narcissist is never going to accept the blame for it, but *you* will feel better about it (and other people might just be a little more understanding of your situation).

So, imagine the scenario where a narcissist is trying to control you, telling you what they think you should be doing, thinking and feeling about a situation.

Let's imagine that Lynda, your stepmother who you have never liked, has just died, widowing her elderly third husband, Al. Your father (her second husband) died years ago, but you stayed in touch with your stepsisters (who you are not genetically related to) out of family duty, and because you have no other siblings.

Lucy, one of your stepsisters, is a Communal Narcissist and, being older than you, has always felt she has the right to order you around. You have had quite enough of Lucy, but have been unable to cut contact with her.

You are dreading the funeral, and would rather not go, but you feel obliged to. In characteristic narcissistic fashion, Lucy has taken charge of the funeral (even though she also had a very poor relationship with her mother Lynda, and rarely saw her more than once a year). She has set up a group chat with you, her other sister and Al. Lucy is fussing about the order of service, the eulogy and the funeral music, and is posting at least 30 messages a day on the group chat.

She begins by telling you to sort out the music, and to run it past her — but every time you make a suggestion, she shoots it down, and tells you to try again. She enlists Al, who has a bit of dementia, to write the eulogy, and when this doesn't come up to scratch, she tells you to improve it, which you do.

She then scribbles corrections on it, adds lots of material about herself, and tells you to redo it. This continues for ten days, with changes constantly being requested by Lucy, which you comply with, even though it is absolutely terrible. Lucy then falls out with the funeral director, and another has to be found. Again, this falls to you.

Lucy wants you, and your dyslexic, autistic, nine-year-old son to each do a reading at the funeral. You hate public speaking, and so you decline, and you also decline on behalf of your son. Lucy is furious, and will not let it go, enlisting Al and your other stepsister to try to convince you to speak. Messaging you privately, she tells you that she doesn't believe that your son really has dyslexia, and that she should know, as she used to be a teaching assistant. She seems completely unable to take on board the fact that your son will be at school that day, and will not even be going to the funeral.

Lucy then decides that you should ride to the funeral in the limousine behind the hearse, with her, Al, her sister, and her sister's husband, Jon. But Jon is the type of man who cannot keep his hands to himself, and has tried to grope you on several occasions through the years. He also once pinned you to a wall (when you were in your early twenties) and tried to kiss you, whilst drunk, in front of Lucy. You decline, saying that you will drive your own car in the funeral procession instead.

Once again, Lucy will not let it go, and privately messages you to tell you that she doesn't want to hear any excuses about your refusal to ride in the limo related to Jon. She tells you that you are being petty and unforgiving, and that you *will* be going in the limousine.

Lucy is a tall woman, with a strong build. She is a lesbian, a feminist and a gay rights activist. She believes that women should be able to do all the things that men can do, and pooh-poohs all traditional ideas that are gendered in any way. She insists, to the new funeral directors, that Lynda's coffin should have all-female pallbearers, even though Lynda was clinically obese and the coffin is made of extremely heavy, solid oak.

Lucy tells you, on the group chat, that you, her, your other stepsister and a few cousins (who she will spring this on, on the day) will be carrying the coffin into the crematorium. You are 45 years old, have a bad back, are only 5 ft tall, and are of very slight build, so you decline, explaining why.

Lucy is furious, and accuses you of being deliberately difficult. She gaslights you that pallbearers 'don't have to be similar heights', that the 'coffin won't weigh too much', and that 'your back will be fine'.

She once again brings up the reading that she wants you to do, the limousine and the funeral music which she wants you to change yet again. And as a final pièce de résistance, she tells you that *your father*, Lynda's second husband, who died when you were just 21, would have *wanted you* to do these things, and would be turning in his grave at your awful behaviour. Again, she does this on a private message to you, so that the others on the group chat don't see it.

So how could you have leveraged this awful behaviour, to get out of this relationship? When Lucy privately messaged you, to insist that you and your son should each do a reading, and that your son isn't really dyslexic, you could have replied with "I will not be doing a reading. Please stop ordering me around and telling me what to do. You have three strikes."

Here you have laid a trap, because a narcissist will rarely respect your boundaries, and will always deliberately try to do the opposite of what you suggest. So Lucy would then have invariably continued with her next message about not riding in the limousine, in which she called you petty and unforgiving.

At that point you could have said "I will not be riding in the limousine. Two strikes." Here you are goading the narcissist into further pushing your boundaries, which they inevitably will do. Narcissists are arrogant. They do not believe that you will stick to your guns, especially if you have been a poor boundary setter in the past.

So Lucy will have immediately continued her campaign, telling you to carry the coffin, and using the emotional blackmail of your father's memory. At that point, you could simply respond with "That was the third strike."

Taking screenshots of the private messages, and posting them on the group chat might be your next move, following it up with a brief, non-blaming message explaining that you won't be attending the funeral.

Here you have outed the narcissist, and imposed the consequence — you not attending the funeral (which you didn't want to go to anyway). The final move would be to limit any possibility for further communication by exiting the group chat and blocking Lucy, and anyone else that you didn't want to speak to about it again.

It may sound easy, but you can only really do this when you are very close to reaching the end of your tether, and you have already perfected the art of not allowing yourself to be re-drawn into any arguments.

Going cold turkey

The final way to leave a narcissist is to just do it, in one hit, unexpectedly. The narcissist will react with rage, and is highly likely to engage in all the bad behaviours described at the beginning of this section (such as the smear campaign) which you will have to be prepared for.

If you are going to do this, you will have to get your ducks lined up. You will have to be able to construct a situation where the narcissist cannot physically see you. You will have to be prepared to block them on all forms of communication, including on social media.

And, if you are in a close orbit, you will have to be prepared for the fact that the addiction you feel to the narcissist, as a result of your trauma bonding, will feel like you have ripped off a limb. You will want to go back to them at times and, ironically, you may find yourself wanting *them* to comfort *you* for the pain you are experiencing. The only way to go cold turkey is to *consistently* maintain no contact with them. The addiction will eventually subside, but it can take months (and sometimes, even years) for those who have escaped close orbits.

12

How to manage a narcissist when you can't leave

In the previous chapter, we looked at different ways to leave a narcissist's orbit — but what if you *can't* leave? What about if you share children with the narcissist, and have to co-parent with them? If you run a business with them, and are trapped (for now)? If you are their adult child, and they are old and alone? If there are various cultural, religious or financial reasons why you feel you can't leave? If they are your boss, and you can't find another job because they are threatening to badmouth you to everyone in your industry? Because they are your client, and you can't find a way to get rid of them? Because your children get on so well with their children, or are their cousins? Because you want to have a relationship with your non-narcissistic parent, but your narcissistic parent is always going to be present? Because they are your neighbour and you can't afford to sell your house and move away?

Your secret weapon

The crucial thing to emphasize here, once again, is narcissist's overriding need for narcissistic supply. This is what ultimately drives all of their behaviours, towards you and everyone else. Keeping this at the forefront of your mind, when dealing with them, is where your power lies. To them, you are simply a source of narcissistic supply. They tease it out of you by getting your attention, preferably through your admiration and adoration. When that doesn't work, they'll create drama and conflict to get your attention, often by roping someone else into the dynamic too. And in lieu of that, they will create situations to make you fearful — the ultimate way to get your attention and feel omnipotent (all powerful).

"Once they trigger you into reacting, things can degenerate very quickly into a slanging match, a row, or a tear-filled encounter — which, of course, is exactly what they want."

But here you have a choice. Now that you are aware of their modus operandi, *you don't have to respond.* When they push your buttons, to trigger your narcissistic supply providing response, you don't actually have to give it.

I'm always struck by the ironies to be found in narcissism. The first irony is the fact that narcissists need to believe that they are special and unique, when in fact, they are pretty much *exactly* the same as all the other narcissists, due to their brain wiring, as you will now understand.

But another irony is that the narcissist needs to be in control, and to feel like they have power over you, and everyone else. But in fact, they *need you*, like addicts need their drug of choice. Who holds the power in that situation? The addict, or the drug dealer? Well, in this situation, *you are the drug dealer — and the drug is narcissistic supply.*

Withholding narcissistic supply

So now you know the key to managing the narcissist in your life. But, like many things, although it sounds simple, it's actually not easy, and certainly not at first. This is going to take practice. It's going to take repeated attempts to get it right. It's going to feel unnatural and contrived. It's even going to feel as if you are being *mean* at times — never a comfortable feeling. And, worse, you are going to have to keep it up *for as long as you know the narcissist.*

I'm sorry to say that this is not something that you can do a few times until you see a positive result, and then stop doing — because it doesn't fundamentally change the narcissist themselves, and they don't actually *learn* anything from it themselves. To them, you will *always* be fair game as a source of narcissistic supply, and their sense of ownership over you means that, given even the slightest opportunity, they will make another attempt to get it from you.

So, how does withholding narcissistic supply actually help you to cope with a narcissist, if it doesn't actually change the narcissist? Well, as you know, the narcissist stores their narcissistic supply in an ever-draining bucket with a hole in it, and they can't let the level of supply drop if they are to keep their protective false persona strong.

So when you stop pouring into the bucket, the narcissist has little choice, in the short term, but to get their supply from *somewhere else* — because maintaining the levels in the bucket is their absolute priority. So, when their initial attempts to goad you into re-starting your supply fail, they give up on you (for a bit) and go off and find someone else to harass/irritate/love bomb/rage at etc.

The problem you have is that, if you have to keep seeing the narcissist, and can't permanently drive off into the distance, leaving them as a speck in your rear-view mirror, you will have to be vigilant *every single time* you see them or communicate with them, so that you are not tricked into recommencing your supply. Because, as you will know, if you have been dealing with a narcissist — once they trigger you into reacting, things can degenerate very quickly into a slanging match, a row, or a tear-filled encounter — which, of course, is exactly what they want.

There are three basic components to managing and coping with a narcissist. You'll need armour, a way to disarm the narcissist, and strategies to manage your fear. It's time to take back your power.

1. Your armour

As you know, the narcissist's false persona is an armour with they hide behind, which keeps them from feeling their own feelings of low self-esteem. But to cope with having a narcissist in your life, you will have to develop your *own armour*. This is your crucial first step, and there are three essential parts to this armour, which we will delve into shortly. They are:

* Knowledge
* Boundaries
* Vigilance

2. Disarming the narcissist

By now you will also be aware of the tactics and weapons that narcissists use against their victims to exploit and use them as sources of narcissistic supply. So you can see why the second essential component of managing a narcissist is *disarming* them. You will need to break into their armoury under the cover of darkness, and render their weapons useless.

3. Managing your fear

Learning how to counteract the physiological fear that your narcissist triggers in you will eventually reduce your reactivity to their behaviours — again, essential if you have to manage them on a long-term basis.

STEP ONE: HOW TO BUILD YOUR ARMOUR

Knowledge

The first essential component needed for your armour is knowledge, specifically about what NPD is, what behaviours you will be subjected to by a narcissist, and why. The good news is that you have already learned most of this from this book so far, although you will probably have to revisit sections until you have completely assimilated it.

Knowledge is a fundamental component of your armour because when a narcissist behaves in a certain way, you need to be able to look at those behaviours from a new perspective. Being able to stand back from the situation and *label* the behaviour you have just witnessed gives your armour immense strength.

So, for example, when a narcissist accuses you of being or doing something, instead of rushing to defend yourself, knowledge will arm you with the ability to stop, and think about what is *really* happening. They may, for example, be 'projecting' (accusing you of being or doing what they *themselves* are being or doing). Or perhaps it falls into another category such as 'gaslighting'.

When a narcissist tries to rope you in by gaining your sympathy, similarly, you could label it as 'playing the victim'. When they try to engage you, by bitching about someone they know you don't like, this might be 'triangulation'.

When you can stop and label the behaviour (in your head), you rob it of its power to hurt you. You realize that it actually has *nothing to do with you*, and that it is simply a tool to get a reaction from you. You realize that this isn't actually personal, and that it is merely the incurable behaviour of a very limited individual.

A summary table of all the behaviours you need to be able to recognize and label, in real time, is given at the end of Chapter 9, on pages 190-191.

The aim is to get to the point where, instead of scratching your head in confusion and ruminating on why the narcissist did or said something, you can simply say "Because they are a narcissist — and that is what narcissists do". When you reach this point, you'll be saving yourself a lot of wasted mental energy — it'll be a blessed relief, trust me.

Boundaries

Many people who find themselves in narcissistic relationships of any sort are either not very good at exerting boundaries, or have inadvertently allowed the narcissist to shamelessly trample all over their boundaries, rendering them useless. This is not to blame the victim — it is the narcissist who is the flagrant boundary violator, after all. But, that said, you can see why learning how to set specific boundaries with the narcissists in your life is such an important component of your armour.

To recap, a boundary is where you end, and another person begins. Setting and sticking to solid boundaries will enable you to protect and take care of yourself. A boundary defines what you will and won't take responsibility for or accept. Boundaries can be physical, professional, personal, emotional, to do with time, or a combination of these. It's sometimes the case that people who have fallen prey to narcissistic abuse are good at exerting certain types of boundaries, but not others. Examples of boundaries include:

- Not hugging your boss
- Not being social media 'friends' with your co-workers
- Not giving your clients your personal mobile number
- Not answering work emails after hours
- Not giving your partner your passwords
- Spending a few evenings a week without your partner
- Wanting the children to knock before entering your bedroom

- Not staying up past 11 pm on work nights
- Not sacrificing your goals or plans to please other people
- Not allowing your partner's mood to affect your own/not feeling responsible for their moods
- Not taking social calls at work
- Not waiting past 8 pm to eat dinner

Let's look at some of the other specific boundaries you may need to exert to keep your narcissist in check, and how the key to dealing with these issues is to *have a plan*.

Time

Narcissists are often late, and will keep you waiting. But instead of just waiting for them, decide *now* on the length of time you will give them before you stop waiting for them. For example, if you are supposed to be meeting your narcissistic sibling in a cafe, you could wait 15 minutes, and if they haven't arrived, leave, and message them, saying something along the lines of 'I waited 15 minutes, but you didn't arrive, so I have gone off to do other things'.

Yes, they will have a fit of rage, bombard you with ranting messages, insist that you return immediately, or play the victim — but you can respond by asking them to be on time from now on. It might take a few goes, but (hopefully) they will eventually learn. And if they don't, you can at least feel good about the fact that you are not just letting them trample all over you anymore.

Your narcissistic boss may regularly expect you to work late, or to respond to their emails or calls outside of work hours. Again, set a boundary, and don't let them cross it. Assert yourself quietly, first by *telling* them what you are prepared to accept, and then by *showing* them — and be prepared to be consistent. If you give in once, you will have gone right back to square one.

If your narcissistic partner likes to wake you up at 4 am if they can't sleep, so that they can chat to you (a surprisingly common issue), and they have continued this, even though you have asked them not to, you might need to make your point in another way, perhaps by sleeping with an eye mask on and earplugs in, or by getting straight up and moving to the spare room, if you have one, and locking the door.

Having a plan, and immediately executing it when a boundary is crossed, is key to teaching the narcissist that you mean business. You might have to get quite creative here.

Physical boundaries

If the narcissist you know likes to turn up to your house (or to events) uninvited, think about what you can do to *prevent* that from happening — or plan exactly what you will do, when it *next* happens. For example, installing a video doorbell, or a peep hole viewer, might be worth the investment, if it means that you are able to not open the door to the narcissist who has 'popped round'. How will you stop the narcissist from turning up to your child's birthday party, for example? Again, a bit of creative thinking, and perhaps some brainstorming with someone supportive, might help with problems like this.

How will you stop your narcissistic flatmate borrowing your clothes, even though you have asked them not to? Would having a lock fitted on your door be enough, or should you impose a consequence on them, if they keep doing it, such as taking the dry cleaning costs off your share of the other house bills? If a narcissist continues to violate your boundaries, even when you have clearly expressed them, thinking up consequences to really make your point can be quite effective.

Learn to stick to your guns

When the narcissist asks you to do something, or to give them something that you don't want to, once you've declined, *do not let them change your mind*, under any circumstances. And remember this — *you don't owe them any explanation at all for saying 'no', and you can be completely unapologetic about it.* This is going to be hard for those of you who are new to it, but it gets much easier with practice.

Even if you become really good at setting and maintaining boundaries, narcissists are likely to keep trying to overstep them every now and then, so this will be an ongoing battle — but an essential one, which will also be useful in other areas of your life.

"Don't be fooled by the occasional reasonable-sounding message or compliment. It simply means that 'Nasty Narcissist' is just around the corner."

Vigilance

Maintaining a high index of suspicion towards your narcissist is another essential part of your protective armour. You already know that the narcissistic abuse cycle has two essential components — Nice Narcissist and Nasty Narcissist, and that it is inevitable that at some point the narcissist will appear to be kind, rational and caring, so that they can rope you in, ready for the next bout of devaluation. So don't be fooled by the occasional reasonable-sounding message or compliment. It simply means that Nasty Narcissist is just around the corner. Do not let them lull you into a false sense of security, ever again.

Gaslighting is also one the narcissist's biggest weapons, and your armour will need to protect you from it. You will have to learn to question *every single thing* a narcissist says to you, because it could easily be a straightforward lie, a rewritten piece of history, a misinterpretation of the truth, or a blatant denial of your reality. When your narcissistic work partner says that they have reviewed a contract and it's fine, don't believe them. When your narcissistic friend divides up the restaurant bill, have a good look at it. When your narcissistic mother tells you that she has had a suspected stoke, check with her doctor. When your narcissistic partner tells you that your joint finances are fine, delve into them more deeply. When your resentful narcissistic sibling says anything at all to you, make your default position is one of disbelief. Of course, sometimes the narcissist *will* be telling the truth — but definitely not always.

STEP TWO: HOW TO DISARM YOUR NARCISSIST

Just as essential as putting on your armour, is taking away the narcissist's power, by rendering their weapons useless. The major ways to do this are by:

- Limiting your contact with them
- Withholding personal information
- Stepping out of the drama triangle
- Dialling down your empathy for them
- Thinking of the narcissist as a toddler
- Appearing fearless

Limit your contact with them

There's no getting away from this one. To give yourself the best chance of managing the narcissists in your life, so that you are not driven completely insane, you are going to have to seriously limit the amount of contact you have with them, to the best of your ability. It stands to reason that the less contact you have with them, the fewer opportunities they will have to bleed you for your narcissistic supply.

Of course, this can be incredibly difficult, and there are many considerations to take into account.

If the narcissist is your parent or sibling or other family member, you are likely to feel immense guilt. You may worry about how other people will view you and judge you, if you do limit your contact. People who have no understanding of the situation are likely to tell you that you should try harder, or learn to forgive, inadvertently gaslighting you on behalf of the narcissist ('But he's your *dad* — you *have* to see him at Christmas'). Of course, the narcissist is likely to try to draw you back, perhaps via these third parties, by playing the victim, by tearfully asking what they have done to deserve this distancing, or by a full on hoover. With all of that said, I can tell you, without doubt, that even with the guilt, this is absolutely worth doing. The less you are in contact with them, the less they can abuse you, exploit you or upset you — and this will enormously improve your life.

It may be harder to do if you work with the narcissist, and again, you may have to get creative. Can you change your work arrangements so that you work remotely on the days that they are in the office? Can you switch into a different role within work, that doesn't require as much contact? Stop eating your lunch in the work cafeteria, and have a sandwich and a walk in the lunch break instead, so that you don't have sit in the same group with them? Can you wear headphones at work, so they can't try to talk to you? Change your shift pattern?

It's not just face-to-face contact that is is going to have to be limited, but all types of contact. Narcissists often like to bombard people with communications in numerous ways, often favouring text or WhatsApp type of platforms, because they can tempt them into giving instant responses. Think about how you deal with this — perhaps muting their notifications, archiving their chats, or blocking them, so that they are forced to use less immediate types of communication (such as email).

If seeing you 'in person' is the best way for them to procure narcissistic supply from you, then video calling of any description is the next best thing for them, followed by speaking to you on the phone. All of these are going to have to be limited wherever possible.

So, next time you get a FaceTime call from them, notice that sinking feeling, and respect it — and *just don't pick up*. And when it comes to phone calls, your aim should be to hardly ever speak to the narcissist on the phone, and when you do, only at a time of *your* choosing. You'll have to severely limit how often you take calls about things which are not emergencies (if you are to avoid conversations which, at best, irritate you for hours or days and, at worst, degenerate into chaos).

It's also important to realize that *indirect* contact on social media also counts as contact. Narcissists are adept at posting things on social media which, on the surface may seem innocent, but that are actually digs, invalidations or irritating assertions of the perfect life or of superiority, which they have aimed directly at you.

Even just the opportunity for them to see what you are up to (or where you are) via *your own* social posts can give them a little hit of narcissistic supply, and can provide them with things to use against you or to gossip about. Narcissists also love to publicly 'like' or comment on your posts (even if they are stonewalling you in real life), which can be very disconcerting.

So, again, you might wish to block them or mute their notifications or feeds. Perhaps you can prevent them from seeing your posts without actually blocking or unfriending them, so that they cannot like or comment on them. If things are really bad, it may even be worth coming off certain platforms altogether. Think about blocking them from the less obvious platforms too — Pinterest and your YouTube channel, for example.

Withhold information, opinions and vulnerabilities

A big part of disarming the narcissist is seriously limiting what they know about you and your life, so that they cannot use these facts to lure you into a difficult conversation, or to badmouth you behind your back. Letting a narcissist know your vulnerabilities is also asking for trouble, as they will be assimilated by the narcissist, and fired straight back at you, with laser precision, when they need some narcissistic supply.

So, when it comes to the narcissist in your life, tell them *as close to nothing* as you can, regardless of who they are. Don't share your plans, news or successes — and hold all worries, failures and any type of sad news equally as close to your chest. Even if the narcissist in your life is your parent or sibling, stay tight-lipped, no matter how serious or important the things happening in your life might be. The narcissist will inevitably disappoint and hurt you with their response — and the sooner you learn to protect yourself from this, the better.

When in the company of your narcissist, be sure to keep all opinions about everything completely to yourself, even if they try to goad you into responding. I recall a story of an elderly male narcissist, who was desperate for supply. When his son and daughter-in-law visited him for dinner, he decided to claim that 'all women who stay out until 2 am want to be raped.'

Completely unaware of the dynamics at play, they both fell for it, and outraged, came down on him like a ton of bricks. The ensuing argument degenerated into swearing and shouting, until the 'hurt' narcissist went off to bed. The couple couldn't drive home because they had drunk too much wine, and were flummoxed when, the next morning, the narcissist behaved as if nothing was wrong, and cooked them a nice breakfast. Take note. The narcissist will do or say anything to get a rise out of you, and your actual opinions and morals are irrelevant to them.

Leave the drama triangle

Remember the three roles in the drama triangle — the victim, persecutor and rescuer? And how narcissists effortlessly assign you roles which they keep switching, as if you are just a pawn being moved around in a game of chess? Well, just being *aware* that you have been pulled into a drama triangle can be enough to enable you to step out of it — infuriating your narcissist, who will realize that they have lost their power.

If you think back to the previous example, the elderly narcissist was clearly the persecutor. His son and daughter-in-law waded in as rescuers of the women he had made claims about, but in so doing, swearing and shouting at him, *they* became the persecutors, and the narcissist, the victim. A highly successful evening all round, narcissistic supply-wise.

Had they noticed the dynamic, they could have simply removed themselves from it, by leaving the dinner table. They could have disarmed the narcissist by *agreeing* with his outrageous assertions, or by deftly changing the subject.

Frankly, in sitting down to dinner with a narcissist (with wine, which reduced their inhibitions), and no idea that they were even *in* a drama triangle, they had set themselves up for a diabolical evening.

Dial down your empathy for them

It's lovely that you are a kind, caring, compassionate person — these qualities are admirable. But your empathy, and possibly your tendency to rush in and save or rescue people, is actually your Achilles heel when it comes to narcissists, and leaves you wide open to being drawn back into the relationship, with all its ups and downs and subtle exploitations. Put plainly, *your* empathy is one of *their* biggest weapons, and it will have to be removed from their armoury.

I'm not telling you to be less empathic with *all* other people, but simply to be so *with the narcissist*. This is incredibly difficult — you'll probably feel like an awful person, and the guilt you may feel at not rushing in to help can sabotage your efforts to be less empathic. You may even feel *cruel* at times.

The key to dialling down your empathic response is *noticing how you feel* when the narcissist plays the victim. Notice how you respond, and what you want to offer to do for the narcissist. Take a giant step back, and ask yourself:

- Could they be playing the victim?
- Am I worried that this time they may not actually be 'crying wolf'?
- What drives me to want to help? A sense of obligation? Moral duty?
- How do I feel about not stepping in? Guilt, shame or fear?

Once you've slowed the chain of events down, by asking these questions, you can make a rational choice. And it is highly likely that, if you refuse to help or be drawn in, your suspicions will be confirmed (when they seek attention from someone else instead of you), that this was another pity play, after all. This does get much easier, the more you do it.

I remember a recent case of an elderly female narcissist, with a chronic lung condition, refusing to get her Covid jab. Her refusal was not because she didn't believe in vaccines, but because (she claimed) she was worried that she would catch the virus from someone in the immunization clinic waiting room. If she caught it, the chances really were that she would be seriously ill, and might even die. Her empathic family wanted to rush in to try to talk some sense into her, but I dissuaded them, suspecting that this

*"Your empathy is one of **their** biggest weapons."*

just another ploy for attention and narcissistic supply. I advised them to nonchalantly say, "You must do whatever you are comfortable with — we will support you all the way," and then just change the subject.

After just a couple days of this she went mysteriously quiet about it, and surreptitiously had the jab a few weeks later. She had clearly (subconsciously) realized that this ploy wasn't working, and she'd have to dream up another way to get her narcissistic supply.

Think of the narcissist as a toddler

There is a good reason why your narcissist's rages resemble a toddler throwing their toys out of their pram — and that is because, emotionally, they are basically stuck in the toddler phase of development. They haven't developed empathy, for starters, and nor are they able to see mummy (or anyone else) as being a blend of good and bad traits (instead seeing people as being either 'all good' or 'all bad', as previously described).

So, whenever they are triggering you, trying to wind you up, scaring you, raging, or trying to get a rise out of you, try to remember this fact. One of the things that I often advise people who are receiving scary, ranting, threatening messages from the narcissist to do, is to copy and paste the narcissist's rantings into a five-year-old's handwriting font. When they re-read it, it suddenly makes a lot more sense. I illustrate this further in Chapter 13, which deals with communicating with a narcissist.

Agree with what you can

This technique is a great way to disarm a narcissist. When a narcissist tries to bait you, by throwing a stone at you, what they want you to do is pick up the stone, and angrily hurl it back at them. They can then do the same, and the stones get bigger and bigger as the insults grow. This volley of back-and-forth stone-throwing is all very satisfying for the narcissist. *But you don't have to pick up the stone, let alone throw it back.*

So, the next time a narcissist tries to do this, if possible, find whatever you can in their statement that you can agree with, and completely the ignore the rest of it.

So, if your narcissistic mother-in-law tries to goad you into justifying yourself, by complaining that your house is too small and that your children need a bigger garden to play in, you could simply say "Yes — big gardens are nice to play in" and then not respond to the rest of the statement. This rather odd strategy would sound bizarre in a conversation with a non-narcissist, but it is unlikely to be recognized as being strange by a narcissist. Instead, they are likely to feel that they have won to some degree, which can have the effect of calming them.

Keep in your mind the image of the stone they have hurled simply dropping to the ground, as you walk away, without picking it up. That stone is now no longer in their armoury. Job done.

Appear fearless

Inducing fear in others is one of the narcissist's go-to tools when they are low on narcissistic supply and, if you have known them for a long time, they will have worked out exactly which of your buttons to press to scare you.

Your narcissist will be highly attuned to how you show your fear, and even small changes in your posture, in the way you swallow and in your breathing rate can give you away, as can micro facial expressions, changes in the size of your pupils and the shakiness of your voice. They may not consciously be ticking these fear responses off as you display them, but they will be registering them on some level.

'Faking it 'til you make it' and doing everything you can to prevent your narcissist from picking up on your fear is a key way to disarm them. Make an active commitment to trying not to show your fear, no matter how terrified you are.

Of course, the best way is to quickly leave the room, or preferably the building. If they can't see or hear you, they can only *imagine* your fear (which although better than nothing, is not the optimal supply they would have been hoping for). Do not delay — the faster you leave, the less fear you will have shown. Once you have left, make sure your phone is turned off for as many hours as possible, so that they cannot perpetuate the drama by contacting you. This is a short-term strategy to simply *hide* your fear — in the next section I explain how to work on your fear response to the narcissist, so that you can terminate it, and eventually even stop it from happening altogether.

STEP THREE: HOW TO DEAL WITH FEAR

Narcissists are adept at finding your Achilles heel and using it to trigger you. Exactly *how* a person experiences this, and how severely they are affected will vary between individuals, but the closeness of their orbit to the narcissist will definitely have a part to play. So, you might feel blind panic, fear and dread, or just tearfulness. Your inner critic, a berating voice in your own head, may kick in, and you will probably find yourself unable to think clearly. Perhaps physical symptoms will be more prominent for you (such as nausea, a racing heart, fast breathing, sweaty palms, chest pain, or even difficulty swallowing). But however you feel when triggered by a narcissist's behaviour, you are likely to be in one of the following four 'self-protection' modes, known as the 'four F's'. They are:

- Flight — wanting to, or actually running away from the problem
- Fight — feeling angry and verbally (or even physically) fighting back
- Freeze — clamming up and saying or doing nothing, paralysed by fear or indecisiveness
- Fawn — trying to appease the narcissist, by agreeing to their demands or being extra nice to them

If these resonate with you, you may have chastized yourself in the past for overreacting to the narcissist, and even felt as though you are 'going mad'. Well, I'm here to tell you that you are not. This is a completely normal, physiological response - a stress response. Allow me to explain.

The unconscious brain perceives the narcissist's actions as an actual threat to your life, and the area in the brain called the 'amygdala' (which is involved with fear) is instantly triggered. It responds by sending signals to the adrenal glands (glands which sit on top of the kidneys), which respond by producing the stress hormones cortisol and adrenaline. These stress hormones cause changes in your circulation, among other things. Your blood pressure rises, your heart beats faster and blood gets diverted away from your brain to your muscles, so that you can fight, or run away. These hormones also cause the other symptoms of anxiety I've mentioned, and all of these are signs that you have gone into one of the four F self-protection responses. This all happens reflexively, and within moments, because this is one the body's inbuilt survival mechanisms.

And, given that blood is being diverted away from your brain, it's no wonder that you lose the ability to think clearly during one of these attacks, making things even worse.

So, what can you do, if this is happening to you, at the hands of your narcissist? How can you terminate this unhelpful stress response?

Terminating your stress response

Awareness

Well firstly, just being *aware* of which of the four F responses you tend to react with can be useful. Think back to the last time the narcissist triggered you — can you remember how you felt, and how you responded? This is likely to be your body's default F response, and is likely to happen the next time the narcissist tries to trigger you too.

So next time, try to bring your rational brain back online *in the moment*, by actively telling yourself which response you are in, and then ticking off what you notice happening physically (eg. I feel like running away, I want to appease the narcissist, my heart is beating fast, my palms are sweating, I am finding it difficult to think clearly). Just doing this can help re-divert blood to your brain and reduce these feelings.

Engage your 'parasympathetic nervous system'

Your body has two systems which work in opposition to each other. When you are triggered by a narcissist into one of the four F responses, it is your *sympathetic* nervous system that has been activated. But very handily, you can deliberately engage your *parasympathetic* system to do the opposite, and calm you down.

There are various ways of doing this, but one of the easiest is the 'physiological sigh' (Spiegel and Huberman, 2023). Firstly, you take a deep inhalation. You then follow that up with another short sharp inhalation, and then you exhale in a deep slow sigh, through your mouth. Repeat this over 5 minutes to get the maximal effect.

Even better, research has shown that if you do this every day for five minutes, even when you are not feeling stressed, your overall mood will be boosted, with greater feelings of joy, peacefulness and energy.

Trick your brain

Another great method is telling yourself, when your stress response kicks in, that you are *not* stressed, panicky or scared, but *excited*. It sounds crazy, but in fact the physiological feelings of fear and excitement are much the same — the butterflies, the racing pulse, the sweaty palms and the breathlessness.

If you tell yourself that you are actually excited, *your brain will believe you* (even if *you* don't believe you), and will change the stress hormone ratios in your blood accordingly (decreasing cortisol and increasing a hormone known as DHEA), so that you actually *do* feel excited. This is called the 'excite and delight' response, and it has been scientifically shown that you can change the 'fight, flight, freeze or fawn' responses into it *just by believing it*. This is a great hack for nervous exam students and public speakers too, because it brings your logical brain back online by re-diverting the blood back to it.

Cull the catastrophizing

When you are constantly fearful of what a narcissist will do next, it's easy to go into a state of hyper-vigilance. You perpetually worry about the narcissist's next moves, and you can lose hours to this mental chess playing. The problem is that the more you think certain thoughts, the stronger the 'neural pathways' relating to these thoughts become, as the brain dedicates more and more neurons to them. And the more neurons you have in a thought pathway, the more powerful these thoughts will be - they will have become ingrained, and reflex — and once triggered, can instantly lead to awful fearful imaginings.

I find this to be particularly common amongst my clients who are divorcing narcissists. The manipulations and ways that a jilted narcissist can weaponize the courts or the children are endless, and quite terrifying. It's no wonder my clients often wind themselves up with such dreadful imaginings.

Picture the scene — an abusive narcissistic father wants to see the children an extra night every week. We are currently at stage one. The non-narcissistic mother's mind instantly goes into overdrive. She might think: This must mean that he is trying to establish a pattern where he sees the children more. He is doing this because he wants to have the children for 50% of the time. This will be terrible for the children, because he will subject them to damaging abuse which the court won't be able to see, because it's too subtle. The court will agree to him having them for half the time. He will refuse to give little Felix his inhaler, because he doesn't believe he has asthma, and just tells him to 'stop breathing like that' during asthma attacks. Felix will die because of this. I will never get over it. I will get debilitating depression, and be unable to look after the other children. My ex will then have the children living with him all the time, damaging them further. They will turn into narcissists, and never speak to me again, other than to abuse me. I will kill myself.

This dreadful train of panicked thoughts can just sweep a traumatized person up, and leave them in sheer terror. Whilst it's true that this is a scenario which could realistically occur, it also might *not*. There are infinite variables here, when it comes to what is going to happen, and they cannot really be predicted. It's totally understandable as to why this mother's brain would hijack her in this way, but this catastrophizing actually doesn't help her at all. She will find herself reacting as though she is at stage ten, in a full-on stress response, when actually she is only at stage one.

> "When you are constantly fearful of what a narcissist will do next, it's easy to go into a state of hyper-vigilance."

Catching yourself when this happens to you, and trying examine each part of your chain of thoughts (to see whether opposite scenarios might be just as likely to happen), can be really helpful here. It is definitely possible, with practice, to terminate these runaway thoughts, so that you don't have to feel the unhelpful emotions that result from them.

Become less easily triggered

Even better than being able to quickly terminate an unwanted stress response is *raising the threshold* at which you (and your amygdala) can be triggered. The problem is that your brain perceives the narcissist's behaviour as an *actual threat* to your life, and so responds accordingly, when in fact its response is disproportionate and unhelpful.

Now this is the bit where you might be tempted to think that I have lost all grip on reality. Because I am going to tell you that having a practice of mindfulness and meditation is one of the best ways to train your amygdala into becoming less trigger-happy. But don't worry — this is actually scientifically validated.

Not only will meditating for 20 minutes a day make you less easily triggered by the narcissist, but it can give you a sense of perspective, and help you to become a master of your thoughts rather than a slave to them. It is one of the most powerful and effective ways to defend yourself from repeated narcissist attacks. I recommend attending a mindfulness-based cognitive therapy (MBCT) course, or a mindfulness-based stress reduction (MBSR) course, to most easily develop the skills.

Here is a little mental strategy that I learned during my MBCT teacher training, for just a flavour of the types of resilience tricks you could discover through a meditation practice.

Become a mountain

Close your eyes and imagine yourself as a vast mountain, made of hard, craggy rock. Think about how the rock of your mountain extends deep down into the earth. Think about how wide the base of your mountain is, and how stable that makes you — how you cannot be moved, because you are so huge and grounded. Now think of the how the summer sun comes up, and how, over the day, it moves around your mountain, lighting up your grass and vegetation. Think about how the rain sometimes pummels the side of your mountain, washing away your soil and streaming down your side, in rivulets. Think about how, in the winter, the peak of your mountain is covered in crisp white snow, and how the howling winds of autumn blow the leaves from your trees. Think about how your mountain, *you*, still stands, regardless of the season, and regardless of the weather.

And consider this, when a narcissist next tries to trigger you: *You are the mountain — and the narcissist is just weather.*

13

How to communicate with a narcissist

There is no getting away from the fact that effective communication with a narcissist is completely different to communicating with a 'normal' person. You have probably already noticed that when you have tried to have any type of communication with your narcissist, whether spoken or in writing, you come away feeling either intensely irritated or completely flummoxed as to what just happened. You will be used to finding yourself trying explain normal basic human emotions to them. You will be drawn into outrageous arguments, and into being guilt tripped. You will be made to feel small and unimportant. And occasionally, you will think they have seen the error of their ways when they seem able to communicate perfectly reasonably, when 'Nice Narcissist' makes another fleeting appearance.

This is another instance when you have to throw out your normal communication rule book and pick up a completely different one — and this one is filled with seemingly the most bizarre techniques. You already know that the first basic premise is that you limit your communication with them as much as you can, by all methods, and spend as little time as possible with them as you can. But this chapter is more about strategies to help you when you have no choice but to communicate with them.

These strategies will help you to reduce narcissistic supply, encourage the narcissist to collaborate with you, and will hopefully make your relationship less one-sided (by occasionally allowing you to get something from it too).

The six golden rules of communicating with a narcissist

1. Use the JADE acronym

When a narcissist tries to get a rise out of you, whether in person, on the phone or via written communication, try to remember not to **J**ustify yourself, **A**rgue, **D**efend (anyone, including yourself) or **E**xplain your actions to them. It takes some practice, but refusing to do this is an essential part of dealing with a narcissist.

2. Use the fewest possible words

The less words you use, the fewer of your emotions come across, and the less ammunition you will be handing the narcissist. This can be incredibly difficult if you are a naturally verbose person, but it's essential. Wherever possible let the narcissist do the talking.

3. Pick your battles

You can't really 'win' an argument with a narcissist in the traditional sense, because they will just keep twisting and spinning half-truths and using illogical rationalizations. The *process* of arguing is what is essential to a narcissist, and their opinions and stances may flipflop back and forth during arguments, because often they have no fixed opinions anyway. Only fight with a narcissist if there is an important issue at stake, that could materially affect you or your family's well-being, if you have absolutely no choice. Otherwise, don't even try to be 'right'. There's no point at all. They'll probably deny the argument ever happened anyway, or rewrite history regarding what did actually happen.

4. Don't hit the ball back

Think of every conversation with a narcissist as being like a tennis match. They will serve the ball, and want you to return it, so that a protracted volley ensues. Let them have their ace. Wherever possible, put down your racket and walk off the court.

5. Be a yellow rock

I describe the grey rock technique in detail on page 209, as a way to withhold narcissistic supply from the narcissist. However, it does come across as very odd to any onlookers, and it might not be practical if you have to maintain a relationship of sorts with your narcissist. This is where the 'yellow rock technique' may be more useful. Essentially, you are doing the same as grey rocking, but just a bit less — you are 'warming up' your grey rock communications a touch. You might make a bit of eye contact with your narcissist, rather than none. You might add the odd pleasantry into your conversation, such as the occasional 'please' and 'thank you'. You might finish a text off with a single 'x' rather than an abrupt ending, or even add a smiley face or a heart emoji, if you can bear it. You'd still want to be boring and relatively monosyllabic, compared with how you are with your non-narcissistic friends, and you'd still want to limit your facial expressions, so that the amount of narcissistic supply you feed your narcissist is reduced just enough.

6. Zone out

Whenever possible, zone out from whatever the narcissist is saying to you, so that you cannot be drawn into a discussion with them. Plan to think about your 'to do' list, or find a pleasant daydream to enter into when with the narcissist, and make the odd agreeable sounding 'uh huh' sound, if necessary. Yes, it's rude, but the alternative is much worse. When they accuse you of not listening, you can always do what they do — and just deny it.

Learn how to placate the narcissist

Placating a narcissist might feel completely wrong when they are behaving badly, but it can modify their behaviour relatively quickly. You can soothe a narcissist by making them feel important and special, as a short-term solution. You may wish to try:

- Thanking them for bringing something to your attention.
- Telling them that you are on 'their side'.
- Agreeing with them. It may be that you can't agree completely with what they have said, but you may be able to find some part of what they have said to agree with, to validate them. For example, imagine your narcissistic sister is criticizing your new flat. Her: "It's too noisy here — you should have moved somewhere quieter — that road is ridiculously busy. No wonder it was cheap — you'd need to be completely deaf to live here…" You: "Yes — the road is busy, it's true…would like a coffee?" Not responding to the rest of her statement, and changing the subject instead can be very effective.
- Praising them. Simply praise things that are true. Make sure your praise is in line with how the narcissist likes to see themselves, and avoid hyperbole (words such as incredible, amazing, wonderful etc.). Be measured and proportionate in your praise.
- Asking for their opinion, and then looking mesmerized by their answer.
- Giving them a bit of control — perhaps let them have the final say or last word on something that isn't too important to you.

- Letting them feel as if they have won ("Yes — you are right. I'd never thought of it like that before…"). Narcissists need to win as much as you need food and water.
- Pretending to be a member of their fan club. Giving your narcissistic boss adoring looks and laughing at their jokes might buy you time, as you look for another job. But remember — it has to be *believable*.
- Dangling a false promise of future narcissistic supply in front of them. Nodding earnestly, and saying "I'll think about it" and "Let me get back to you on that" are excellent ways to shut down a conversation with a narcissist, under the guise of taking whatever they have said to you seriously. The false promise of future narcissistic supply is better than none, after all.

Tips when standing up for yourself

Avoid starting a sentence with 'no'

If you are working on asserting your boundaries with the narcissist, just know that using the actual word 'no' can be like a waving red rag at a bull. 'I decline', 'I won't be doing that' or 'I will be unable do that' might be better, less inflammatory ways to say 'no' to a narcissist.

Use 'yes and' instead of 'but'

Narcissists can't bear being invalidated, so using this communication tactic can work quite well with them. If your narcissistic colleague is arguing with you about why *they* should have the Christmas period off again this year instead of you, think carefully about how you respond.

"I hear your point of view, *but…*" really means that you *don't* hear their point of view, and are actually dismissing it. This is bound to further inflame a narcissist. However, if you were to say, "I hear your point of view, *yes, and* [insert your position]…" you sound much more agreeable.

Call them out

This advice is commonly given out as being a good communication strategy to employ with narcissists, but I really do think it is of limited value. Perhaps it may be of use if you have a narcissist with quite a bit of insight into their behaviours, or with someone who is not very high on the spectrum of narcissism (perhaps at a seven). Phrases like "Don't tell me what to feel", "You are ordering me around again" and "Do you hear yourself?" might be worth a try — but personally, I wouldn't bother — you'll probably realize that you might as well be talking to a brick wall.

How to persuade a narcissist to do what you want

Use 'we' instead of 'you' or 'I'

Sometimes narcissists respond well to collaborative pronouns, like 'we' and 'us'. Narcissists hate to be alone, and need other people desperately, so reminding them that you are with them can help calm them down, as it's almost a little promise of narcissistic supply. "*We* need to sort out the holiday schedule for the children", is better than "*You* need to sort out the holiday schedule for the children" and "*We* are agreed that the deadline is next Monday" is better than "I agree with the deadline of next Monday".

Flatter them

Do you want to get your narcissistic mother-in-law to bake the cake for your daughter's birthday party? Do you want your narcissistic brother to tile your bathroom? Well, make sure they know how amazing they are at caking baking and tiling, then. The *more people* you can also (legitimately) claim appreciate their skills, the better. Bear in mind that this will only work for things they *are* actually good at — their real strengths. If you need the narcissist to do something, this is worth a try, but not if they are in the middle of a rage.

"When you made that carrot cake last year, no one could stop talking about it. In fact, Roger brought it up again the other day. We've so many people coming to the birthday party, and having your cake as the birthday cake would elevate the whole event. Everyone would be delighted if you would consider doing it. I just can't think of a better way to treat our guests…"

"I've been raving about your tiling to everyone for years. I keep going to people's houses and seeing their bathrooms, and I have to say, what you can do is in a completely different league. Because it's the guest bathroom and so many people will see it, I just really want it to be right, you know? I don't suppose you'd be able to help out with this? I wasn't sure whether to ask you, but everyone says I'd be mad not to at least try!"

"You have always been good at encouraging Felix with his football. Would you take him to his match on Wednesday?" "You are so good at persuading people to do things — everybody says so. Would you be able to speak to Amelia's teacher about letting her dropping Drama?"

Catch them in good behaviour

Training a narcissist to behave themselves can be a bit like potty training a toddler. When the toddler successfully uses the potty, you make a huge fuss, and look thoroughly delighted, thereby encouraging them to do it again, next time. This positive reinforcement is more effective than telling them off when things don't go the way you wanted them to.

Whilst a narcissist, *unlike* a toddler, will get narcissistic supply from negative attention, like being told off, they do tend to *prefer* praise for good behaviour, and respond well to it.

So, when your narcissistic boss lets you leave the office on time, give them a huge appreciative smile, and loudly tell them how brilliant it is of them to let you go, so that everyone in the office knows how generous they are being. It might seem contrived and false to you, but the narcissist won't see this, as they bask in your appreciation and positive attention. It may take a few goes but, eventually, you may find that being forced to work late becomes a thing of the past. But make sure you keep praising them, *every single time* for letting you go. Everything is transactional to a narcissist, as you know, so you might as well play the same game as them.

Use the hamburger method of persuasion

Here you sandwich your request, the burger, in between two compliments (the bread).

Bread: "You are so much better than I am at dealing with the builder. He really respects you and listens to what you say, and clearly is in awe of you, even though he tries to hide it."

Burger: "We'd be so much further on if we could discuss which flooring to have with him this week. I know you can't wait to get it all finished so we can have that party. Shall we arrange a time for him to speak to you?"

Bread: "I think he really needs your input, because he knows you've got such a good eye for this kind of thing."

Note the use of the collaborative word 'we' in the burger, and the explanation as to why it would be in the narcissist's interest to meet with the builder (so that they can show off the house by having a party, once it's finished).

Note also how the narcissist is given ownership of the compliment in the bread sections by using the word 'you' ("*you've* got such a good eye for this sort of thing…")

Again, when complimenting, you do have to use things which are actually true for your narcissist (or at least things that *they* believe to be true).

Use 'would you' instead of 'could you'

Narcissists are contrary, practically by definition. They often like to be overly literal in conversations to this end, so avoiding asking them to do something using the word 'could', might make them less likely to wriggle out of doing it.

You: "Could you put the rubbish out, dear?"

Narcissist: "Yes."

The next day:

You: "Oh. I see you didn't put the rubbish out."

Narcissist: "You didn't ask me to. You just asked me if I 'could' do it."

"*Would* you put the rubbish out, dear?" might increase your chances of them actually doing it. (If you are lucky).

Tell them why it would be in their best interests

Narcissists are selfish. They only do things that will benefit them and give them narcissistic supply, whether that supply is gained immediately, or in the medium or long term. So, how will the thing you want them to do make them feel special, unique and superior? How will it gain them positive attention? How will it enable them to put someone else down, 'get one over' on someone else, or cause a bit of conflict? How will it give them a way to win, or make them feel like they are being seen to be altruistic?

Narcissists are also often drawn to things which are cutting edge — they often like the newest phone or the latest fad so, if what you want happens to concur with this, then you might be onto a winner. ("Let's get an electric car — we'd be the first on the street, and it'll really annoy your brother, who is always going on about how about environmentally friendly he is…")

(Some narcissists are *inverted* snobs though, and get more attention from doing just the opposite. There is no shortage of wealthy narcissists who drive beat-up cars and wear scruffy clothes, for attention. "He's so humble and down to earth. You'd never know he was an investment banker from just looking at him…").

Make them think it was their idea

This one is self-explanatory, but it may involve you having to gaslight the narcissist a bit, which you may find very uncomfortable. But remember, you are dealing with a very limited individual, and as long as it is for the common good, this might actually be okay.

"I've been thinking about what you said ages ago, and you were right. A maths tutor for Felix is a good idea after all. I should have got one organized when you first mentioned it, but shall we go ahead and find one now?"

Shame them

If all else fails, you can try to shame a narcissist into doing what you want, if refusing will make them look unreasonable to others. "I'm just worried about how other people are going to view you when they find out about this." "Jane and Dave just can't understand why you won't agree. I just don't know what to say to them, especially as they hold you in such high regard." "But what if you lose your reputation over something this small? Is it really going to be worth it?" "Isn't it going to look much better for you to agree? That way you can look like the bigger person." These are the sorts of truths that might make a narcissist do what you want, because they want to avoid feeling shame, and desperately need to look good to others.

How to communicate with a narcissist in writing

You already know that narcissists procure their really top-grade quality narcissistic supply from in-person, face-to-face interactions. Here they can (not necessarily consciously) pick up on the tiniest of visual and auditory signals, and use them to inform them of what to say and do next, to get even more supply. A minuscule flaring of the nostrils. A slight stiffening of the shoulders. Involuntary dilation of the pupils. A barely noticeable gulp. A momentary clenching of the jaw. All of these are gifts to a narcissist, which although not quite as good as unfettered adoration, will do very nicely indeed.

You can see why you might feel safer limiting your communication with them to the written word — but here you have another set of potential dangers. Narcissists love to triangulate people and play them off against one another, and emails and all forms of instant messaging are a fantastic way to do just that. A trigger-happy narcissist in a rage will violate your boundaries, and forward your communications to anyone they can. Your employer, your spouse, your kids, the police — no one is off-limits, and you will be portrayed as the perpetrator.

Even more concerning, if you happen to be in a dispute with a narcissist that reaches court, you can fully expect to hear your own words being read back to you in front of a judge.

Perhaps you feel that I am being over-the-top here. After all, you may be thinking that your narcissistic sister, deeply unpleasant and devaluing though she may be, could *never* have a reason to drag you to court. But the harsh truth is that narcissists often do. They challenge wills, they accuse people of fraud, they allege violence and they divorce using the courts. That boundary dispute with your narcissistic neighbour, that false allegation of harassment, that unfair dismissal claim — all can escalate in ways you couldn't have dreamed possible.

All the tips in the previous section apply when you are communicating with a narcissist in writing, with the addition of some other techniques that will help you to dodge the inevitable traps that are being laid, whilst maintaining your boundaries. So, when you have received a written communication from a narcissist, make sure you follow these steps, *before you respond.*

1. Notice how you are feeling

Have you been thrown into the fight, flight freeze or fawn stress response, described on page 248? It's quite likely that your brain will misinterpret the situation as one that poses a genuine risk to your life, and cause you to react as if you are being attacked by a lion. But in doing so, blood is being diverted away from your cerebral cortices — the logical, thinking areas of your brain, so you can't actually think clearly.

Notice whether you feel angry, and want to fight back (fight), or panicked, and wanting to run away from the problem (flight). Or do you feel frozen with indecision (freeze)? Perhaps you feel like apologizing and placating the narcissist (fawn)? Is your heart racing? Are your palms sweating? Do you feel sick? How is your breathing? Is it possible that you have been triggered into a physiological response, which is completely over-the-top, and preventing you from thinking clearly? If so, you may wish to take a time out and use the strategies in Chapter 12 to calm you, and bring your brain back online, completely away from the letter or message.

2. Remember that you are dealing with a toddler tantrum

When it comes to re-reading the narcissist's communication, you will definitely benefit from viewing it from the perspective from which it was written — that of a raging, small child. A powerful tool for visually reminding yourself of this would be to copy and paste the letter into a five-year-old handwriting font, before re-reading it. Here's a typical narcissistic email from a mother to her ex:

"You either pay me an extra £500 per month or I go for sole custody of the girls — which I have been advised will be a given, with a case as strong as mine. You need to get help. Sort yourself out. You are unravelling, and are unfit to parent. Expect to hear from my lawyer. As usual it is left to me to take the moral high ground."

It's a bit less scary when you see it transformed below, I'm sure you'll agree.

You either pay me an extra 500 pounds per month or I go for sole custody of the girls — which I have been advised will be a given, with a case as strong as mine. You need to get help. Sort yourself out. You are unravelling, and are unfit to parent. Expect to hear from my lawyer. As usual it is left to me to take the moral high ground.

3. Translate the letter

Once the letter is in its new child's font, you will need to forensically break it down into all the narcissistic behaviours that I summarized in the table on pages 190-191. To remind you, a few of the things to identify are:

Gaslighting
Lying
Rewriting history
Projection
Manipulation
False allegations
Threats and blackmail
Playing the victim
Denial
False justifications
Blame-shifting
Shame-dumping
Grandiosity/superiority/knowing best
A need to win

Sense of entitlement
Devaluations
Lack of empathy
Inability to apologize
Exploitation
Seeing people as only all good or all bad
Selfishness
Boundary violations
Jealousy
Schadenfreude
A need to be in control
Triangulation
Rules not applying to themselves
Hypocrisy
Rage
Aggression
Pseudo-logic
Word salad
Contradictions
Toxic positivity
Invalidation
Stonewalling
Instilling fear
Future faking

With these in mind, let's now break down our short excerpt:

- You either pay me an extra 500 pounds per month or I go for sole custody of the girls. Here we see threats, blackmail, instilling fear, aggression, rage, a need to be in control, exploitation, sense of entitlement and manipulation.

- *which I have been advised will be a given, with a case as strong as mine.* This demonstrates gaslighting and a need to win.

- *You need to get help. Sort yourself out. You are unravelling, and are unfit to parent.* This is gaslighting, together with false allegations. We also see projection and shame-dumping — she is actually saying, "*I* need to get help. Sort *myself* out. *I* am unravelling and unfit to parent.

- *Expect to hear from my lawyer.* Here we see more threats and manipulation.

- *As usual it is left to me to take the moral high ground.* And finally, here is grandiosity and superiority, pseudo-logic, and playing the victim.

4. Formulating a reply

Now that you know what you are actually dealing with, you can consider what really needs responding to. Whatever response you do give should be in 'grey rock' style, using the communication tips given earlier in this chapter. Perhaps a good response here would simply be "*Any further communications regarding maintenance/alimony should be via your lawyer, and will not be responded to directly.*"

The key points for written communication are:
- Don't respond in the heat of the moment
- Decode what the narcissist is saying to you
- Write as little as possible
- Don't JADE (justify, argue, defend or explain)
- Don't expect them to understand a rational, logical explanation

- Don't hit the ball back — walk off the court
- Show no emotion (grey or yellow rock)
- Minimize niceties
- Assert your boundaries
- Imagine that you are writing for a court

14

The wider implications

So there you have it — the unvarnished truth about the many, many narcissists in our midst.

We've talked about how differently the various types of narcissist superficially present themselves to the outside world, but how, underneath, their behaviours are so very similar. I've explained exactly how we can be unwittingly lured into the Narcissist Trap, and why escape is so difficult. I've detailed escape plans, and laid out options for coping, if you have no choice but to remain in the trap.

We've discussed that curious, but crucial, concept of 'narcissistic supply', the fuel that constantly needs topping up so that a narcissist can stay feeling emotionally safe — and I've relentlessly hammered home how *everything* that a narcissist does is driven by this need to procure this fuel.

So where does all of this information leave *you*? Perhaps you are feeling relieved that some of the difficult people in your life have turned out to be fairly easy to understand, after all. Or perhaps this book has left you devastated by an unwanted realization about someone you love. I'm so sorry, if that's you.

It may be that your mind is swinging wildly between two realities — the notion that the person in question most definitely is a narcissist, followed by the opposite belief. You may be feeling utterly confused at these times — that you must have made it up, that you are wrong, or even that *you* must be the narcissist, instead of them. Guilt at making these judgments may weigh heavily on you. This is the psychological phenomenon of 'cognitive dissonance' — the brain can't comfortably hold two opposing beliefs at the same time, and so it chooses just one. But now that the scales have fallen from your eyes, the brain finds itself vacillating between its various realities — Nice Narcissist or Nasty Narcissist? Put upon victim or perpetrator? True or feigned love? It's disconcerting and very difficult to experience — but it does eventually resolve.

You now understand how damaging a narcissistic relationship can be. It can destroy a person's sense of self-worth and self-belief, deeply affecting how they live their life, in so many ways. It can leave a person in a close orbit completely bankrupt — emotionally and financially.

You may have gained a sense of how vampiric these relationships can be — how victims can feel as though they have been violated at their very core. At its worst this can feel like 'soul rape'. So many people crawl away feeling like ghosts — transparent figures of no substance. But narcissists are not mystical beings with supernatural powers. They are not 'in league with the devil' or 'evil' — although it certainly can feel like it, if you are locked in a battle with one. I feel that it's important, if you are a victim of narcissistic abuse, to try not to give them this added power through your words — they are powerful enough as it is. But I accept that you may disagree with me here.

Allow me to briefly remind you here of how most narcissists are made — through how they reacted to a childhood that was difficult in some way, or one in which they were over-idealized. Remember little Lina, our Closet Narcissist, and her shopkeeper father, who she was expected to adore above all else? Remember Jonathan, who as a child was invalid and unseen unless he constantly achieved? Oonagh, whose critical, mean-spirited, alcoholic father drove her away from her life in rural Ireland, but not before the damage had been done? And Marcus, the child who had been so badly wanted that he was placed on a pedestal and constantly and excessively praised, with all the best intentions in the world? These children did not *choose* their fate — although how much power they have *as adults* to change their behaviours is a matter of much debate. One thing is for sure though — most narcissists do *not* choose to change.

In this book I have mentioned the children of narcissists — those unfortunates who were not *lured* into the Narcissist Trap, but who were *born* into it, and I believe they deserve special consideration here.

Narcissistic parenting is very bad for children — very bad indeed. You already know that it can lead to children becoming narcissists themselves, passing narcissism on through subsequent generations, propagating havoc and abuse. But those children of narcissists who are lucky enough to escape, without becoming narcissists *themselves*, are very likely to attract (and be attracted to) further narcissists, as adults. Around half the people who come to me for help to leave their narcissistic partner describe having a narcissistic parent. These children can go on to endure a lifetime of narcissistic abuse from various narcissists, whose teeth just happen to fit their childhood wounds.

In fact, I was one such child. I was born into a home of narcissism, but for decades, I had no idea that that was where I was. My childhood was a very tricky one — a warm, loving, sociable mother who died slowly and painfully from cancer when I was thirteen, and a father who I pretended not to be related to. At his best, in private, he was cold and distant, at his worst, full of rage. I would creep around, hoping to avoid his wrath. I would even justify his criticisms, his put downs and his ridiculing as being normal for a first-generation South Asian immigrant. And incredibly, I used to blame *myself* for the inevitable beatings that I lived in fear of.

At school, however, I thrived — surrounded by friends, kind teachers, fun and hilarity. I believe that it was probably this life-affirming and validating school experience that saved me from becoming a narcissist myself. At school I was seen, accepted and liked for who I was, and I was even allowed to laugh without repercussions.

However, laughing was very definitely not something my father would tolerate at home, and he would turn on anyone who did it, spitting venomously "Yes, you have your fun — God will pay you back — *with interest.*"

Things were different when out in public, however. He would speak in a completely different, congenial way, and chuckle every now and then (if there was an audience), doing a passable impression of normality to anyone who didn't know him.

In some ways I was lucky — he was so obviously toxic behind closed doors that it became difficult to miss that the problem lay with him. Of course, I eventually came to understand that he was a Devaluing Narcissist — but it still took four decades for me to learn to accept his limitations without hoping for change, whilst ensuring that I no longer put myself in harm's way.

If it was this hard for *me*, in the face of such *obvious* abuse, you can see how confusing it must be for the children of the three other types of narcissist. It's no wonder they can spend whole lifetimes being thrown off the scent, by their narcissist's adoring fan clubs and enablers, whilst experiencing abuse so much more covert, but no less damaging, than my own. You may remember Laura from the introduction of this book — the Texan lady I met on a plane, who, in her sixties was still trapped by the demands, expectation and put downs of her narcissistic mother. Her story, as an adult child of a narcissist, is far from unique.

So, how did this upbringing affect me in later years? Well, aged eighteen, at medical school, I started to attract a different type of friend to my genuinely nice school friends. They were superficially gregarious and fun-loving; mainly quirky 'outsiders' with unconventional backgrounds or a difficult parent, usually passing themselves off as hyper-intelligent. These mutual attractions felt to me like an inescapable gravitational pull — and until my own 'awakening' I had no idea how toxic these relationships, which continued to form for years, were. I had thought I was safe, because they were superficially nothing like my dad — but I was wrong. Although these people *outwardly* seemed very different to the narcissist I grew up with, in fact the patterns of behaviour and psychological abuse turned out to be strikingly similar.

So, although I could subconsciously spot and avoid Devaluing Narcissists, like my dad, the Closet, Exhibitionist and Communal varieties could lure me into their traps with ease. As a result, I have had to eject myself from multiple narcissists' orbits in my life — but these days, even though I still occasionally get sucked in, I can get out much more easily.

But let's hone in on exactly how narcissistic parents affect their children in their crucial formative years, because after all, this is where each narcissist can do the most damage — to the very people who are utterly dependent on them.

In earlier chapters I have touched upon the way that narcissists see their children as being *extensions of themselves,* and how this inability to view them as being separate from themselves leads to problems. They are not seen, heard, or validated for who they actually are, as individuals with their own personalities, talents and wants — and instead are expected to want what their narcissistic parent wants. Their preferences, even if they were to be acknowledged, are irrelevant. If these children grow up not to be narcissists, they learn to squash their needs, or to not have any at all. They learn to put other people's needs above their own — a recipe for future co-dependent relationships, with abusers, narcissists, substance addicts or those with chronic illnesses.

This inability to see themselves as separate from their children also leads to narcissists being especially poor at tolerating 'imperfections' in their children. Woe betide the teenage daughter who is slightly overweight. The son with ADHD or autism. The child who has asthma, with that annoying breathing that they exhibit during what must be a 'feigned' asthma attack. An imperfection in their child equals an imperfection in *them* — and as you know, narcissists need to believe that they are special, unique and superior, because the only alternative is to feel utterly worthless and defective.

But there's also a unique, seemingly paradoxical dynamic going on with their children, which adds an extra layer of complexity. Because, at the same time as being unable to see them as separate from themselves, narcissists will also subject their children to all the other abusive behaviours that they subject everyone else to.

A narcissist's children are *objects* which belong exclusively to them, and so can be used in whatever ways serves the narcissist — as admirers, confidants, servants, or even as punchbags. In divorce, they will be used as weapons against the other parent. And although narcissists often outwardly play the role of 'fun' dad or mum, their children will receive no empathy from them (unless there happens to be an audience).

A narcissist's children are also sources of *direct* narcissistic supply, in all the usual ways — they give the narcissistic parent attention and adoration, they place them on a pedestal, they allow them to exert power and control over them, they engage in their dramas and conflict and they live in fear of them.

"At the same time as being unable to see them as separate from themselves, narcissists will also subject their children to all the other abusive behaviours that they subject everyone else to."

But narcissists also use their children as *indirect* sources of narcissistic supply too — to obtain fuel from onlookers. Remember how Jonathan, our headmaster, couldn't tolerate his son Max being gay, until he found a way to use it to procure narcissistic supply for himself, in becoming a national school LGBTQ advocate? How, even though he didn't want him to play the piano, he would applaud him loudly at concerts, and happily take the glory for his talents?

And Marcus got immense narcissistic supply from the admiration of the mums who came to watch him coaching his stepson Janis's football team, in deliberately tight-fitting shorts and T-shirt. His outward persona of 'perfect stepdad' was much admired in the process. And Lina used her lavish children's parties simply as a way to gain the admiration (and jealousy) of others.

Let's face it — who hasn't cringed at a 'Disney Dad's' over-the-top public displays of affection for their child, like Marcus and his stepson, Janis? Who hasn't encountered a 'perfect mum' who seems far too good to be true, and who parades her immaculately dressed, perfect children around for all to admire? Who hasn't been at a school concert, play or sports event where a narcissistic 'tiger mom' is applauding their exhausted, overachieving child just a little too loudly?

A narcissist's child has another important function to perform, because they also actually form part of the narcissist's false image — that of the perfect parent with the happy family. If you are the adult child of a narcissist you'll be used to having to turn up to various functions, with your own children in tow, to fulfil this role.

And allow me to briefly remind you of what happens when there is more than one child being reared by a narcissist (and often their hapless, enabler co-parent). Here the narcissist will use a variation of 'triangulation'; the dynamic of the 'golden child, the scapegoat and the invisible child'. In this situation the scapegoat child (who can do no right), and the invisible child, find themselves ferociously competing for the narcissist's positive attention, desperate to usurp the golden child (who can do no wrong in the narcissist's eyes). Typically, this goes on forever, even when the children are grown up.

My clients who have had multiple children with their narcissistic partners instantly recognize this toxic triangulation, and the fact that, when it comes to their children, narcissists very definitely *do* have

SUPRIYA MCKENNA

favourites. It's patently obvious to them that their narcissistic co-parent's love for their children is unequal and entirely conditional.

Sadly, even though the golden child may have *appeared* to have largely escaped the abuse, they will, as an adult, most likely, become a narcissist themselves. And, having idealized their narcissistic parent and been rewarded for it with praise and love, they commonly end up as the child who eventually inherits all the family money, leading to yet more tension with their adult siblings. As far too many people will know, narcissistic parents are even adept at delivering blows from the grave.

So, what are the wider implications of narcissism in families? I've already mentioned how narcissism propagates through the generations, creating more and more narcissists to wreak havoc on yet more innocents, in years to come — and how *multiple* innocents will be trapped in every single narcissist's orbit. Put simply, the more prevalent the problem of narcissists in families, the greater the impact on everybody else.

I wonder — how many people who are being bullied at work are actually trapped in a narcissist's orbit? What percentage of workplace bullying is actually *narcissistic abuse*? What proportion of employment disputes result directly from narcissistic behaviours? How many narcissistic judges and lawyers, who themselves hail from narcissistic families of origin, are out there, exploiting victims, wielding power, destroying innocent people's lives *and getting away with it*?

I've already described how the non-narcissistic children of narcissists are extra susceptible to being further abused in adulthood, as they are easily lured into another narcissist's trap, through the subconscious pull of the familiar. They often end up with narcissists as partners, as a result. But how much *domestic* abuse is actually *narcissistic abuse*? How many 'coercive controllers' are actually narcissists, exhibiting a much wider set of behaviours than coercive control on its own (which would be easy to identify, if anyone cared to look)?

And what of the fact that narcissistic parenting leads to 'attachment' issues — difficulties in forming secure loving, trusting bonds with others in adulthood, in the offspring of narcissists? Has this contributed to the statistics showing that, in the UK at least, the proportion of married people is declining, and the proportion of singletons increasing? And with divorce hitting one in two marriages, I wonder what proportion of divorces actually involve a narcissist, given their limitations when it comes to having mutually fulfilling, reciprocal relationships?

Sadly, the children of narcissists often also go on to develop mental health issues, such as depression, anxiety, eating disorders, self-harming behaviours and substance addictions. In a world in the midst of a mental health crisis, I cannot help but wonder what proportion of it is related to familial narcissism, hidden behind closed doors.

Just how significant a factor is narcissism in all these various societal problems? We'll probably never know, and certainly not until the prevalence of NPD in our populations can be properly determined.

But what we do know is this: one narcissistic parent will *inevitably* cause damage to all of their children, in one or more of the ways above, if the children spend enough time with them, and don't have the damage limited or reversed by other healthy relationships. I'm afraid it really is that bad.

But on that depressing note, let's now widen our beam, and take a brief look at how narcissism affects society at large — arguably the most important thing of all, when it comes to the not so small matter of the human race.

The 'super-narcissists'

So, let's talk about the 'super-narcissists'. The ones who make it to the very top of the tree in their professions, to a degree where they affect entire countries and economies. Where their narcissism has an effect on a global scale. The narcissists with massive worldwide companies. The ones who are world leaders. The narcissistic politicians.

You now know that narcissists aren't really driven by the desire to 'make their countries great', or to make the lives of people better. You know that they don't really care about the welfare of the planet, or the environment. They are driven by the need for narcissistic supply, period.

The super-narcissists are just like all the other narcissists — except that their orbits extend all the way out to include society at large — millions of people they have never even met will be sucked in by their gravitational fields, and their lives will be profoundly affected by them.

If you live in a country which happens to be run by a dictator, you are off the hook here — you didn't choose your leader, and to overthrow them would likely mean risking your life and the lives of your family.

"Millions of us in the world have been **collectively** lured into the narcissist trap, and have paid the price."

But millions of us in the world have been *collectively* lured into the Narcissist Trap, and are paying the price. The super-narcissists in politics use exactly the same methods as their less successful counterparts to suck us in to their traps, and to get us to willingly vote for them.

They love bomb us, and charm us. They shapeshift, appearing to become exactly what we think we need. They future fake, making pledges that they have no intention of delivering, and they promise to rescue us from whatever our biggest collective pain points are.

Once in position, and doing a terrible job, they keep us in their trap by weakening us, largely by confusing us. Gaslighting is the commonest tactic used — they'll tell us that things didn't actually happen the way we think they did. They'll refuse to take responsibility, by blame-shifting and projecting their own behaviours onto others. They'll employ toxic positivity — telling us that things aren't as bad as we think and that we should pull together and look on the bright side. They'll answer questions using pseudo-logic — giving barely plausible answers, with great conviction, and stonewalling questions they don't want to answer. Their enablers will stand steadfastly beside them, loudly and vocally lending their unwavering public support.

And whilst all of this is going on, they will break their own laws and rules (as they clearly do not believe that they should apply to *them*). When they are nearly exposed, they will lie, and minimize or justify their behaviours, as all narcissists do. When they do get properly caught, and threatened with abandonment, they go into full-on hoovering mode. They apologize to the masses, having seen the error of their ways, and promise to do better. They beg their enablers for their continued support, using flattery, renewed love bombing and bribes. They guilt trip the electorate, and play the victim to excuse their 'mistakes'. And they make yet more enticing false promises, until we give them yet another chance.

All of this is incredible narcissistic supply to a super-narcissist, of course — a permanent cocaine-like high. They feel omnipotent, superior and clever as they run rings around, quite literally, millions of people, feeding off the attention, the drama and the conflict.

Journalists will point out their contradictions and lies, with outrage and confusion, and the internet will go radioactive as people react in the same way as the journalists. *But why would they do that?* People will ask, angrily. *But surely that is just a lie? But how can they justify doing that? But how can that be in the nation's best interests? But surely that's illegal?*

And when the leader is about to be voted out, or forced to resign, they will react as all narcissists do when facing a deep narcissistic injury to their false persona — with unbridled fury and rage.

But a super-narcissist's rage doesn't just threaten to hurt the people who happen to be in their close vicinity. They can incite violence and start wars, and do. Frighteningly, some of them have nuclear codes at their disposal. It's no exaggeration when I say that the effects of a super-narcissist's rage can be far reaching, and quite literally a matter of life and death for millions.

Eventually, inevitably, the super-narcissist's power will wane. They may be voted out by their disillusioned former fans, in which case they may refuse to go, and try desperately to cling on to power. To admit defeat would dissolve the false persona they need so badly to maintain, to protect them from their own true feelings about themselves — so they will deny the reality of their downfall, for as long as they can.

Perhaps their departure will be as a result of being forced to resign. Here rage is likely to make another appearance, and they will blame others, refuse to take any responsibility for their actions, or continue to deny that they ever even happened, sourly accusing others of participating in a 'witch-hunt' against them.

And once again, public outrage will ensue, and opinions will go round and round in circles about their behaviour, which seems so odd and difficult to explain. Except that it isn't *at all* inexplicable — as you now know.

Wouldn't we, collectively, all save ourselves a lot of angst and mental energy if we understood what was *really* going on? I think we would. Shouldn't there be mandatory testing for personality disorders in those standing for high political office? I think there should. Narcissists *cannot* care about others, other than in the context of what they can do for them. That on its own should be enough to discount them from running our countries — and from deciding the fate of our beautiful, yet ailing planet.

I end this strange journey into the mis-wired minds of narcissists with you here, and I thank you for your company. I do hope that this book has been enlightening, and that it has made sense of a thing or two that might have been troubling you. My wish is that perhaps it will also play a part in enabling you to detoxify your life, by helping you to recognize and manage the narcissists within it, and that *that* might even make you happier.

And if you *have* recognized that you have fallen into the Narcissist Trap and that you want to escape, I wish you well with your endeavour. I'm rooting for you, every step of the way.

Glossary

Term	Definition
Altruistic Narcissist	Another name for Communal Narcissist
Blame-shifting	Narcissists cannot take the blame for their actions (except in the rare instances when doing so will give them narcissistic supply) and so pass the blame onto others with lightning speed, to avoid feeling shame.
Closet Narcissist	This type of narcissist (also called the 'Vulnerable', 'Introverted' or 'Covert' Narcissist) shies away from the limelight, and comes across as quiet, shy and self-effacing. They often try to feel special by association, by attaching themselves to a person, cause or object that they hold up as being special. They often play the hard done by victim.
Co-dependency	A type of relationship addiction characterized by preoccupation and extreme dependence – emotional, social and sometimes physical – on another person. Co-dependents feel responsible for the feelings and actions of their loved ones. The partners of narcissists, alcoholics, substance abusers and those with chronic illnesses are often co-dependents. They characteristically put the other's needs ahead of their own.

THE NARCISSIST TRAP

Term	Definition
Cognitive Dissonance	This occurs when a person is holding two or more contradictory thoughts or beliefs in their minds at the same time. This creates an uncomfortable sense of confusion, which the brain resolves by choosing just one of the beliefs to believe, discarding the other by denying it, minimizing it or justifying it.
Communal Narcissist	Also called the Altruistic Narcissist. These narcissists prop up their self-esteem and sense of specialness by giving to others. They obtain admiration, attention and a sense of specialness ('narcissistic supply') from good works and deeds. They need others to see them as being the most generous, the most caring, or the most kind person they know.
Covert Narcissist	Another name for a Closet, Vulnerable, or Introverted Narcissist.
Cycle of 'Idealize' and 'Devalue'	The initial stage of a relationship with a narcissist is the 'idealization' phase, also known as 'love bombing'. The next stage is the devaluation stage, where the narcissist puts down their victim. This cycle (Nice Narcissist/Nasty Narcissist) repeats, over and over, causing Trauma Bonding.
DARVO	Defend, Attack, Reverse Victim and Offender. This is a classic narcissistic strategy to shift the blame, by playing the victim, so the focus is shifted from their wrongdoing on to your alleged bad behaviour.
Deletions	Information that the brain filters out that is not in line with your beliefs, or your view of the world. You do not become consciously aware of this information, as a result.

Term	Definition
Devaluations	Put downs through being critical, ridiculing, or demeaning. The devaluations usually increase so slowly that the victim may not notice, so becoming the proverbial 'frog in boiling water', so staying in the relationship.
Devaluing Narcissist	Also called the 'Toxic' or 'Malignant' Narcissist. They exhibit many of the other more general narcissistic behaviours too, but what is more prominent in this type of narcissist is that they devalue, criticize, and demean others in order to inflate their own sense of self-worth.
Distortions	The brain distorts how we view reality, in line with our own personal prejudices resulting from former experiences. The brain magnifies or diminishes our perceptions of things, resulting in 'distortions'.
Drama Triangle	Karpman's drama triangle is a description of conflict in social interactions. There are three roles within the triangle – victim, rescuer and persecutor. In narcissistic relationships the narcissist moves themselves and others around the triangle, to take up different roles at different times. This perpetuates and continues the drama.
Euphoric Recall	The tendency for the human brain to remember past events in a positive light, rather than in a negative light, by filtering out the bad bits. Seeing the world through rose-tinted spectacles in this way can lead to victims staying with their narcissistic abusers.

Term	Definition
Exhibitionist Narcissist	Also known as 'Grandiose' or 'Overt' Narcissist. They are extroverted and superficially charming. They can appear haughty and arrogant, and give off an air of superiority. Many are financially successful in their chosen fields, but some are not, and prefer to exploit others financially instead.
False Self or False Persona	Narcissists outwardly project a 'false self', which they cannot maintain without attention from others (which comes in the form of drama, conflict and adoration). This false self is highly convincing and at odds with the underlying emptiness. Many refer to this outward image as a 'mask', which can temporarily drop when the narcissist feels threatened or abandoned.
Fight, Flight, Freeze or Fawn Response	When a human brain sees a threat, which it perceives as a threat to life, the amygdala, a part of the brain, gets activated. Narcissists are good at triggering this response in their victims, so that without even thinking, the person is thrown into an instinctive fight, flight, freeze or fawn response. The release of various stress hormones, such as cortisol and adrenaline means that blood is diverted away from the cortex (the thinking part of the brain) to other areas of the body, such as muscles, so that they can fight harder or run away. Some victims may freeze and do nothing, and others may 'fawn', doing whatever their perpetrator wants, in order to stay safe.
Financial Abuse	A form of abuse commonly employed by narcissists. Other types include emotional, physical and legal abuse.

Term	Definition
Flying Monkey	One of the narcissist's fan club. Named after the flying monkeys in *The Wizard of Oz*, who do the evil bidding of the wicked witch, they abuse the narcissist's victim on their behalf, spying on them and spreading lies about them.
Gaslighting	The act of undermining another person's reality by denying facts, their environment, or their feelings.
Generalizations	Another way that the human brain filters out incoming information, by making automatic assumptions, based on the person's past experiences eg. 'all nurses are kind'. (See also deletions and distortions.)
No Contact	If at all possible, the victim of a narcissist should have no contact at all with the narcissist. However, if they share children, are still living under the same roof, or if they are involved in a joint business venture, this may not be possible. If it is possible, however, then they should block the narcissist from all methods of contact (including phone, email, social media, messaging apps and texts).
Golden Child	The child who is being idealized by the narcissist, who is treated differently to the other children in the household, as if they can do no wrong.
Grandiose Narcissist	Another name for an Exhibitionist or Overt Narcissist.

Term	Definition
Grey Rock Technique	A communication technique to minimize the amount of narcissistic supply one gives to a narcissist, by giving no emotional response at all. The ways in which this can be done include reducing eye contact, making the voice flat and boring, speaking slowly, ignoring inflammatory statements and reducing facial expressions.
Hoovering	The term given to the narcissist's tactic of sucking the victim back into the relationship, so that they can continue to use them as a source of narcissistic supply. It occurs when they suspect that they are about to be abandoned.
Idealization	Also called love bombing. Idealization occurs when the narcissist puts their victim on a pedestal, and treats them well. It is inevitably followed by 'devaluation'.
Intermittent Reinforcement	The technique used by narcissists to keep their victims hooked to them by giving them unpredictable, varying, wins and losses in the cycle of idealization and devaluation.
Introverted Narcissist	Same as a Closet Narcissist.
Love bombing	Also called 'idealization'. The initial stage of a relationship with a narcissist.
Malignant Narcissist	Another name for a Devaluing or Toxic Narcissist.
Mask	The mask is the outward projection of the narcissist's false self. But when the narcissist does not get enough narcissistic supply the mask can drop, to reveal their true nature. See also False Persona.

Term	Definition
Narcissistic Abuse	Abuse carried out by someone with NPD. This is mostly covert emotional abuse, but physical abuse can also be a feature.
Narcissistic Collapse	The deep depression that some narcissists go into, when they suffer a narcissistic injury. Unlike true depression, they can quickly recover from it as soon as they get enough narcissistic supply.
Narcissistic Injury	This occurs when the narcissist's outer bubble is punctured; when the protective suit of armour, the false persona, is penetrated by some external event. It could be a perceived personal slight which brings on the injury, or any situation in which things do not go the narcissist's way. It leads to a severe loss in narcissistic supply, which results in narcissistic rage, or a narcissistic collapse.
Narcissistic Personality Disorder	A diagnosable personality disorder, as defined in the Diagnostic and Statistical Manual of Mental Disorders (DSM-5).
Narcissistic Rage	Intense fury as a consequence of narcissistic injury.
Narcissistic Supply	Narcissists need 'feeding' attention, in some form or other, to maintain the fragile image that they present to the world. This external validation is 'Narcissistic Supply'. Without narcissistic supply those with NPD are forced to feel their own sense of unworthiness and shame. Almost everything a narcissist does is with the aim of securing narcissistic supply.

Term	Definition
Object Constancy	The ability to believe that a relationship is stable and intact, despite the presence of setbacks, conflict, or disagreements. Narcissists have not developed this ability, so they cannot see you as somebody they love and someone who has angered them, at the same time.
Overt Narcissist	Another name for an Exhibitionist or Grandiose Narcissist.
Passive Aggression	Examples are silent treatments, lateness, procrastinating on jobs, sabotaging another's work, name calling and insults re-framed as jokes.
Projection	A psychological defence mechanism unconsciously used by many people, but by all narcissists. Anyone who finds it difficult to accept their failures, weaknesses, poor behaviours and own less flattering traits may unwittingly use projection as a way of feeling better about themselves, by accusing another person of exhibiting those traits or carrying out those behaviours. Essentially, they are assigning the imperfect or flawed parts of themselves to other people.
Projective Identification	If a victim has been gaslit for years, it is quite common for them to take on, believe and identify with whatever it is that the narcissist is projecting onto them. This is called 'projective identification'. They come to believe what the narcissist is telling them about themselves.
Pseudo-logic	A typical narcissist's communication style which includes contradictions, irrational conclusions, and false logic.

Term	Definition
Rescuers	Rescuers need to rescue others to feel needed and to matter. A narcissist will exploit this trait time and time again, in order to pull the target into the Narcissist Trap, by playing the victim.
Scapegoat	The child of a narcissist who is blamed, shamed and can do nothing right – the golden child's opposite number.
Shame-dumping	Giving away ('dumping') feelings of deep shame to others, so that a person does not have to feel the shame themselves – characteristic of narcissists.
Spectrum of Narcissism	Narcissism exists on a spectrum. Those at the lowest end of the spectrum are not narcissistic enough, and are attractive to narcissists. Those at the opposite end of the spectrum are the narcissists, who are blind to the needs and feelings of others, and concerned only with meeting their own needs to feel special. The middle part is the healthy zone.
Toxic Narcissist	Another name for a Devaluing or Malignant Narcissist.
Toxic Positivity	A form of invalidation, where only positive thoughts and attitudes are allowable. This means that any negative feelings are 'wrong' and therefore invalid.
Trauma Bonding	The neuro-chemical addiction of a victim to the narcissist, as a result of the cycle of idealization and devaluation.
Triangulation	Where the narcissist brings a third person into the dynamic, to play one off against the other in the triangle.

Term	Definition
Vulnerable Narcissist	Another name for a Closet, Covert, or Introverted Narcissist.
Whole Object Relations	The capacity to integrate the liked and disliked parts of a person into a single, realistic, stable picture, instead of alternating between seeing the person as either all-good or all-bad (as narcissists do).
Word Salad	The nonsensical style of communication from a narcissist after they have descended into a narcissistic rage – illogical and ranting in nature, with very loose associations between ideas.
Yellow Rock Technique	A version of the Grey Rock Technique, in which the communications are warmed up slightly, perhaps through the addition of the occasional emoji, or by using a slightly more friendly tone. Useful if communications might be seen by a court, or if you have no choice but to maintain communication with a narcissist.

ABOUT THE AUTHOR

Dr Supriya McKenna is one of the best known names (and voices) in the field of narcissism. A former family doctor, she is the author behind the Amazon number one bestseller *Divorcing a Narcissist: the Lure, the Loss and the Law* (with legal contributions from UK family lawyer, Karin Walker). She narrates the internationally bestselling audiobook of the same name.

Recognising a huge need for education in UK family lawyers, in 2020 Supriya conceived the groundbreaking guide, *Narcissism and Family Law: a Practitioner's Guide*, now affectionately referred to by lawyers as 'The Red Book'. She wrote this in parallel with Karin, during Covid lockdown.

Supriya has trained thousands of family law professionals in narcissistic personality disorder. She works directly with those who have fallen victim to narcissistic abuse and produces and hosts the top 5% podcast *Narcissists in Divorce: The Narcissist Trap*. Her resources can be found on her websites, thelifedoctor.org and doctorsupriya.com, and she regularly posts insights on Twitter, Instagram and LinkedIn.

A speaker and media commentator, Supriya started her writing career whilst working as a young doctor, when she regularly contributed health features to magazines such as Cosmopolitan and Marie Claire. She continues to write features and articles for various well known publications to raise awareness of this personality disorder.

Printed in Great Britain
by Amazon